D1518929

POPULATION AND ECONOMY IN CLASSICAL ATHENS

This is the first comprehensive account of the population of classical Athens for almost a century. The methodology of earlier scholars has been criticised in general terms, but their conclusions have not been seriously challenged. Ben Akrigg reviews and assesses those methodologies and conclusions for the first time and thereby sets the historical demography of Athens on a firm footing. The main focus is on the economic impact of that demography, but new conclusions are presented that have profound implications for our understanding of Athenian society and culture. The book establishes that the Athenian population became very large in the fifth century BC, before falling dramatically in the final three decades of that century. These changes had important immediate consequences, but the city of the fourth century was shaped in fundamental ways by the demographic upheavals of its past.

BEN AKRIGG is Associate Professor in the Department of Classics at the University of Toronto. He is co-editor, with Rob Tordoff, of *Slaves and Slavery in Ancient Greek Comic Drama* (Cambridge, 2013).

CAMBRIDGE CLASSICAL STUDIES

POPULATION AND ECONOMY IN CLASSICAL ATHENS

BEN AKRIGG
University of Toronto

CAMBRIDGE
UNIVERSITY PRESS

CAMBRIDGE
UNIVERSITY PRESS

University Printing House, Cambridge CB2 8BS, United Kingdom

One Liberty Plaza, 20th Floor, New York, NY 10006, USA

477 Williamstown Road, Port Melbourne, VIC 3207, Australia

314-321, 3rd Floor, Plot 3, Splendor Forum, Jasola District Centre, New Delhi - 110025, India

79 Anson Road, #06-04/06, Singapore 079906

Cambridge University Press is part of the University of Cambridge.

It furthers the University's mission by disseminating knowledge in the pursuit of
education, learning and research at the highest international levels of excellence.

www.cambridge.org
Information on this title: www.cambridge.org/9781107027091
DOI: 10.1017/9781139225250

© Faculty of Classics, University of Cambridge 2019

First published 2019

A catalogue record for this publication is available from the British Library

Library of Congress Cataloging in Publication data
NAMES: Akrigg, Ben, author.
TITLE: Population and economy in Classical Athens / Ben Akrigg.
OTHER TITLES: Cambridge classical studies.
DESCRIPTION: New York, NY: Cambridge University Press, 2019. | Series:
Cambridge classical studies
IDENTIFIERS: LCCN 2019002566 | ISBN 9781107027091 (alk. paper)
SUBJECTS: LCSH: Athens (Greece) – Population – History. | Athens (Greece) –
Economic conditions. | Athens (Greece) – History – To 1500.
CLASSIFICATION: LCC HB3632.5.A84 A35 2019 | DDC 304.60938/5–dc23
LC record available at https://lccn.loc.gov/2019002566

ISBN 978-1-107-02709-1 Hardback

CONTENTS

TABLES

ACKNOWLEDGEMENTS

This book has had a long gestation and I have incurred a commensurate number of debts.

The ultimate origins of this work lie in my Cambridge PhD thesis, completed as part of the Cultural Revolutions in Classical Athens project funded by the AHRC. The thesis was supervised by Robin Osborne, the director of that project. No student could ask for a wiser or more supportive adviser. I also owe profound thanks to the other members of that project, especially the core group of Simon Goldhill, Elizabeth Irwin, Julia Shear, Claire Taylor, and Rob Tordoff; and to the many others from Cambridge and further afield who attended seminars, especially Peter Fawcett. The thesis was examined by Peter Garnsey and John Davies, who provided invaluable feedback.

I also owe my thanks to the following people:

All the habitual denizens of the graduate common room of the time in the Faculty of Classics at Cambridge, without whom life as a PhD student would have been much more miserable, including especially Ellen Adams, Elton Barker, Jenny Bryan, Emma Buckley, Ashley Clements, Tom Lambert, Polly Low, and Abi Price.

The staff of all the various libraries without whom this project would have been impossible: the library of the Faculty of Classics at Cambridge; the Cambridge University Library; the Institute of Classical Studies and Joint Library of the Hellenic and Roman Societies; the library of the British School at Athens; the London Library; and University of Toronto Libraries.

My colleagues in the Department of Classics at King's College London from 2004 to 2006, especially Hugh Bowden, Lindsay Allen, Carlotta Dionisotti, Rebecca Flemming, Claire Holleran, Catherine Morgan, Henrik Mouritsen, John Pearce, and Dominic Rathbone.

Acknowledgements

My colleagues past and present in the Department of Classics at the University of Toronto, especially Eph Lytle, Dimitri Nakassis, and Victoria Wohl.

The members of the inconsistently labelled but consistently supportive and inspiring group of ancient Greek historians and political theorists meeting around the American Midwest: Greg Anderson, Matthew Christ, Judith Fletcher, Sara Forsdyke, Adriaan Lanni, James McGlew, Eric Robinson, Bernd Steinbock, Bob Wallace, and above all Kurt Raaflaub.

Michael Sharp, for his untiring patience.

My parents, for encouraging and supporting my interest in the ancient world almost for longer than I can remember.

Kate, for making everything better.

Anything valuable or insightful in what follows is due to one or more of these people; everything that is mistaken or muddled is my own.

ABBREVIATIONS

Abbreviations are generally those used in the *Oxford Classical Dictionary*, including those for authors and texts. Abbreviations of classical periodicals, however, follow those in *L'Année Philologique*, and of corpora of inscriptions, those of *SEG*. An addition to these rules is:

CEH   W. Scheidel, I. Morris, and Saller, R. (eds) (2007). *The Cambridge Economic History of the Greco-Roman World*. Cambridge: Cambridge University Press.

CHAPTER 1

INTRODUCTION

This book has two aims. The first is to provide an account of the historical demography of classical Athens: that is, the size and structure of its population, and how these changed over time. The second, more important, is to show why such an account is necessary, and to persuade the reader that this subject, dry and technical as it might sometimes appear, is an important part of the history of the city.

At one level, the latter aim is a superficially simple matter of filling a gap in the existing scholarship. The only previous account to deal with the population of classical Athens as a whole remains Gomme's little book, published in 1933. This remained the standard account for more than 50 years. Since the 1980s, the field (such as it is) has been dominated by the work of Mogens Herman Hansen, whose best-known and most important contribution is *Demography and Democracy*. In the three decades since this book appeared, Greek historians have shown little inclination to engage with Hansen's work. Instead, the tendency has been to cite 'Hansen 1985' as though it really were the last word on Athenian demography.[1] It is important to say here that my goal is not to challenge Hansen's conclusions: if anything, this account puts them on a firmer foundation than they had before. However, it is often overlooked how narrow Hansen's focus was in this book (its subtitle – *The Number of Citizens in the Fourth Century BC* – is precise and accurate). Furthermore, it is often underappreciated how difficult it is to draw wider conclusions on the basis of his work.

There is more to it than just supplementing Hansen, however. I hope to show just how dramatic the story of Athens' historical

---

[1] Rhodes 2010, 162; Morris 2009, 114–5 with note 41; Bresson 2016, 409.

1

demography is (how great the numbers involved were, and how significant the extent of change was), how that demography can be an indispensable tool for explaining and understanding what was happening in the *polis*, and why it should not be the sole preserve of a small number of specialists in (mainly) political history.

Most if not all, of the existing interest in the size of the population has come from political historians. This is not so surprising. Much of the continuing fascination with classical Athens derives from its status as a democracy. One of the key factors in understanding and appreciating that democracy is the extent to which its citizens participated in its institutions. Clearly, how many citizens there were makes a great deal of difference to what we think about both the breadth and depth of that participation. This is what motivated both Gomme and Hansen and their interlocutors, Jones and Ruschenbusch. Barry Strauss' account is meant to explain the context for the post-Thirty recovery of the democracy. Sinclair provided an appendix on the number of citizens in his account of democratic participation. More recently, and in a rather different way, the size of the citizen population has been important to Edward Cohen and Josiah Ober. Recent studies of individual demes have given some attention to the populations of those demes.[2] While these accounts do provide some wide illumination, the focus remains on political history.

But the evidence for the detailed operation of democratic institutions is mostly fourth century in date: oratory, the Aristotelian *Athenaion Politeia*, and many of the relevant inscriptions. Detailed accounts therefore tend to concentrate on this period, and with them much of the interest in citizen numbers. The most thorough attempt to look at the size of the population in the fifth century since Gomme, by Cynthia Patterson, was concerned primarily with the context of the passage of Pericles' citizenship law in 451/0, and essentially took 431 as an end point.[3] An important consequence of this focus on democracy has been that precisely the period when Athens experienced a major exogenous demographic shock – during the Peloponnesian War – has been

---

[2] Gomme 1933; Hansen 1985; Strauss 1986. Sinclair 1988, 223–4; Cohen 2000; Ober 2008. Demes: Moreno 2007, 37–76 (Euonymon); Kellogg 2013 (Acharnai).

[3] Patterson 1981.

neglected.[4] A further consequence has been that the question of how many *non*-citizens were living in Attica remains relatively under-explored.

More recently, demography has become increasingly important as a topic within Roman history, with increasingly sophisticated approaches and arguments being developed.[5] Interest in cliometric arguments has not been restricted to demography. Aside from perennial discussions of trade and money supply, a great deal of attention has been given to questions about the existence or otherwise of economic growth. Although this concern had been present before, new impetus was given to addressing it by the appearance of the *Cambridge Economic History of the Greco-Roman World*.[6]

As the editors of the *Cambridge Economic History* made clear at the start of their introduction, this volume was meant not only to summarise the current state of research, but to influence its future direction. For the most part this was entirely welcome, as at the start of the twenty-first century there was clearly a need to move (finally) beyond the dominant primitivism–modernism and substantivism–formalism debates of the twentieth century. To a certain extent the present volume, in so far as it deals with demography and has a substantial quantitative element, can be seen as in line with the priorities of the editors as they laid them out there, and as they have developed since. The comparative projects of Morris and Scheidel, in particular, would be impossible without quantification.[7] Demography is given a prominent treatment by Scheidel's contribution to the *CEH*. His first footnote is revealing of the status of the historical demography of Greece compared to

---

[4] On the apparent exception provided by Hansen 1988, 14–28, see 142–143 below.

[5] The key article here, on the problems of studying the structure of Roman populations, is Hopkins 1966, on which see 16–17 below. See De Ligt and Northwood 2008 for signs of movement out of what once appeared to be an intractable morass; Hin 2013 develops one of those avenues eloquently and in detail, and with wider significance than her title suggests. Concern about the proper ways to approach and model economic behaviour in the ancient world, and in particular the usefulness of the concept of economic rationality, is a key concern of, for example, Rathbone 1991. For the scope of the historical demography of ancient Rome and its empire, and a useful general summary, see Scheidel 2001b; also Parkin 1992 for a positive assessment. A majority of articles in Holleran and Pudsey 2011 are concerned with Roman questions.

[6] *CEH* 2007. Earlier concern with growth: Saller 2002;

[7] For subsequent work of these three, see for example Saller 2012; with much greater ambition and scope, Morris 2010, 2013; Scheidel 2017.

its Roman counterpart: work published in subsequent years has if anything sharpened the contrast.[8] However, I should argue that the aims pursued here are not quite the same. By stressing the importance of economic growth and questions of economic performance rather than structure, they are obliged to take an extremely long view and emphasise long-term trends, over the course of which tiny incremental changes can, cumulatively, become significant. In looking at classical Athens, I am taking a very small region over a relatively short time period, less than two centuries, where such long-term trends may not be visible and may not in fact help us to understand what was happening.

The emphasis on quantification (sometimes apparently for its own sake) and growth and suggestions of long-term improvement in living standards can make the *CEH* and the work that has been done in its wake appear to be very much a 'modernist' project. A focus on a single city could be seen as primitive antiquarianism (of the sort derided, famously and justifiably, by Finley); some readers may prefer to see it, at least in its emphasis on the particular, as instead postmodern. My own view is just that Athens really was an important place, and one that deserves to be seen in its own terms. Accusations of Athenocentricism often hold weight, but they can cut both ways. If we cannot generalise from Athens to the rest of Greece (and often we cannot), then neither should we generalise from Greece as a whole to Athens. Part of what made Athens unusual was the sheer size of its population, and so a proper understanding of the historical demography of Athens is crucial.

That is not to say that historical demography holds the key to all understanding of Athens. There is an important and revealing little passage to this point in De Ste Croix's *The Class Struggle in the Ancient Greek World*. Although this is not quite a work of economic history as such, De Ste Croix was obviously concerned with economic themes. De Ste Croix did not himself make a case against the construction of economic models (of the types which were then being used by historians of other periods) for studying ancient history. But his explicit reason for dismissing the validity

---

[8] Scheidel 2007, 38 note 1.

4

of such approaches was that 'a very able article' by the medieval historian Robert Brenner had dealt 'admirably with various types of "economic model-building" which try to explain long-term economic developments in pre-industrial Europe primarily in terms either of demography (Postan, Bowden, Le Roy Ladurie, and North and Thomas) or of the growth of trade and the market (Pirenne and his followers), disregarding class relations and exploitation as primary factors'.[9]

There is little point in going over what became known as the 'Brenner debate'.[10] What is important here is that Brenner's position (which, like De Ste Croix's, argued forcefully that class interaction was *the* primary factor in explaining historical development – in Medieval Europe, in this case) was very far from winning universal acceptance. Some of the resistance was no doubt motivated principally by differences in political stance; but there were real problems with Brenner's account. De Ste Croix was aware of the immediate responses to Brenner's article – but had nothing to say about them except, in a footnote, that they were of 'very uneven value'.[11] This is an entirely reasonable view, but expressed like this, it neatly tarred the valuable contributions with the brush of the mediocre and the poor, without his having to engage with them in detail. While Brenner's ability is not in question, I am not as admiring as De Ste Croix of his method of dealing with those who had proposed alternative models for explaining economic development. In particular, I shall be arguing in favour of a position which is not, in the end, all that dissimilar to that expressed by one of Brenner's principal targets, Michael Postan.[12]

From an external perspective, a problem with De Ste Croix's argument is that he too is in fact engaged in a form of the 'model-building' he despises: using class, instead of population and resources or commercialisation, to explain development and change. As De Ste Croix hinted, the Middle Ages have proved to

[9] De Ste Croix 1981, 83, referring to Brenner 1976.
[10] The relevant articles from *Past and Present*, in which the debate was chiefly conducted, are collected in Aston and Philpin 1985.
[11] De Ste Croix 1981, 552 note 2a.
[12] Postan 1973a; Postan 1973b.

be a particularly hotly contested battleground of competing models for explaining change. The crucial point in this context, however, is that, as Hatcher and Bailey more recently argued, none of the traditional 'supermodels' which have been deployed has ever managed to deal a knockout blow.[13]

Hatcher and Bailey observed that demographic models initially emerged as a counter to simplistic 'modernising' assumptions, but managed to attain a hegemonic status in medieval history. It was this situation which Brenner sought to shake up with his explicitly Marxist account. The 'Brenner debate' fought out in the pages of *Past and Present* failed to produce a clear winner, which in turn (and with some irony) allowed the re-emergence of the commercialisation model, albeit now in more sophisticated forms. But the greatest strength of each of these single-issue models – simplicity and ready appeal to intuitive understanding – has proved to be their greatest weakness, as each also involved too great a level of abstraction to be reconcilable with the ever-increasing detail of scholarly understanding of the medieval world. In this context, Badian's penetrating observation about the grand narrative that is presented in *The Class Struggle in the Ancient Greek World* – that the areas of weakness in its argument occur precisely in the times and places about which we are best informed – is particularly telling.[14]

Variations on the observation that 'if the only tool you have is a hammer, it is tempting to treat everything as if it were a nail' have been illustrated by historians of the economies of ancient Greece in recent decades as well as by anyone. Without straying too far into the realms of caricature, Finley's *The Ancient Economy* (in so far as it is about economic history at all) tries to explain everything in terms of status relations, for which De Ste Croix substitutes class relations. More recently, we have seen Cohen's *Athenian Economy and Society* explain the important changes in its subject in terms of the emergence of a fully marketised economy and private banks. Loomis saw the key determinant of *Wages, Welfare Costs and Inflation in Classical Athens*

---

[13] Hatcher and Bailey 2001.
[14] Badian 1982.

as being the available money supply. Loomis' project derived from Schaps' attempt to collate the commodity price data from the ancient world; Schaps' own treatment of *The Invention of Coinage and the Monetization of Ancient Greece* is an overtly (and sophisticated) commercialist account of important changes in archaic and classical Greece. Important recent contributions to the economy of classical Athens include Moreno's *Feeding the Democracy* and Bissa's *Governmental Intervention in Foreign Trade in Archaic and Classical Greece*. Athens is given due attention in more general works such as Ober's *The Rise and Fall of Classical Greece* and Bresson's *The Making of the Ancient Greek Economy.*[15] Greek, and especially Athenian, economic history is thus at present approached largely in terms of commercialism and marketisation. In part, this is a continuing reaction to Finley. Along with the strategic thrust of the *CEH* in favour of emphasising economic performance and trying to quantify growth, there is a danger here of a swing back in Greek history to an unreflective modernism, where the valuable lessons of the substantivism–formalism debate are lost. However, by suggesting that demography is an important part of the economic history of Greece and of Athens, I do not want to suggest that this is a better hammer. I am not arguing for the superiority of historical demography over approaches that emphasise other factors more; it would be a disaster if, having dragged ourselves away from the substantivism–formalism debates, we should simply start to refight the Brenner debate.

Having said all of that, I still want to maintain that close attention to historical demography can help us understand classical Athens, and in more ways than it has been used in the past. This includes its political history: at the very least, there is scope for progress in pulling together those accounts that deal with issues related to population size over relatively restricted periods. Barry Strauss' intuition – that demographic change must be an important part of the explanation for the course taken by Athenian politics in the immediate aftermath of the Peloponnesian War – can be

[15] Cohen 1992; Loomis 1998; Schaps 2004; Moreno 2007; Bissa 2009; Ober 2015; Bresson 2016; Harris, Lewis, and Woolmer 2016.

justified even if one does not accept the detail of the arguments he makes to this end.

However, we can go further than this too. Athens was not just a set of political institutions, nor is its continuing fascination due solely to its democracy. All of its achievements and failures were, whatever else can be said about them, products of a particular context and background. The number of Athenians, the structure of the population, and the fact that both of these were not static but susceptible to change (and sometimes dramatic change) are in themselves an essential part of that context. The emphasis in this volume is on the relationship between demography and economic history. That the two are connected may seem obvious, but the connection is rarely made explicit by ancient historians. I hope to show that active consideration of the relationship can have interesting results. Even if the detailed conclusions advanced here are not found convincing, I hope to show that the subject is worth pursuing.

Chapter 2 begins with a general consideration of the population structure and how ancient historians have tried to get to grips with ancient populations. In Chapters 3 and 4, I look at the evidence for the absolute size of the citizen and non-citizen populations at various times in classical Athens. In Chapter 5, I consider the evidence for and scale of change in the population over the course of the fifth and fourth centuries. In Chapters 6 and 7, I suggest some important implications of the picture of Athens' population that emerges from the earlier chapters; Chapter 6 deals primarily with simple and obvious issues of aggregate consumption, while Chapter 7 tries to draw slightly more complex connections between population and wider social, political, and economic themes.

CHAPTER 2

POPULATION STRUCTURES

Introduction

This chapter will discuss the structure of the population of classical Athens. The main focus will be on age structure, although at the end of the chapter, I shall turn briefly to a broad question of sex structure (that is, whether there was ever a significant imbalance between the numbers of men and women). In both cases, I shall concentrate here on the native citizen population. The free resident non-citizen (metic) and servile populations, both of which were of considerable size for most of the fifth and fourth centuries, present their own special challenges and will be discussed separately (in Chapter 4).

Population structure has on the whole received less attention from would-be historical demographers of Athens than the size of the population. I give it a more detailed treatment here for two reasons. The first is that, for reasons that will become apparent, the age structure of the population is fundamental to almost any attempt to derive demographic data from the information in the literary and epigraphic sources. This fact has of course been clearly recognised by most of those who have sought to quantify the population. Most influential here is Mogens Herman Hansen, whose position on this issue has been widely accepted.[1] One of the key points I want to make here is that the details of the conclusions Hansen and others have reached were even less firmly based than they realised, and that we can in fact do better. The second, which has not always been fully appreciated by Greek historians, is that

---

[1] Golden 2000 provides a summary; this is, admittedly, in the context of a volume produced in Hansen's honour, but in fact Golden cannot be accused of exaggerating: see note 1 in Chapter 1.

issues of structure are of considerable intrinsic interest and importance – and potentially more so than discussions that are limited to
the overall size of a population.[2]

Why Does Age Structure Matter?

In the first place, age structure matters because attempts to quantify the size of the Athenian population have started – almost
inevitably – from the scattered figures surviving in written
sources. These texts deal overwhelmingly with two of the most
ideologically central fields of citizen activity: war and politics.
We have various (and variously helpful) figures referring to
Athens' armed forces, both in their entirety and, more often, to
the forces involved in specific campaigns. We also have a fair
knowledge of the institutions of the classical democracy and their
operation, especially for the fourth century, and so can draw
reasonably detailed inferences both about how many people
those institutions would comfortably have accommodated, and
about how many people would have been required to operate
them successfully and sustainably.

This matters here because both front-line combat and most
political roles were primarily the responsibilities of men of particular age groups. Military field forces were usually made up of
relatively young men (probably those in their twenties and thirties:
see 72–73 below); council service was limited to those over the
age of 30. At the extremes, ephebes (at least after the late fourth-
century reform of the institution) were those aged 18 and 19,
whereas the *diaitetai* or 'arbitrators' were those in their
sixtieth year. It is not surprising, then, that epigraphic records of
those who served as councillors or arbitrators and those who
trained as ephebes have played a prominent part in demographic
discussions of the citizen body. Having some idea of the proportion of the total male population which consisted of 18-, or 30-, or
60-year-olds would obviously be both interesting and important if
it could be attained.

---

[2] Robert Sallares provides an exception (Sallares 1991, 48). The point has been more
widely accepted by historians of Rome: see Hin 2013, 101–257.

This also helps to account for the fact that political history has been the main driver of investigation into Athenian demography. The very first page of Gomme's 1933 treatment provides a clear example of the prevailing view:

That it [the subject of population] is of great importance we cannot deny ... chiefly because it would, obviously, add so much to the vividness and truth of our picture of Greece, and of Athens in particular, if we could give even approximate answers to three questions

of which 'perhaps the most interesting question' concerned

the peculiarities of the Athenian constitution: if the assertion of the oligarchs in 411 that no more than 5,000 citizens ever attended the ecclesia was not wildly untrue, what proportion was that of the whole number? And what proportion of the whole were the dikasts?[3]

Gomme's sentiments were echoed over 50 years later by Hansen in the preface to his *Demography and Democracy*:

The most amazing aspect of Athenian democracy is the degree of participation. Every year the Athenians convened 40 *ekklesiai* which were regularly attended by no less than 6,000 citizens. On the ca. 150–200 court days thousands of jurors were appointed by lot from a panel of 6,000 citizens aged thirty or more. The council of five hundred was manned with citizens above thirty of whom only a few took the opportunity to serve twice in the *boulē*. And ca. 700 other magistrates were elected or selected by lot. This massive participation must, of course, be related to the total number of citizens.[4]

Both Gomme and Hansen were absolutely right, of course: it really is important for political historians to have some sense of the size of the citizen body in the democracy, whatever the style of their approach. Most of the explicit investigation into numbers has, it is true, been carried out by historians of Athens who have prioritised the study of institutions: it is important to mention Peter Rhodes here.[5] The size of the citizen body and the extent of participation in those institutions is also fundamental to the rather different answers presented to the question 'how did the Athenian democracy work?' in the work of Josiah Ober.[6] Almost immediately,

[3] Gomme 1933, 1–2.
[4] Hansen 1985, 6.
[5] Rhodes 1988.
[6] Ober 2008.

however, each of them (along with everyone else who has shared their interest) ran into difficulties in addressing this issue.

How Can Age Structure Be Established or Estimated?

The main source of those difficulties turns out to be that direct evidence for the age structure of the population of classical Athens is completely lacking. This may seem slightly surprising, as there has in some quarters been a great deal of discussion of the evidence for age structure in the ancient world in general, and we are used to classical Athens being relatively well documented. That there is effectively no literary evidence should perhaps not be surprising, at least on a moment's reflection: no author in antiquity would have been interested in this kind of issue in anything like the detail that would allow us to make useful inferences. The failure of epigraphic and archaeological sources in this area may need a little more explanation, however.

A lot of attention used to be devoted to tombstones from the Roman world which recorded ages at death. It has been established, albeit not without effort on the part of the sceptics, that such data do not in fact reveal much, if anything, about age structure, as opposed to practices of commemoration.[7] The historical demography of Athens has been simplified by, and perhaps has even benefitted from, the fact that Athenian grave monuments generally do not record age at death. The obvious exception, that of Dexileos, is a genuinely rule-proving one.[8]

The use of human skeletal material is the other obvious recourse, and Angel's study (which is still often cited) of material from Attica can even be seen as the start of the discipline of palaeodemography.[9] However, there are in practice severe difficulties in making use of this kind of evidence, which account for its absence from most discussion of classical Athens. In summary,

---

[7] Hopkins 1966; the case had to be made again in Hopkins 1987 and Parkin 1992. The evidence of tombstones is not necessarily useless for demography, however: see Hin 2016 on using Hellenistic and Roman gravestones from Attica to investigate migration into Athens and its effects.

[8] Dexileos: *RO* 7B.

[9] Angel 1945.

there are two main areas of difficulty. The first is that it is usually very difficult to assess the relationship between any given archaeologically excavated assemblage of skeletal material and any once-living population. The second is that actually deriving a chronological age at death of an adult from his or her skeleton is very much more difficult, imprecise, and uncertain than the forensic archaeologists in television detective programmes make it look. This is the case even in ideal circumstances where the skeleton is complete and undamaged; when, as often, it is not, then the problems are compounded. Ever more subtle and sophisticated techniques, especially of statistical analysis, are allowing the claim that palaeodemography is dead (with no pun intended) to be resisted, but we are not yet in a position where it can make decisive, or even helpful, contributions to Athenian demography.[10] This is not to say that further study of skeletons will be useless. On the contrary, it will in the future surely be a vital part of establishing the parameters (including disease and diet) which largely determined age structure. However, for the present at least, human skeletal remains cannot add much, if anything, definitive to the historical demography of Athens.

In the absence of useful direct evidence, we need an alternative, and in practice this means that we need to find an appropriate comparative model for classical Athens. Again, this has been clear to most scholars. It is therefore precisely here that much of the discussion has centred. It is worth surveying the highlights of previous discussion, and Gomme's account provides a good starting point.

Gomme's solution to the problem of age structure seems at first glance to be unsophisticated to the point of crudity. His frequently quoted estimate of 43,000 for the size of the citizen population in 431 derives from his analysis of the army figures provided by Thucydides for Athens at the outbreak of the Peloponnesian War (at 2.13.6, a passage about which we shall have much more to say later). In the main text of his book, he simply multiplied this number (which was offered as a figure for men aged 18 to 59) by

---

[10] Hoppa and Vaupel 2002 present an optimistic assessment of the potential for future contributions from palaeodemographic research, but they also illustrate the value of research on age structure independent of the skeletal material.

4 to give a total population figure, inclusive of women and children. Assuming for the moment that there was no serious imbalance in the sex ratio, this could be taken as equivalent to saying that the 18- to 59-year-olds comprised 50 per cent of the male population, with the 0- to 17-year-olds making up the bulk of the remainder, with only a very small number of men aged 60 and over.

In a substantial note at the end of the volume, however, it is revealed that there was a careful argument behind Gomme's adoption of this 'multiplier'.[11] Beloch had already used a census for Italy in 1881 to establish a multiplier of four as appropriate for Roman history. Gomme noted that Beloch's choice of date for the comparative model was meant to avoid the distortion caused by emigration from Italy to the United States and by heavy casualties in the First World War. Athens in 431, however, had been subject both to emigration and war casualties, and so Gomme, quite rightly, thought that the issue deserved some more detailed attention. He therefore tabulated data from a number of European nations in the late nineteenth and early twentieth centuries, with the intention of illustrating a number of different population structures, birth and death rates, rates of increase, and degrees of industrial development. It was only after consideration of these data that he concluded that the right multiplier for Athens was, after all, four.

A. H. M. Jones – who was also led into this subject principally by the study of Athens' political systems – had a number of problems with Gomme's treatment of Thucydides. In particular, he was critical of the way in which Gomme dealt with what seemed to Jones, as it did to many other commentators before and since, a 'startlingly' large overall number of hoplites and an extremely large garrison force. I shall return to Jones' arguments later on, but what matters here is his rejection of Gomme's answer to the issue of age structure, and his alternative suggestion that the age distribution of the Athenian population was likely to have been similar to that proposed by Burn for Roman Africa under the principate. If Burn's model applied to Attica, and taking the

[11] Gomme 1933, 75–83.

14

14,000 cavalry and hoplites of the field army to be the men aged 20 to 39 (which is what Jones suggests), then the 40- to 59-year-olds (Jones' interpretation of Thucydides' 'oldest') would have numbered fewer than 7,000. The 'youngest', or the 18- and 19-year-olds, would have numbered well over 2,000. The garrison force would therefore have contained around 9,000 citizens, and (consequently) around 7,000 metics. That seemed to Jones to be a 'not unreasonable' number of metics.[12] Jones based this suggestion on a pair of inscriptions from the late fourth century, one revealing that in c. 330 BC there were about 500 ephebes, and another that in 325/4 there were 103 arbitrators. Although these figures too were 'startling' when compared to those for England and Wales in the mid-twentieth century, they accorded quite closely with what Burn suggested:

> The main conclusion from his statistics, applied to Athenian figures, is that the Athenians suffered a uniformly high death rate from the age of 20 to 60, so that *of 500 young men of 20 not many more than 100 survived to be 60 forty years later.* Having reached about 60 a man was, it appears, so tough that he might easily live another 10 or 15 years. There are no ancient statistics of the child death rate, but it was probably at least as high as that of adults. The population would therefore have been very young, with a high percentage of children.[13] (emphasis added)

As we shall see, in the end Jones' conclusions about the number of citizens of hoplite status in Athens in 431 were not all that different from Gomme's. Gomme thought that there were about 25,000, Jones 23,000 – but Gomme's figures also included those unfit for active service, while Jones' did not. This may have contributed to the failure of this aspect of Jones' interpretation to make much impact. However, Jones' argument was different in an important respect. In adopting a whole comparative age structure, rather than just confirming what was the right 'multiplier' for the militarily active population, Jones allowed for *further* use of the model for addressing questions other than those of simple population size, as he hints at the end of the passage quoted above.

Jones' account also has one important similarity to Gomme's. Like Gomme, his first recourse when starting to think about the

---

[12] Jones 1957, 82–3.
[13] Jones 1957, 83.

historical demography of Athens was to adopt the work of a historian of Rome. It is not surprising, perhaps, that the *next* important step in the historical demography of Athens was also driven by a Roman historian.

In 1966, Keith Hopkins published an important and influential article (though not always, as we shall see, influential in the way the author intended), 'On the probable age structure of the Roman population'. Hopkins' aim in this piece was ostensibly limited and largely negative. Previous accounts of the population of the Roman empire had attempted to calculate an average life expectancy at birth, and at later ages on the basis of the ages given on Roman tombstones. Hopkins argued that this evidence, while it produced superficially plausible results, could not in fact be used, because the distribution pattern of ages at death suggested by the tombstones was at best highly improbable and often downright impossible. Essentially, this was because the tombstones reflect primarily habits of commemoration rather than death rates, and there is no available means of correcting the distortions that this implies. The temptations exerted by the size of the data set that the tombstones appeared to provide, however, meant that more than 20 years later Hopkins and others were obliged to restate and elaborate the argument.[14]

Although he acknowledged Jones' advice and help in the writing of this article, Hopkins demolished the underpinning of Jones' argument about the age structure of the citizen population of Athens. Burn's suggested age distribution pattern, employed by Jones, was based on a combination of census data from India in 1900 and the Roman tombstones. While Hopkins conceded that Burn's article was 'by far the most sophisticated and serious discussion of Roman mortality', it was nonetheless one of his principal targets: 'his method and his presentation of data are open to grave objections'.[15]

Central to Hopkins' argument was the use, in place of a comparative model from any modern society (and ultimately both Gomme and Jones had used modern data), of the first set of

[14] Hopkins 1987, Parkin 1992, 5–27.
[15] Hopkins 1966, 250; referring to Burn 1953.

empirical model life tables. These were tools developed by the United Nations for use in countries where detailed census data and accurate vital event records were not available, and which provided models of age structure that could be used by ancient historians. According to Hopkins, 'the most important aspect of this argument is that the "truth" of the inscriptional evidence is "tested" by reference to the external standard of the UN model life tables'.[16] And it was this aspect of his work – the appeal to modern demographic models – that proved to be of most interest to, and the greatest influence on, Greek historians: not least, perhaps, because they had no data set like the tombstones available to them in the first place.

In fact, the precise timing of Hopkins' article was slightly unfortunate. At the time when he was writing, the UN model life tables were effectively the only set available. As Hopkins was perfectly well aware, they had already come in for considerable criticism, and their use was soon to be discontinued.[17] In the same year as Hopkins' article, however, another set of life tables was published: Coale and Demeny's Regional Model Life Tables.[18] These were more satisfactory, in terms both of the quality of the empirical data from which they were derived, and in the statistical methods by which they were derived.[19] Hopkins himself observed in a later article that the Coale–Demeny tables were superior to the UN tables he had used.[20]

Greek historians proved to be enthusiastic followers of Hopkins in the limited sense that they adopted the use of the UN model life tables, but in doing so they missed not only the appearance of the Coale and Demeny tables but the point of what Hopkins had gone on to say in his original article:

Our attention therefore should no longer be directed to different aspects of inscriptions, but rather a more general assessment of the applicability of these model life tables and to an analysis of the determinants of mortality, both in Rome in particular, and in general. To do this more accurately and sensitively we need

[16] Hopkins 1966, 264.
[17] Newell 1988, 134.
[18] Coale and Demeny 1966; a revised second edition was issued in 1983.
[19] Newell 1988, 131–9.
[20] Hopkins 1987.

life tables based on the total range of existing historical material and the critical construction of theories explaining population growth.[21]

Important work in the 1980s on Athens, particularly by Cynthia Patterson and Robin Osborne on the fifth century, employed the UN tables not just as appropriate comparative models but essentially as predictive models for the classical Athenian citizen population.[22]

It was of course Mogens Herman Hansen who took what was to be the next and still more influential step in his *Demography and Democracy*. He started this account of the Athenian citizen population in the fourth century by considering seven 'general problems of historical demography and historical method'. Each of these questions was an important one, although it turned out that some of them could be answered quite straightforwardly. Most of them can be discussed in Chapter 3, but I want to focus here on the third in Hansen's list: 'which is the proper analogy to be used when we make assumptions about the age distribution of adult male Athenians?' Note the 'adult' males: Hansen was only interested here in citizens.[23]

Like Patterson and Osborne, Hansen followed Hopkins in rejecting the use of any modern population as an appropriate analogy for any ancient population, and in preferring instead to use a set of model life tables. However, he used the Coale–Demeny tables in place of the old UN tables.[24]

Apart from the quality of the data on which they are based, one of the principal advantages of the Coale–Demeny tables over the UN tables was in their greater flexibility. With the original UN tables, once a mortality level has been chosen, there was only one life table available. In effect, the choice of a given average life expectancy at birth determined the age distribution of the whole (model) population. Clearly, though, it is possible for populations with the same level of mortality overall to have different age distributions. One such population may suffer from relatively

---

[21] Hopkins 1966, 264.
[22] Osborne 1985, 43–4; Patterson 1981, 42.
[23] Hansen 1985, 7, 9–13.
[24] Hansen 1985, 11; a new set of UN tables was published in 1982.

high mortality among adults, but another among children – to take a very crude example of the potential for difference.[25]

When they created their life tables, Coale and Demeny were aware of this problem and tried to provide some more flexibility. Instead of providing a single pattern of age distribution for each level of mortality, they generated four sets of models, each with a different age pattern. Each set was named for a 'region': North, South, East, and West (hence 'regional' model life tables).[26] The 'West' model was the one recommended by Coale and Demeny for use when there is no reliable information available on the age pattern of mortality in a population. Hansen duly followed this recommendation and adopted the West model, although he also noted that for his purposes (where the margin of error was so wide) it would have made relatively little difference if he had chosen one of the others.[27]

The Coale–Demeny tables were the best option available at the time, and remained so for some years to come, especially for those who, like ancient historians, were not specialists in demography. Hansen can hardly be blamed for putting them to a purpose which was after all very close to the one for which they were designed in the first place: providing a plausible set of figures for situations where the recording of actual statistics was inadequate. However, even at the time of their first publication in the 1960s, these tables were not immune to criticism, and the confidence that Hansen

---

[25] Newell 1988, 134.

[26] The choice of names makes sense when the empirical basis for each region is considered. The North family of models was derived from life tables from Sweden, Norway, and Iceland, where mortality among infants and older adults (over 45) was relatively low, while adult mortality at earlier ages was relatively high. This seems to have been a result of a high incidence of tuberculosis, although life tables from all three countries between 1890 and 1940 were excluded because exceptionally high tuberculosis mortality caused major deviations in the mortality rates in the ages 5 to 40 during these years. The East tables were derived from data for Austria, Germany, Czechoslovakia, north and central Italy, Hungary, and Poland. The pattern here was quite different, with high mortality in infancy and over the age of 50. The South tables were derived from life tables for Spain, Portugal, and southern Italy, and showed high mortality for those under 5, low mortality from about 40 to 60 and high mortality again over 65. The West region represents effectively an 'average' pattern of mortality. It was derived from the tables that remained after those showing the distinctive age patterns of the East, South, and North regions had been removed. On the derivation of all four regions, see Coale and Demeny 1983, 11–12.

[27] Coale and Demeny 1983, 25; Hansen 1985, 16.

expressed in them was not altogether justified. In practice, as we shall see, this did not matter very much for the validity of Hansen's own conclusions, but it has implications for those who have followed him in the adoption of this particular model for reconstructing the population of Athens.

After choosing Model West, Hansen still needed to choose a mortality level and a growth rate in order to select the appropriate age distribution (or stable population – see 25 below). It is at this point that Hansen was on the weakest ground. Like Jones before him, Hansen appealed to the work of Roman historians in establishing the credentials of his model for age distribution in Athens:

Recent studies in the population of the Roman empire suggest that the demographic structure of the Mediterranean world in the early centuries AD resembles the European demographic system ca. 1500–1750. Roman life expectancy at birth was in the region of 25 years, and the natural increase of the population was very slow, in most cases probably less than ½ per cent per year ... On the reasonable assumption that the demographic structure of Greece in the fourth century BC was basically the same as the demographic structure of the early Roman empire, we must adopt an age distribution of adult males which fits a life expectancy of ca. 25 years and a growth rate of 0–½ per cent per year.[28]

So from Coale–Demeny Model West, Hansen selected males, mortality level 4 (life expectancy at birth 25.26 years), and growth rate 5.00 (annual increase of ½ per cent).[29] The awkward figure for life expectancy is a consequence of adopting the 'male' model rather than the 'female' one. Demographers are more interested in women, so the round numbers for a given mortality level are applied to them. The tables reflect a higher life expectancy at birth for women than men for a given mortality level but do not differentiate otherwise. Hansen would have lost nothing by applying Model West, females, mortality level 3, with a life expectancy of exactly 25, to the male citizens of Athens. Still, in the end, this probably was as good a model as any available to Hansen for looking at the age distribution of the Athenian population. But his arguments for adopting it gloss over many serious problems and potential objections. Some of these problems have no easy

[28] Hansen 1985, 10–11.
[29] Hansen 1985, 10–11.

solution, but they are important and must be addressed openly. Otherwise, any calculations that are performed on the basis of the model will appear to be more firmly based than they have any right to.

One obvious problem is the analogy with the Roman empire. It seems reasonable to say that the demographic structure of the Roman empire was more like that of early modern Europe than it was that of nineteenth-century Europe. But this is a weaker claim than it appears to be. All it amounts to is that populations that existed before what has conventionally been termed the 'demographic transition' resemble each other much more closely than they do populations that are undergoing or have undergone that transition. As Newell put it:

The classical description of the theory [of demographic transition] . . . is roughly as follows. 'There are a series of stages during which a population moves from a situation where both mortality and fertility are high, to a position where both mortality and fertility are low. Both before and after the transition population growth is very slow. In between, during the transition, population growth is very rapid, essentially because the decline in mortality tends to occur before the decline in fertility.'[30]

However, although transition theory remained at the centre of much demographic study for a long time, and to a certain extent it still does, it is clearly highly problematic in this simple formulation.[31]

In fact, and again this was a feature of the revolution in historical demography that Hansen is trying to take advantage of, the basis for his assumptions has, if anything, gotten less firm. Since it was first formulated in the 1940s, demographic transition theory has come under attack on a number of fronts. In this context, what is most important is that no single explanation for the transition can be identified, and the connected observation that the move from a 'pre-transitional' to a 'transitional' and/or 'post-transitional' structure happens at different times and in different ways in different places. For example, in France, the decline in fertility seems to have started before, or at least simultaneously with a decline in mortality, rather

[30] Newell 1988, 10–11.
[31] Newell 1988, 11; Golden 2000, 28–9.

than following it, as in the classical theory. The old assumption that the demographic transition in Europe was in some way provoked by the Industrial Revolution is now untenable – the transition began long before any technological developments could have had notice-able demographic effects. As a result, it is impossible to assert absolutely that all ancient populations must have been pre-transitional just because they were ancient.[32] It is perhaps worth noting that, although she does not put it in these terms, Patterson comes close to suggesting that fifth-century Athens was undergoing some kind of demographic transition.[33]

It still seems certain, however, that Athens did basically have what can be described as a pre-transitional (high-mortality, high-fertility) population regime. The size of the city of Athens and density of occupation will have exposed the Athenian population to density-dependent diseases, which will have increased mortal-ity. As the population of Athens seems to have been increasing through the fifth century, the losses incurred will have to have been made up somehow. Inward migration is one possibility (and one ignored, incidentally, in traditional transition theory), but the number of citizens seems to have increased by reproduction, too.[34] After the citizenship law of 451/0, especially, immigrants would have found it hard to join the ranks of citizens, so a high level of fertility seems likely to have prevailed.

In any case, the relevance of bringing the Roman empire into a discussion of fourth-century Athens is not immediately apparent. But Hansen's choice of analogy seems to rest almost entirely on his 'reasonable assumption' that the demographic structure of fourth-century BC Greece was 'basically' the same as that of the early Roman empire.

There are two related problems here. One is fairly obvious, that it is surely impossible to talk about *the* demographic structure of the early Roman empire. One of the results of the 'revolution' in historical demography to which Hansen referred in his preface was to make it clear that demographic structures can vary enormously even within quite small areas, let alone an area as huge and diverse

---

[32] Wrigley 1969, 146–202; Newell 1988, 10–12.
[33] Patterson 1981, 70–1.
[34] Traditional transition theory and migration: Newell 1988, 11.

as the Roman empire. To be sure, this variety of structures could be averaged out to give a (theoretical) 'typical' structure for the whole empire. But the chances of any single area within the empire (such as Attica) having a population structure that matched this average template would be small, and even if it did, the similarity would only be coincidental. Saying that fourth-century Athens had a 'basically similar' population structure to that of the Roman empire is almost meaningless. As Hin puts it, also in the context of a discussion of model life tables, 'both age-specific mortality and life expectancy at birth are shaped by disease ecologies that vary by time, place and other criteria. The Roman empire is therefore too large an entity for aggregate analysis'.[35]

The second problem is that Hansen appeared to overstate the extent of our knowledge about the demography of the Roman empire. The rhetorical advantage of using the example of Rome when addressing ancient historians of Greece is obvious. His reference to 'recent studies' and confident assertion about Roman life expectancy at birth give the impression that we are better informed about the demographic structure of Roman populations than we are about Greek ones. This was not the case in 1985, and even now the situation is not greatly improved, in spite of an increasing level of interest in demography among Roman historians.[36]

Putting 'Roman' life expectancy at 'in the region of 25 years' was reasonable at the time, and could still be considered likely. But the figure was not based on Roman data. Rather, the argument is that life expectancy at birth must have been somewhere between 20 and 30, and 25 is simply the mid-point in this likely range of plausible figures.[37] A population where life expectancy at birth was below 20 years over the long term would have had difficulty reproducing itself, and would rapidly have declined in numbers. There is no indication that such a decline occurred across the Roman empire. On the other hand, if life expectancy at birth had been much greater than 30 years, then this would seem to imply a much lower level of mortality, and especially infant mortality, than was plausible given the available standards of medical care and the likely prevailing

[35] Hin 2013, 123.
[36] Hin 2013, 169–71.
[37] Parkin 1992, 84.

disease regimes – and it would make the Roman empire exceptional, if not unique, among comparable pre-industrial societies.
However, it is possible that life expectancy at birth was as high as
30 years or even, in some circumstances, higher: an observation
which, it is only fair to say, has been given extra credibility by more
recent work in the historical demography of the Roman world.
A good example is provided by Hin's summary of her discussion
on mortality rates, and the importance she continues to place on
comparative data and modelling. It is also worth noting that Hin's
formidable erudition and expertise in the techniques of demography
were still deployed first in an intervention about the size of the
population of Italy in the last two centuries BC.[38]

Many of the limitations on what can be said about Roman
demography were clear to Hopkins even in 1966, and 'recent
studies' had, 20 years later, done relatively little to alter the
picture. Hansen was perfectly justified in making similar assumptions about classical Athens, but the validity of those assumptions
derived not from any work by Roman historians but from comparative data from other, better documented human populations
and what we know about human reproductive biology (which
probably has not significantly altered in its fundamentals over
recorded history).

As for the rate of growth of the population, Hansen's claim that it
was very slow over the period in which he is interested is not
obviously true of the fourth century (any more than it was
for Patterson when she made a similar claim about the fifth; see
144–145 below). In the end, however, he goes for an annual rate of
½ per cent – which in reality is not all that slow. A population that
could sustain growth at that rate would have doubled in less than
140 years, or the time between the battles of Plataea and Chaeronea.
It is only slow by comparison with the other models provided by
Coale and Demeny, where ½ per cent per year is the slowest growth
rate allowed for.

So much for the parameters of Hansen's analogy. But what
about the model he actually went on to select? To a greater extent
than his predecessors, Hansen acknowledged that the use of model

---

[38] Sallares 2002, 271; Hin 2013, 170.

life tables in general, and the ones he was using in particular, did present some problems, and that all his later calculations which start from it 'must be taken *cum grano salis* and we must always allow for a certain margin of error'.[39]

Specifically, he pointed out that the Coale–Demeny models apply only to stable populations (that is, closed populations with constant birth and death rates). A stable population is not to be confused with a stationary population (one that is of a constant size, neither increasing nor decreasing). The overall size of a stable population may be changing very rapidly, but doing so at a constant rate. A stable population may also be stationary, but a stationary population does not have to be stable. A situation could be envisaged where the rates of fertility and mortality were both changing at the same time in ways that effectively cancelled each other out, so that the total size of the population remained unaltered.

The Coale–Demeny models do not take account of the effects of migration. This is not much of a problem for Hansen, given that he was talking about the total number of Athenian citizens, as they constituted a closed population – at least they did most of the time. Events like the enfranchisement of the Plataeans or the Samian isopolity did not happen very often in the fourth century, even if the registration of citizens became lax during the Ionian War, and the number of citizens losing their rights cannot have been very great before 322.[40] However, this remains something to bear in mind when considering the age distribution of citizens actually resident in Attica, even though the detail may be unrecoverable. Moreover, no population is ever really stable. Hansen pointed out that the models are an abstraction in which 'the effects of war, famine and epidemics have been smoothed'.[41] Nonetheless, he is confident enough in their utility to carry on using them. The only explicit justification is that the age distribution he adopts is not all that different from those calculated by other scholars.[42] It is implicit, however, that the level of abstraction is not so great that the model is not reflective of an underlying long-term pattern of age distribution.

---

[39] Hansen 1985, 12.
[40] Figueira 1991, 235–8, on the registration of citizens during the Ionian War.
[41] Hansen 1985, 12.
[42] Especially Ruschenbusch 1979, 1981, 1984; see also Rhodes 1988, 271–7.

In fact, Hansen considerably underestimated (or at least under-stated) the problems involved in the adoption and use of his model. Hansen adopted the Coale–Demeny models in the absence of empirical data for the age structure of ancient popula-tions, and because the demographic statistics available from more recent periods did not provide a valid comparison. What Hansen neglected to mention was the way in which the Coale–Demeny models were created in the first place. Model life tables of this kind are derived by extrapolating from empiri-cal demographic data for historical and contemporary popula-tions. The only empirical data that were considered sufficiently reliable to use as the basis for this process came from countries that carried out periodic censuses of their populations and that maintained continuous registers of vital rates. Inevitably, this means that almost all of the data used by Coale and Demeny were European in origin and recent in date. The earliest material that they felt confident about using came from the latter part of the nineteenth century, and most of it from the twentieth. All of this evidence comes from populations where mean life expec-tancy at birth was above the mid-thirties. No data from high-mortality populations could be used, because the data from such populations, where they were available, were not recorded suffi-ciently accurately. Thus the ultimate basis for the Coale–Demeny models was the same evidence that Hansen *rejected* as inap-propriate for comparison with ancient Greece.

That this might pose some difficulties for their employment by historical demographers of periods earlier than the nineteenth century was observed shortly after the publication of the first edition of the Coale–Demeny tables (as used by Hansen) in 1966. Hollingsworth, for example, observed that 'the tables are in fact based upon populations where the expectation of life at birth was between 35 and 70, and so the mortality schedules calculated for expectations of life at birth of 20 to 35, which are important for historical demography in Western Europe because they are what is usually found before 1800, are really only extra-polations of observation'.[43]

---

[43] Hollingsworth 1969, 343; also quoted by Parkin 1992, 81 note 30.

A defence of the use of model life tables could be mounted along the lines suggested by Parkin:

> Demographic principles are of universal application, and tables for high mortality can be calculated from lower mortality by regression. But this is not the whole answer, since age patterns can change over time, though not so significantly as to render the results from the model life tables invalid. The criticism remains, however, a valid one. But there is every reason to believe that the demographic pattern of age structure and mortality trends that the Coale–Demeny tables illustrate are broadly applicable to ancient populations, and are at any rate the best source of information available ... so long as it is remembered that the results given in such tables are smoothed estimates of population structure and average life expectancies and are not exact reconstructions of historical reality ... then the tables produced are an invaluable tool in the study of pre-industrial populations.[44]

It should also be noted that Coale and Demeny themselves did not think that their model life tables *would* be appropriate for use in all situations:

> There is no strong reason for supposing that the age patterns of mortality exhibited in these [life tables] cover anything like the full range of variability in age patterns under different circumstances ... The question of what is the pattern of mortality in a population of an underdeveloped area is essentially unresolvable ... By the time a population has reached the stage where age-specific mortality rates can be measured with confidence, the level and age pattern of mortality may have changed, so that the pattern of mortality during the underdeveloped period may never be known.[45]

This contradicts Hansen's belief that the Coale–Demeny tables represent 'models of *all* possible (stable) populations at 24 different mortality levels' (emphasis added).[46]

For model life table extrapolation to work, it has to be assumed that age-specific mortality will vary in predictable ways across all the possible range of levels of mean life expectancy at birth. That it can vary in more than one way is reflected by the fact that Coale and Demeny felt the need to generate four different families of tables. But as they pointed out, these families do not cover 'anything like' the full range of potential variability. One major

---

[44] Parkin 1992, 81–2.
[45] Coale and Demeny 1983, 25.
[46] Hansen 1985, 11.

problem is that in high-mortality populations, infant mortality rates can vary substantially wholly independently of adult mortality rates.

In a Roman context again, Scheidel argued this case pointedly for the benefit of classicists in an article in *JRS* in 2001 – but the observation itself was not a new one even then.[47] Göran Ohlin, for example, pointed out originally in the 1960s that where life expectancy at 15 was the same, life expectancy at birth could vary by up to ten years. Wrigley and Schofield also highlighted that infant and childhood mortality rates could be either much higher or much lower than model life tables would have suggested from the adult mortality rates in the populations they were looking at (parishes in sixteenth- and seventeenth-century England).[48] The recognition of the potential weakness of model life tables in this regard was another part of the very 'revolution' in historical demography of which Hansen was trying to take account. Up to a point, it could be argued that this particular problem was not fatal for Hansen, because he is only interested in adult mortality rates; but the point is that the hypothesis that underlies the derivation of all the life tables is indemonstrable.

Life tables face another problem as a result of this derivation from recent low-mortality populations. The higher mortality of pre-transition societies was mainly a result of the high incidence of endemic infectious diseases. Many of the most dangerous diseases have individual age-specific impacts. The obvious consequence is that the age structure of a population will be in large part reflective of the dominant disease regimes – which, of course, are wholly different in post-transition societies. Scheidel, in particular, has stressed the importance of this for the use of life tables, reaching the depressing conclusion 'that model life tables cannot reasonably be expected to capture or even credibly approximate the demographic experience of high-mortality populations'.[49]

Even Scheidel, though, has been confronted with the fact that we do not often have a better alternative to the use of model life tables, and he concedes that 'they will always be "good to think

---

[47] Scheidel 2001a, 6.
[48] Ohlin 1974, 66; Schofield and Wrigley 1979. Both also cited in Parkin 1992, 83 note 36.
[49] Scheidel 2001a, 11.

with"'.[50] They provide examples of and checks on what is possible and plausible – or at the least a firmer starting point for discussion than the kinds of round-figure guesswork in which Gomme engaged. Saying that Hansen's model almost certainly overstates infant mortality and underestimates adult mortality is, surely, a great deal more helpful than just complaining about the inadequacy of our evidence. Parkin's comment here can be allowed to stand: 'the cautious and informed use of model life tables can help us to gain a greater understanding of the population and of the society of the ancient world, in ways that have hitherto been unattainable because of the lack of direct and realistic data in ancient populations'.[51]

In recent years, it has, it is true, become obvious that as they stand the Coale–Demeny tables cannot be used as realistic models for high-mortality populations. That does not, however, mean that we are left with no better options. One obvious recourse would, for example, be to deploy the Coale–Demeny tables themselves in a more flexible manner that better reflects the reality of historical high-mortality populations. As one of his examples of child mortality varying independently of adult mortality, Scheidel notes that Wrigley et al. found that in England in the 1680s, mortality up to age 15 corresponded to Model North Level 8 (in which life expectancy at birth, both sexes averaged, is around 36); while adult mortality was close to level 2 (in which life expectancy at birth is just over 21).[52] Scheidel cited this in a footnote to an argument designed to puncture the certainty of ancient historians who rely too much on the use of the Coale–Demeny models, which is fair enough. His source, however, presents this observation slightly differently, and more positively: that parts of the Coale–Demeny tables actually matched observed reality quite closely. The implication is that a model combining those parts could be created and used. In a model population with this pattern of mortality, average life expectancy for males would be a shade under 30. This is (just) within the parameters established by Hansen for classical Athens, and may in fact not be wholly

---

[50] Scheidel 2001a, 26; Woods 2007, note 64.
[51] Parkin 1992, 90.
[52] Scheidel 2001a, 6 note 25.

implausible. Purely for the sake of argument, we could accept this as an additional model to see what difference it would make to our interpretation of the evidence. This is not to say that the model would be an exact fit, only that it might be closer to the reality, and perhaps even better to think with. At the least, it widens the pool of possible comparisons.

Another alternative would be to use different kinds of model life tables. More recently, and again primarily in a Roman (and Hopkins-inspired) context, Robert Woods proposed two alternative sets of models which seek to describe the experiences of high-mortality populations better than the Coale–Demeny models, and these too could help us to think more effectively and realistically about the age structure of the Athenian population.[53] In either case, we could use them to see how much difference they would make to the credibility of Hansen's arguments.

For the sake of illustration, I provide in Table 2.1 a comparison of stable populations based on three different model life tables. All three age distributions here are stable populations with an annual growth rate of 0.5 per cent, a rate chosen here for the sole reason of making comparisons easy. 'Hansen's model' is based on Coale and Demeny's Model West, males, mortality level 4 (average life expectancy at birth 25.26). The 'Coale–Demeny hybrid' model uses age-specific death rates for ages up to 15 from Model West, males, mortality level 8 (average life expectancy at birth 34.89), and for ages over 15 from Model West, males, mortality level 2 (average life expectancy at birth 20.44). The 'Woods Southern Europe model' uses that model with an average life expectancy at birth of 30.

A number of observations can be made here. While neither of these alternative models is necessarily at all close to representing the actual age structure of Athens at any time in the classical

[53] Woods 2007. These models are different from 'empirical' model life tables such as the UN tables and the Coale–Demeny model tables. They are relational model life tables, created using the Brass two-parameter system. Definitions can be found in Newell 1988, 130–66. The difference lies in the way in which they are derived, from a mathematical relationship between variables rather than from empirical data. The practical implication is that they can be used to generate a vastly more flexible range of models. Further discussion focused on the use and limitations of the Woods model in a Roman context may be found in Hin 2013, 110–23.

2.1 *Comparison of model life tables for Athens*

Age	Hansen's model	Coale–Demeny 'hybrid' model	Woods Southern Europe model
0	3.53	3.02	3.12
1	10.49	10.70	9.86
5	11.51	12.08	10.68
10	10.76	11.42	9.91
15	10.05	10.67	9.31
20	9.21	9.66	8.57
25	8.31	8.58	7.75
30	7.41	7.51	6.96
35	6.52	6.46	6.23
40	5.61	5.43	5.57
45	4.73	4.44	4.95
50	3.86	3.50	4.37
55	3.01	2.63	3.81
60	2.20	1.83	3.20
65	1.46	1.14	2.48
70	0.84	0.60	1.68
75	0.38	0.25	0.96
80	0.12	0.07	0.46
85+	0.02	0.01	0.13

period, they both answer most, if not all, of Scheidel's criticisms of the model life tables previously used by ancient historians, and they account for substantially lower child mortality and higher adult mortality than any of the high-mortality regional models in Coale and Demeny. A closer look at the numbers, however, suggests that Hansen's model did not seriously mislead him when it came to quantifying the fourth-century citizen population. On Hansen's chosen model, 20- to 39-year-olds make up 37.06 per cent of the population; in the hybrid model, they are 37.64 per cent; in Woods' Southern Europe model, they are 35.08 per cent. For 20- to 59-year-olds, the figures given by the respective models are 50.86 per cent, 50.04 per cent, and 51.41 per cent. These are very small discrepancies compared to the level of uncertainty in the figures in the ancient evidence. This exercise also indicates that Gomme's use of relatively recent population statistics did not necessarily have very seriously misleading consequences when he settled on his rule of thumb to multiply the militarily active age groups by four. In any case, there is no reason to dispute Hansen's quantification of the Athenian citizen population on the basis of military mobilisation figures. This accords with intuition, too. If Hansen's age structure model overestimated child mortality but underestimated adult mortality, he would have thought that there were more older men and fewer younger men in the active age groups than there were in reality, but the total would not necessarily have been much different.

The other key group for Hansen's argument is the 40-year-olds who provided the bulk of new *bouleutai*. Again, all three models show similar numbers: they make up about 1.2 per cent of the male population. In fact, Hansen's argument would actually be strengthened by the adoption of either of the other two models. On his model, 40-year-olds make up slightly more than 1.2 per cent of the male population; on both the others, they are slightly less than 1.2 per cent. So, on those models, a given number of 40-year-olds would actually imply an even greater total population (or to put it the other way around, a larger total population would be needed to provide the necessary number of 40-year-old men). In any case, Hansen's model may be suspect in detail, but in practice the conclusions he reached with it were sound.

What that does not mean, however, is that the model is actually a good one, in the sense that it reflects the actual age structure of the fourth-century citizen population or that it can be used for the interpretation of other kinds of evidence or for other arguments. For the quantitative arguments Hansen was developing, it may not have mattered which model for age structure he used, but there are important differences between them. This amplifies a point made by Rhodes in his commentary on book 2 of Thucydides, where he notes that in spite of Hansen's criticisms of the use of Mitchell's figures, his own chosen model was not that different.[54] All of the models cited by Rhodes are, however, potentially vulnerable to the criticisms levelled by Scheidel.

[54] Rhodes 1988, 277.

The importance of this is best illustrated by the ratio of 'ephebes' (men of 18 or 19) to 'arbitrators' (men in their sixtieth year).[55] On Hansen's model, the ratio is 3.7:1. On the hybrid model, it is 4.6:1. On the Woods model, it is 2.6:1. Note that this highlights the scale of difference between the two alternative models: from this perspective, Hansen's model occupies a middle position between them. With its relatively benign environment for children but brutal regime for adults, only the hybrid model would match the 5:1 ephebe to arbitrator ratio accepted by Jones on the basis of the inscriptions from Euonymon. According to Hansen's model, and still more the Woods model, the inscriptions cannot be a straightforward reflection of demographic reality, or at least not one that can be generalised for the whole of Attica from a single (albeit large) deme at the end of the fourth century.

The Sex Structure of the Citizen Population

In *Goddesses, Whores, Wives and Slaves*, her fundamental work on women in the classical world, Sarah Pomeroy argued for a significant imbalance in the sex ratio of the 'citizen' population, in favour of males.[56] There are some grounds for believing that if such an imbalance existed, it would have been particularly acute around the end of the fifth century. The key passages are as follows:

The adoption of a niece by the wealthy Hagnias in 396 BC may have been a result of the dearth of young men and the surfeit of unmarried women following the disastrous events of the second half of the Peloponnesian War. (1975, 68)

The dating of the adoption to 396 BC is argued by Davies [1971] pages 78, 82–3. Her inheritance should have facilitated finding a husband, but there is no proof that she married.

(1975, 236 NOTE 44)

---

[55] All the model life tables actually provide data on age-specific death rates for five-year cohorts; in practice, ancient historians have (usually implicitly) derived single-year cohorts for 18-year-olds and 59-year-olds by taking them to be equivalent to 10 per cent of the 15- to 24-year-olds and 55- to 64-year-olds, respectively, which provides a very close approximation. The ephebe to arbitrator ratios presented here are strictly the ratios of 15- to 24-year-olds to 55- to 64-year-olds.

[56] Pomeroy 1975, 68–70.

In normal times, when citizen men outnumbered citizen women, there were not enough brides for each man to be able to marry. In unusual periods – for example, during the last quarter of the fifth century BC, when the male population had been depleted by the many years of war and by the loss of a huge contingent of soldiers in Sicily – some men had legitimate relationships with more than one woman.

(1975, 70)

Harrison [1968] 16–17 gives the ancient evidence, but does not totally accept it.

(1975, 236 NOTE 47)

The principal problem here is one of quantification. It is possible that men generally outlived women in classical Athens, and that Pomeroy is right to claim that 'the sex difference in longevity alone would be responsible for a large ratio of men to women in the population', but it is rather unclear how much difference this would have made in practice.[57] Given the inaccuracy and imprecision of the figures we have for the male part of the population, and the likely parameters for an imbalance in the sex ratio, it seems easiest to assume that the number of women in the citizen population was roughly the same as the number of men.[58] Greater precision cannot really be obtained, and for the present purposes nothing of value would really be achieved by trying.

Pomeroy's grounds for believing in a severely imbalanced sex ratio are shakier than she was prepared to admit. Hignett, whom she cited in support of her notion that 'in normal times ... there were not enough brides for each man to be able to marry', makes no such claim. What he says is that 'the obvious gainers from the [Periclean citizenship] law were the unmarried women of Athens, since it improved their chances of obtaining husbands', which is not the same thing as saying that there was a shortage of Athenian men for them to marry before or after the law – just that the pool of potential rivals was restricted after it.[59]

Similarly, what Pomeroy goes on to say about the last quarter of the fifth century, and men having relationships with more than one woman, is supported by reference to Harrison, who 'gives' the evidence, but does not 'totally accept it'. The reason for

---

[57] Pomeroy 1975, 68.
[58] Hollingsworth 1969, 292; Newell 1988, 27–31.
[59] Pomeroy 1975, 70; Hignett 1952, 346.

Harrison's reluctance is clear: the ancient evidence for this phenomenon is extremely poor. In his discussion of the existence (or otherwise) of laws enforcing monogamy in Athens, Harrison refers to the stories 'that Sokrates was married both to Xanthippe and to Myrto, a granddaughter of Aristides, at the same time, and that Euripides had two wives at the same time'. The sources for these stories are not exactly impressive, however: 'the former story occurs in Diogenes Laertius [2.26], where it is given on the authority of Aristotle. There is no hint of it in Plato and Xenophon. The latter is from Aulus Gellius [15.20]'.[60]

Harrison observes that both of these stories may well in fact be apocryphal. In both stories, it is claimed that the Athenians passed a decree that allowed men to have two wives at once. However, Harrison notes that if Diogenes is reproducing at all accurately the terms of the decree, then technically what was being allowed was *not* that a man could have two wives at once but that a man who was married to one woman could have children by another. The implication is that 'the children of the second union would have all the public rights and duties of full citizens ... [but f]rom the fact that their mother was not a γυνὴ γαμετὴ we can probably conclude that they would at least have been at a disadvantage [with respect to family law and inheritance] over against the "married woman"'.[61] Harrison is prepared to believe that the decree really was passed, and for the reason quoted by Diogenes – that Athens was (perceived to be) in danger of a shortfall in population. What is not made explicit is either whether this was a response to an actual or perceived imbalance in the sex ratio, or, crucially, when this decree was passed. Harrison is reasonably happy to accept that it was 'during the stress of the Peloponnesian War', but there is no explicit justification for this in either story. If we accept the stories, then the decree must have been passed before Euripides' death in 407/6; the major manpower losses happened after 413 and the Sicilian Expedition. This narrows the likely window for the passage of the decree, if it really was a response to a shortage of men; but during that window, Socrates, Euripides, and Myrto would all have been

---

[60] Harrison 1968, 16–17.
[61] Harrison 1968, 17.

rather elderly. We might wonder why they are the only people about whom these stories are told. The earlier major cause of increased mortality was the plague, but there is no reason to suggest that it disproportionately affected men (of whom, in any case, Pomeroy thinks there would have been a surplus before it struck). It is also notable that both stories have obvious motives: in Euripides' case, to explain his alleged misogyny, and in Socrates' case, to link him with Aristides 'the Just'. In terms of timing, there seems no particular reason to locate the decree in the Peloponnesian War rather than, for example, after the Egyptian disaster of the 450s.

I do not in fact think that the evidence is sufficiently compelling to make us believe in the decree at all, or, even if it was passed, that it really reflected an imbalance in the sex ratio of the citizen population. It is worth noting that Plutarch also retails the story about Socrates and Myrto (in his *Life of Aristides*, 27), but observes that Panaetius had refuted it 'sufficiently' in his work on Socrates. Clearly, Plutarch was not convinced either. Overall, I do not think that the evidence is sufficient to persuade us of a significant imbalance in the sex ratio, and it seems reasonable to assume that the number of women was roughly the same as the number of men at the beginning of the Peloponnesian War.

That conclusion in itself may suggest that Pomeroy was right to suggest that girl children were more likely to be the victims of exposure and infanticide than boy children. In between the two passages quoted above, Pomeroy noted that the 'natural mortality of infants in classical Athens was so high as to preclude the wholesale practice of infanticide', but that nonetheless 'it was practised to some extent' and 'that more female infants were disposed of than male'.[62] Young men were more likely to be killed or to emigrate. Precisely this absence of evidence for an excess of women, especially women of marriageable age, has been used to support the idea that the Athenians chose not to rear as many girl children as boys.[63]

The extent to which infanticide was practised in Greece has, of course, been a subject of long-running debate.[64] It is worth

---

[62] Pomeroy 1975, 69.
[63] Golden 1981.
[64] Bresson 2016, 51–4, provides a useful summary with further references. Golden 1981 and Ingalls 2002 present different views, specifically on classical Athens.

observing that almost all of the clear evidence for infanticide as such in Greece comes from the Hellenistic period, or the very end of the classical period at the earliest. The earliest literary evidence comes from Aristotle, who can, however, be quoted both by those arguing for widespread infanticide and those arguing against it.[65] The lack of a clear consensus about how common infanticide was may just be due to variations across time and space. While it seems probable that infanticide was always a possibility in the Greek world, its frequency was surely different in different circumstances.

Bresson has suggested plausibly in this context that the possibility of temporarily decreasing the incidence of population control measures, including infanticide, and thus of increasing the effective birth rate, may help to explain how classical Greek cities were able to sustain high levels of military casualties; on the other hand, intensification of those measures could help prevent a population outstripping its economic resources.[66] Athens' population was able to grow rapidly during the early part of the fifth century, absorb heavy casualties before and during the Peloponnesian War, and then recover and grow again through the fourth century. This may be an indication that infanticide was relatively rare in this particular classical city, as well as being a reflection of the city's relative wealth.

[65] So Ingalls 2002, 248 (against); Bresson 2016, 51 (for).
[66] Bresson 2016, 54.

CHAPTER 3

POPULATION SIZE 1: CITIZENS

Introduction

In this chapter, I look at the evidence for the size of the citizen population in Athens in the classical period and comment on its interpretation. We have already seen that it has primarily been an interest in the political history of the democratic city that has driven interest in the number of citizens.[1] In later chapters, the main focus will be on the total population, inclusive of the women and children in citizen families, and of their slaves, and of the free non-citizen residents of Attica, the metics. The citizen population is treated separately here, because most of the evidence we have for numbers of people in particular groups concerns citizens. There are specific issues concerning that evidence and its interpretation that can be addressed most simply in isolation. Moreover, as will become clear in Chapter 4, assessments of the size of non-citizen groups often have to be framed in terms of their size relative to that of the citizen population.

Hansen's *Demography and Democracy* has to be our starting point.[2] This book represents by far the most systematic and sophisticated attempt to grapple with these issues, certainly as far as the fourth century is concerned. Still widely accepted as the standard account of Athenian historical demography, as we have seen, it inevitably forms a focus of discussion in this chapter. As Hansen describes it in his preface, his project arose out of his unwillingness to trust the assumptions that previous historians had made about the Athenian population.[3] Hansen himself resists, to an impressive

[1] Gomme 1933, 1–2; echoed in Hansen 1985, 5–6.
[2] Hansen 1985.
[3] Hansen 1985, 5.

degree, any tendency to make easy assumptions of his own. Each stage in his argument is carefully argued – and most of the arguments are persuasive. It is worth emphasising that in broad terms, Hansen's conclusions and many of his detailed arguments about 'the number of Athenian citizens in the fourth century BC' can be accepted and need only to be briefly summarised here. However, there are some points that need additional comment and further exploration. In particular, the extent to which a similar approach can be applied to the fifth century is important, especially as Hansen himself clearly thought that it could not.[4] But we can start by following Hansen into the fourth century.

Hansen and the Fourth Century

Hansen began his account by considering seven 'general problems of historical demography and historical method'. These were:

1 What does it mean to say 'in the fourth century, the total number of adult male Athenian citizens was x thousand'?
2 What are the demographic peculiarities of a legally defined citizen population as against a geographically defined population?
3 Which is the proper analogy to be used when we make assumptions about the age distribution of adult male Athenians?
4 Did the Athenians themselves know the exact number of citizens?
5 How can the information we have about army strengths be used in calculations of the entire citizen population?
6 Can information about squadrons of triremes manned with Athenians be used in calculations of the total number of citizens?
7 Is it possible to use information about grain supply and grain consumption to say anything about the number of citizens?[5]

Each of these is an important question (although some are quite specific, and not really very general), but they do not all require lengthy answers.

I discussed in Chapter 2 how we should answer Question 3. Questions 1 and 2 are closely related to one other, as both address the basic demographic issue of how the term 'population' is to be defined. Clearly, a distinction can be drawn between 'all the

---

[4] Hansen 1981; 1982.
[5] Hansen 1985, 7.

citizens of Athens' and 'all the citizens of Athens actually normally *resident in Attica*'. It is quite possible, even likely, that there were at various times during the classical period significant numbers of Athenian citizens who were, for various reasons, normally resident elsewhere. Ultimately what is meant by 'population' will depend on the interests of the person asking the question and their reasons for wanting an answer.[6] For many historical purposes, the greater interest lies in quantifying the number of citizens who were normally resident in Attica and so immediately available for military and political activity, and who were directly engaged in economic production and consumption. It is not surprising that this is where Hansen's own focus lies. Most of our evidence concerns precisely those citizens who were politically and militarily active. While the distinction is theoretically important, then, it is not an issue that needs to detain us here any longer than it detained Hansen.

There is, nonetheless, an important series of questions to do with the numbers of citizens who left Athens to take part in colonial foundations and (possibly) cleruchies. The complexities are illustrated by the case of Chalkis in Euboea.[7] Herodotus describes at 5.77 how a cleruchy was established (in 506 BC) which involved 4,000 Athenian citizens. This would obviously be demographically significant, but the cleruchy seems to have come to an end in 490 (Herodotus describes the departure of the cleruchs, who appear not to have returned, at 6.100). Even during the years that the cleruchy existed, it is not entirely clear that the cleruchs had moved permanently from Attica. The passages of Herodotus are usually interpreted to imply that the cleruchs were permanent residents on the lots of land they were apportioned, as for example by Jones, who interpreted 5.77 and 6.100 as 'proving' the point.[8] However, Moreno infers from exactly the same passages that 'most or all of the Athenian cleruchs resided *in Athens*, and not in the cleruchy at Chalkis'.[9] Jones' reading seems to me

---

[6] Hansen 1985, 8–9; Newell 1988, 9–10.
[7] Jones 1957, 166–78; Graham 1983, 166–210; Figueira 1991, especially 201–17. Moreno 2007, 77–143.
[8] Jones 1957, 175.
[9] Moreno 2007, 94.

a more natural one, but Moreno is surely right to stress the proximity of the cleruchy to Attica; probably we should imagine frequent traffic to and fro across the straits rather than sporadic mass movements. Either way, the line between the total number of citizens and the number of citizens in Attica is blurred. This should be kept in mind throughout what follows.

Hansen's arguments that the answer to Questions 4 and 7 is basically 'no' are convincing. It is hard to imagine circumstances in which it would actually have occurred to anyone in classical Athens to ask how many citizens there actually were in total – as opposed to the number who were available to perform some military or financial services for the city – and there is certainly little indication in contemporary sources that it did. This may have changed after 322, however. Van Wees has argued that the census carried out by Demetrius of Phaleron (which on his account would have been held in 317) would have involved such a comprehensive count, owing to the unusual political circumstances that made it necessary.[10] Even so, the task would surely have been nearly impossible. Carrying out censuses to a useful level of accuracy strains the abilities of advanced modern state bureaucracies, even where there exist both an established tradition of such censuses and consistent records of vital rates (without which census data are hard to evaluate).[11] In classical Athens, the tools and expertise simply did not exist. There appears to have been no central register of citizens; the practical usefulness (for demographic purposes) of the records maintained by the individual demes in the form of the *lexiarchika grammateia* would have been extremely limited, even if those purposes had been part of their function.[12] Peter Fawcett has suggested that the registers would have been used for taxation records (or at least records of who was liable for certain taxes). This makes sense, and might have made the records more useful for census purposes, but the evidence he cites (including Demosthenes 50.8, where the reading of 'demarchs' is not wholly secure) is rather slight.[13]

---

[10] Van Wees 2011; see note 33 below.
[11] Hollingsworth 1969, 20–34; Newell 1988, 13–21.
[12] Osborne 1985, 72–3; cf. Rhodes 1981, 494–8.
[13] Fawcett 2016, 176.

'Information' about grain supply and consumption is no more abundant than that for population; in practice, attempts to quantify aggregate grain consumption for classical Athens tend to start from attempts to quantify the population and then move on to discussion of likely rates of per capita consumption.[14] There are no ancient figures for the amount of grain Athenians ate in a year.[15] The quantity of grain that Attica could produce in an 'average' year is difficult to assess, owing to persistent controversy over the agricultural strategies employed and so the 'carrying capacity' of the land – which is itself affected by the population density.[16] In any case, it is well known that Athens imported grain in substantial quantities in many, if not all, years during the classical period, and Attica's carrying capacity did not mark an upper limit to or an approximation of its actual population. This might not matter if there were reliable figures for the total amount of grain that was imported to make up the shortfall, but such figures do not exist either. There is of course some evidence for the scale of food imports, but it is at least as problematic to interpret as the evidence for population size. Where there are figures for grain distributions (from one-off 'gifts' from overseas), a major problem is that it is not clear – to say the least – that every citizen received a hand-out.

Hansen's own attempt to formulate an answer to the question is this:

All attempts to calculate the size of the population of Attica from the annual consumption of grain, produced and imported, must in my opinion be rejected because (a) it is extremely difficult to calculate the amount of grain produced in Attica; (b) it is impossible to calculate the total import of grain; and (c) the calculations made so far have been based on a consumption of wheat, whereas the sources indicate that the basic constituent of the Athenians' diet was barley.[17]

---

[14] So, for example, Garnsey 1988, 89–90; Whitby 1998, 109–14. Most recently: Moreno 2007, 28–31; Oliver 2007, 76–87; Bissa 2009, 171–2.

[15] Foxhall and Forbes 1982 underlies all more recent attempts to get to grips with the issue; see also Moreno 2007, 31–2; Bissa 2009, 173; and 183–187 in Chapter 6. O'Connor 2013 also documents the reliance of subsequent scholarship on this article, and has important comments on the methodology employed; but his concern is with the rations for active-duty soldiers and sailors, not the population at large.

[16] Sallares 1991, 73–84; Forsdyke 2006; Halstead 2014, especially 33–47.

[17] Hansen 1985, 43.

Hansen's point (c) has been comprehensively addressed in more recent accounts; unfortunately, this is the least important of the three.[18]

From Hansen's list of seven general questions, then, we are left with the two about Athens' military strength. For much of the classical period, Athens was of course best known for its naval capability, and the fleet employed a significant proportion of the city's available military manpower. Hansen's question 6 is therefore an important one. However, the answer is still effectively 'no'. In his conclusion, Hansen neatly summarises one of the essential points: 'when we use information about Athenian navies for calculations of the number of citizens, we must assume that no Athenian squadron was ever manned exclusively with Athenian citizens. On the other hand, some Athenians must have served in any squadron sent out from Athens'.[19]

While it is widely (if still not universally) accepted that a full-strength trireme crew of the fifth and fourth centuries was in the order of 200 men, of whom around 170 would have been rowers, it is unknown in any given case how many of these men might have been Athenian citizens, and how many would have been non-citizen residents of Attica (slaves and metics) and/or 'foreign' mercenaries. Nor is it always clear that the ships in any given squadron or fleet were actually fully manned, although Wallinga's claim that 'even in the Athenian navy undermanning was habitual' is surely overstating the case.[20] Given that the whole point of the trireme design was to pack as many rowers into the hull as possible, it seems rather unlikely that many would have been sent out seriously undermanned; one fully crewed ship would have been vastly more effective than two half-crewed ones.[21] Most of Wallinga's arguments to the contrary are addressed by Gabrielsen.[22] Wallinga's observation about the versatility of the trireme design (that it could act, without major alteration, as an

---

[18] Garnsey 1988, 105; Keen 1993; Whitby 1998; Moreno 2007, 3–33; Bissa 2009, 169–91; Bresson 2016, 405–14.

[19] Hansen 1985, 65–6; the full discussions of trireme crews are on 21–4 and 43–5.

[20] Wallinga 1993, 174. See, for further scepticism, Tilley 2012, 123.

[21] Morrison, Coates, and Rankov 2000, 107 note 1.

[22] Wallinga 1982, 1993; Gabrielsen 1994, 109, 249 note 11. Papalas 2012, 105–7, responds to Tilley's scepticism (note 20 above); much the same ground is being covered again.

effective troop-carrier as well as a fighting ship) is a good one in itself, but this still seems more likely to have been a useful secondary benefit to large-scale users such as Athens than something that was appealing to small cities. Wallinga is quite right to observe that there must have been occasions when triremes could not have been fully manned, and it is impossible to argue with his conclusion that 'we must realise that numbers of ships in the traditions of the Aegean world cannot be translated into manpower in any simple way, and can even less be taken as a yardstick for actual naval power'.[23] However, his quotation from Thucydides 6.50.2 cannot bear the weight that he puts upon it, which is to establish a position that trireme fleets were effectively never fully crewed. Nor are his arguments that differences in ship performance within a single fleet can only be explained by differences in levels of manning (as opposed to the quality or experience of individual crews, or the physical qualities of the ships and their construction) particularly convincing. In practice, it seems reasonable to accept that Athenian fleets were generally sent out with reasonably complete crew complements, except in those circumstances where the intention was to find full crews elsewhere.

On the other hand, there is so little information about the manning of Athenian warships that this is less important for demographic purposes than it might appear. If we were absolutely sure that every Athenian trireme to leave the Piraeus were crewed with exactly 200 men, then this would of course be of potential interest for the total size of the male population of Athens *if* every one of those men had been a long-term resident of Attica. Because at least some of the crew were certainly slaves and metics, the data would still be of very limited value for assessing the numbers of citizens. While that would be disappointing for Hansen, it would be less so for other questions. Nonetheless, it is certain that, at least when Athens' ambitions were at their height and when the money was available, significant numbers of mercenaries were employed in the fleet too. Under the fifth-century empire, this would presumably have included, but not been limited to, men from those

---

[23] Wallinga 1993, 182.

allied cities that had no fleets of their own.[24] There were times when the number of mercenaries must have been small, for lack of money to pay them; unfortunately (but hardly unexpectedly), these are not usually the times when we have important or useful information about fleet sizes.

All of which leaves us with Hansen's fifth question: how can the information we have about army strengths be used in calculations of the entire citizen population? It is worth noting that the phrasing of the question takes for granted that this evidence is going to be useful at least in some way. This is less surprising when one considers the list of the categories of evidence that are available, which is Hansen's next subject. It is also only fair to point out that Hansen is under few illusions about the quality of this kind of evidence, and his careful discussion, here and elsewhere, of the methodological issues provides a convincing answer to this question.

Before looking in more detail at this answer, it is worth looking at Hansen's useful summary of the evidence that we *do* have, which he breaks down into seven (again) categories:

Our sources [for the number of citizens in fourth-century Athens] can be subsumed under the following seven headings. (1) Rough estimates of the total citizen population, mentioned in passing. (2) Counts of all citizens in connection with a change of the constitution. (3) Army figures giving the number of citizens called up and/or sent out on a campaign. (4) Naval figures stating the number of triremes (quadriremes) launched, and sometimes how they were manned. (5) The number of recipients when grain or money was distributed among the Athenians. (6) Epigraphical evidence for the number of ephebes. (7) The number of citizens required to run the council of five hundred constitutionally.[25]

This list refers explicitly to the sources Hansen had for the fourth century, but it is just as applicable to the whole of the classical period. For anyone even vaguely familiar with the historical demography of other times and places, however, this list makes depressing reading, especially as it deals only with the citizen population – which is relatively *well* documented. It is instructive (and mildly alarming, from the point of view of the ancient

---

[24] Morrison, Coates, and Rankov 2000, 107–26; Gabrielsen 1994, 105–10; Graham 1992, 1998.

[25] Hansen 1985, 26.

historian) to compare this list with the one provided in Hollingsworth's book on historical demography.[26] There is nothing here that will give us any of the crucial data of vital rates. There are no first-hand census data, only more or less dubious reports of alleged censuses whose purposes, even if they actually took place, are not clear. What Hansen regards as the most promising kind of source, the army figures, are likewise not original documents but reports in the writings of historians of varying (but mainly poor) reliability. The perils of putting too much weight on such figures were vividly illustrated by David Henige.[27] Although no explicit mention is made of Athens at this point in Henige's book, these pages should make uncomfortable reading for anyone trying to use *Demography and Democracy*. However, complaining about the inadequacy of the sources does nothing to improve their quality.

Before moving on, though, the absence of archaeological data from the list deserves some mention. This absence is not entirely the result of prejudice or ignorance on the part of historians of classical Athens. Rather, the current state of the available archaeological evidence does not allow it to be usefully employed to answer the kinds of questions that historians tend to want to ask about the population of Athens. One obvious response to this would be that perhaps those historians might want to cultivate an interest in questions that *can* be answered. I hope that what follows will show that there is actually some point in pursuing these particular text-based questions a little further. However, at the end of this chapter, I shall return to the existing archaeological data.[28]

The seven categories laid out by Hansen are not of equal value; his own conclusions in the end depend principally on his

---

[26] Hollingsworth 1969, 42–4.

[27] Henige 1998, 287–8.

[28] Scheidel 2008, 49–54, reached a similar conclusion for Roman Italy; Hin 2013 is (probably rightly) optimistic about the potential of skeletal and environmental data, but even in the case of republican and early imperial Rome, most of the work lies in the future; for classical Athens, aspirations are almost all we have available. Hin's chapter 8 provides a useful consideration of both the use and limitations of surface survey data for issues of population size in republican Italy; such data are, of course, vastly more abundant for Italy, and have important implications for historical interpretation (as in Launaro 2011); again, almost nothing like them exists for classical Athens (for the exceptions, see 84–88 below).

categories 3, 4, and 7: the army figures (which are supplemented by and interpreted in the light of the figures for naval mobilisation, which are less precise and harder to evaluate), and the operation of the Council of 500.[29] Most of the additional material in the other categories (1, 2, 5, and 6) turns out in fact to be of little or no value in this context, and needs only to be summarised briefly.

Under the first category, of 'rough estimates of the total citizen population, mentioned in passing', there are in fact only two items: Aristophanes *Ecclesiazusae* 1131–3 and Demosthenes *Against Aristogeiton* 25.51. Neither can be pushed at all as sources of demographic data; both seem in fact to fall into a larger category of cases where a figure of either two or three myriads is used as a conventional big number for a total citizen body, in practice meaning nothing more than 'lots'.[30]

The second category, 'counts of all citizens in connection with a change of the constitution', also contains only two items: the two episodes in question are those of 322/1, when an oligarchy was established by Antipater, and under the rule of Demetrius of Phaleron (i.e., between 317 and 307). During the former, political rights were restricted only to those Athenians who possessed property worth at least 2,000 drachmas. As a result, many citizens were disfranchised. The story is reported in both Diodorus Siculus (18.18) and Plutarch (*Phocion* 28). The problem is that they disagree on the number of citizens disfranchised; Diodorus puts the figure at 22,000, while Plutarch puts it at 12,000. There is no way to tell which (if either) is right. There is no indication as to the number of citizens who *retained* their rights as citizens in Plutarch; Diodorus, however, gives the figure as 9,000.[31] In the context of Hansen's discussion and his debate with Ruschenbusch, the passage assumed greater (apparent) importance: Plutarch's figure is apparently more consistent with a total citizen population of 20,000; Diodorus' only with one of nearer 30,000. Once these round figures are abandoned, however, the significance disappears. That is not to say that these passages are uninteresting in every respect – that the threshold was at 2,000 drachmas may be

---

[29] Hansen 1985, 65–9.
[30] Hansen 1985, 26–7.
[31] Hansen 1985, 29–30; see also note 33 below.

significant, as is the simple fact that thousands of citizens did not meet it. Van Wees has argued more recently that both figures are ultimately derived from Demetrius' census, and so are not of any value for the size of the population independent of those figures.[32]

The latter episode is reported in a fragment of Ctesicles preserved in Athenaeus (6.272c):

Ctesicles, in the third book of his annals, says that at Athens during the one hundred and seventeenth Olympiad a review of the inhabitants of Attica was carried out by Demetrius of Phalerum, and that there were found to be 21,000 Athenians, 10,000 metics, and 400,000 slaves.

There are a number of problems with interpreting this passage, but two immediately stand out. First, there is no clear indication as to the *purpose* of the census, which would affect both the interpretation of the figures and the likelihood of their bearing some relationship to reality. There is not a large number of possible alternatives, but nonetheless censuses carried out for reasons of taxation, military mobilisation, and eligibility for political participation would be subject to different biases and sources of inaccuracy. Second, there is the figure for slaves, no fewer than 400,000. Almost no one would now accept this figure; it seems far too high, not only relative to the size of the free population but relative to the land area of Attica. And if we cannot accept that figure, perhaps we should not have any more confidence in those for citizens and metics. This is not to say that this passage is without any value. On the contrary, it is very revealing about *perceptions* of the structure of the population of late fourth-century Athens. But it is surely of, at best, limited use as direct evidence for the actual size of that population.[33]

The fifth category in Hansen's list, 'the number of recipients when grain or money was distributed among the Athenians', contains a small number of items. The problem with these is

---

[32] Van Wees 2011.

[33] Hansen 1985 argues that the figure for citizens must be consistent with his general picture of the fourth century; Hansen 1988, 10–11, discusses his figure for metics. Van Wees 2011 suggests that 'Demetrius' census figure deserves more serious attention than most ancient numbers and we should take seriously the possibility that in fourth-century Attica the slaves really outnumbered the free by some margin' (112). Van Wees' arguments, however, do not challenge Hansen's view on the number of citizens in the fourth century before 322 (nearer 30,000 than 20,000).

that, even where the numbers quoted seem to be credible in themselves, they are rather low. Hansen's crucial observation was that in no case is it necessary to infer that *every* citizen was able in practice to benefit from the distributions.

The sixth category of evidence in Hansen's list is the ephebic inscriptions. Hansen concluded that in the 330s and 320s there were on average about 500 ephebes every year.[34] Given that the ephebes were trained in the skills needed by peltasts and other light-armed troops, as well as those needed by hoplites, that the hoplite equipment of the late fourth century was less elaborate and less expensive than it had been in archaic and early classical periods, and that the irreducible minimum equipment of spear and shield was now provided to every Athenian ephebe on the completion of his training, Hansen saw no reason to doubt that Athenians from all of the Solonian property classes participated in the ephebeia.[35] On the other hand, he still found it unlikely that *every* citizen took part, in spite of the fact that this is what is implied by the Aristotelian *Athenaion Politeia*, and seems to be explicitly stated by Lycurgus.[36] The Lycurgus passage is slightly problematic for Hansen's argument, since the orator claims that every citizen swears an oath when their name is entered into the *lexiarchikon grammateion* of their deme and becomes an ephebe. The problem is not completely insuperable, however. Lycurgus may just be exaggerating. Alternatively, it could be observed that his emphasis here is on the swearing of the ephebic oath, rather than on the completion of the full course of military training described by Pseudo-Aristotle, and that the two need not have been inextricably linked.

Some men would simply have been physically unfit. Perhaps more significantly, the number of ephebes provided by individual demes seems in a number of cases to have been significantly fewer than their bouleutic quota, but the demes in question had no difficulty filling that quota.[37] This rather implies that not everyone

---

[34] Hansen 1985, 47–50. He discusses additional material in 2006b, 33–8, but does not alter his basic conclusion.
[35] Hansen 1985, 48–9; Rhodes 1981, 503.
[36] *Ath. Pol.* 42. *Lyc.* 1.76.
[37] Hansen 1985, 77–9.

who served as a *bouleutes* had necessarily previously been an ephebe – especially since not everyone who had been an ephebe would have survived to the age of 30. Hansen thought it a 'reasonable assumption' (49) that 'at least a fifth of the ephebes would die before the age of 30'. This is actually a rather more pessimistic view of early adult mortality than is suggested by his model of age distribution; the figure of a fifth is presumably instead derived from his belief that that was roughly the proportion of the members of the *boulē* in a typical year who would be serving for a second time, and is meant only to imply that the figures for ephebes and *bouleutai* can be directly compared.[38] This might be problematic, except for the facts that Hansen argued that the average age of the *bouleutai* was likely to be closer to 40 than 30, and, as we have seen, that early adult mortality was perhaps higher than Hansen thought (although still not quite that high). In any case, the crucial point for Hansen was that it is not possible to tell exactly what proportion of the citizen population participated in the ephebeia (and were commemorated in inscriptions), and so the ephebic inscriptions are not much help with assessing the total number of citizens. This remains a sound conclusion.[39]

Hansen and Army Figures

Hansen's key conclusions about the size of the Athenian citizen population therefore depend on two main foundations: the operation of the institutions of the democracy, especially that of the Council of 500, and the cumulative evidence for Athens' military potential in the fourth century.[40] Although Hansen does not present it this way, the latter should perhaps be seen as more important. There is a danger for the political historian of circular reasoning in using the democratic institutions for demographic arguments. The size of the Athenian citizen population is interesting in part because of what it would mean for the scale of participation in democratic institutions; to derive information from the

[38] Hansen 1985, 31–64.
[39] See also Hansen 2006a for recent discussion; again, this does not seriously affect the original conclusion.
[40] Hansen 1985, 67–8.

operation of those institutions for demographic purposes requires assumptions to be made about the scale of that participation. This is true even for the operation of the Council of 500, which superficially appears to be a straightforward case because of the lower age limit on service and the restriction to two terms of service. While strict application of these rules would impose an absolute lower limit on the size of the citizen population, such a minimum figure is of limited use in helping towards a realistic total without some indication of how many people actually served on the Council and how many did so twice. While there is *some* evidence relevant to these questions, none of it is definitive.[41]

It is not surprising, therefore, that Hansen devotes so much attention to the army figures in the written sources. In finding himself having to use these figures, he was in essentially the same position as all his predecessors in the field, but his handling of the difficulties in their interpretation is uniquely detailed.

There are a number of problems – some obvious, some less so – involved in the use of army figures for historical demography. It is clearly not possible straightforwardly to infer the size of a population from the size of an army that is fielded by that population. And even before that stage is reached, we have to consider whether or not the army figures we have are at all accurate in the first place. There is nothing intrinsically more trustworthy about a figure given for the size of an army than there is any of the alleged population figures in the sources which have already been rejected. Sometimes the numbers in ancient sources are so large that they cannot possibly be credible. Most infamous in this regard is surely Herodotus' figure for the size of the Persian force available for the invasion of Greece in 480. There really is no way that Herodotus' figures here (a total of more than 5,000,000) can be true. It would be futile to try to infer anything at all about the size of the population of the Persian empire from this (except that the Greeks thought that it was big).

But this is an extreme example, whose falsity is easily revealed. The trouble is that not all such figures are so obviously ludicrous, and assessing their worth is rather harder. One such case is considered

---

[41] Hansen 2006b has a summary, with references.

briefly by Hansen.[42] This is Diodorus 15.29.7, where it is claimed that in 378 (actually placed by Diodorus under 377/6), the Athenians voted to levy 20,000 hoplites and 500 cavalry, and to man 200 ships, in order to make war on the Spartans. The figure for *hippeis* seems unremarkable.[43] The figure for hoplites is extremely large. Athenian field armies of the fourth century seem usually to have been of the order of 5,000 or 6,000 hoplites.[44] The only way that the 20,000 figure could be right would be if it included pretty much every man in Athens who owned hoplite equipment and was even notionally capable of bearing it. We might compare Thucydides 2.13, where at the beginning of the Peloponnesian War, Athens could apparently deploy 13,000 hoplites for field service, with another 16,000 metics and old and young citizens for garrison duty, along with over 1,000 cavalry. On the other hand, ownership of hoplite equipment could have been more widespread within the citizen population at the end of the fourth century than it had been in the fifth, especially if that equipment had become less elaborate over time. But if that 20,000 is supposed just to be a paper, rather than an effective, strength, then it is not too wildly implausible – or at least not obviously so, even if it would have taken a colossal effort actually to muster this many men. Indeed, if this passage is supposed to reflect the total number of men of hoplite status in Athens in the early 370s, then it would be crucial evidence for the size of the Athenian population at the time, better in this respect than most of the army figures we have (where a major problem is trying to work out what proportion of the whole population is represented).

Of course, 20,000 does look like a rather suspiciously round figure; whether we should think that this is the fault of Diodorus, his sources (at this point in the early fourth century, more than usually dubious), or a rather overenthusiastic and over-optimistic Athenian assembly is not clear. But a more serious problem seems to arise with the 200 triremes. Not all the 40,000-odd men that were needed to crew such a fleet would have had to be Athenian, however, and if 20,000 hoplites could be found, then presumably there would have been a few thousand men without hoplite arms to

---

[42] Hansen 1985, 40.
[43] Spence 1993, 83–5.
[44] See 53–55 below.

provide at least a minimal Athenian presence on each ship. So again, although it would imply a quite prodigious effort on the part of the Athenians, the manpower demands of a fleet of this size do not on their own seem obviously to demand quite the dismissive approach that Hansen adopts.[45]

The snag that fatally undermines confidence in this passage is in the ships themselves. Twice in the 370s, we are told the size of Athenian fleets. One occasion is a little later in Diodorus (15.34.5), when Chabrias has command of 83 triremes in an action off Naxos. The other is in Xenophon's *Hellenica* (6.2.21), where Timotheus is given command of 60 ships to help Corcyra. Significantly, he was fatally hampered (12.13) by his inability to find full crews for even this number. He was replaced by Iphicrates, who was able to scrape together a fleet of about 70 ships.

This rather gloomy picture from the literary sources of Athens' naval capability in the 370s is amply confirmed by the epigraphic testimony. *IG* ii² 1604, the earliest surviving inventory of the curators of the shipyards of Athens, suggests that in the mid-370s there were barely 100 hulls available, and not all of those would have necessarily been fully seaworthy or have had all their equipment. A fleet of two hundred triremes in 378/7 was clearly way beyond the resources available to the Athenians. And once again, when one figure can be shown definitely to be in error, it rather casts doubt on the others with which it is associated – in this case, the 20,000 hoplites. But if Diodorus 15.29.7 existed in isolation, it could not be so easily dismissed. This should be kept in mind whenever army figures are under discussion.

If this passage cannot be taken seriously, how much more weight can really be placed on any of the other figures Diodorus or anyone else gives us? The passages cited by Hansen for the fourth century are these:

- Xenophon *Hellenica* 4.2.17: 6,000 Athenian hoplites and 600 cavalry at Nemea in 394
- Diodorus 15.26.2, with 32.2: 5,000 hoplites and 500 cavalry sent to Thebes in 378

---

[45] Hansen 1985, 40: 'The size of both the army and the navy here is simply out of the question.'

- Polybius 2.62.6: 10,000 soldiers (*stratiotai*) sent to Thebes in 378, plus 100 triremes launched
- Diodorus 15.63.2: 12,000 men sent to the Peloponnese in 369, including 'young men' (*neoi*)
- Diodorus 15.84.2: 6,000 Athenian soldiers at Mantinea in 362
- Diodorus 16.37.3: 5,000 Athenian infantry and 400 cavalry at Thermopylae in 352
- Diodorus 18.10.2 and 11.3: all Athenians up to the age of 40 mobilised; 40 quadriremes and 200 triremes launched; 7 (out of 10) regiments (*phylai*) sent to Thessaly, amounting to 5,000 infantry and 500 cavalry, supported by 2,000 mercenaries; all during the Lamian War in 323.

Of all these passages, only one is taken from the works of an author who was alive at the time of the events being described, and Xenophon was not actually present at the battle of Nemea. Worse, he was not even at Athens but with the army of the Spartan king Agesilaus as it returned from Asia, with which he would fight against an army including Athenian troops at Coronea later the same year. It might reasonably be asked how well informed he was about the Athenian order of battle at Nemea. If one wanted to be generous, one could imagine that he could have spoken to Spartans who were present at the earlier battle; and, further, to think that they would have been in a position to estimate reasonably accurately the strength of the forces that opposed them. Or, alternatively, Xenophon could at a later date have been informed by an Athenian source who was willing to talk to him (and also possessed accurate information). But the passage itself does not inspire confidence in Xenophon's concern for accuracy in these matters:

The army opposing these contained the following numbers of hoplites. There were about 6,000 from Athens and, so it was said, about 7,000 from Argos; the Boeotians (since Orchomenus sent no troops) only produced 5,000; 3,000 came from Corinth, and from the whole of Euboea at least 3,000.

Xenophon goes on to deal with the cavalry and, even more vaguely, with the light-armed troops.

Our confidence is even further dented when we look at his order of battle for the Spartan side at 2.16. This is expressed in similarly vague terms, and manages to omit completely the Tegeans, whose presence is attested at sections 13 and 19. The latter passage implies that they were present in reasonably large numbers.

Polybius and Diodorus were much more remote from the events they describe than was Xenophon. If we want to make use of the numbers they quote, we have to make a number of assumptions: that *their* sources were in a position to obtain accurate information, and that they took the trouble accurately to record it. Still, leaving aside the impossible figures of Diodorus 15.29.7, the rest of Hansen's sources do present a consistent picture of Athenian military deployments throughout the fourth century. Partial mobilisations of 5,000 or 6,000 men supported by a few hundred cavalry are common; but, at a push, a full force of some 10,000 men could be fielded for operations outside Attica. This is consistent, argues Hansen, with the picture presented by what he considers the most important single piece of evidence: Diodorus 18.10.2 and 11.3, the Athenian military effort during the Lamian War in 323.[46]

This passage clearly represents the most detailed piece of evidence we have for the fourth century. It is less obvious that it is also the most reliable. However, it does seem that at the beginning of book 18, Diodorus is drawing on a different principal source from that which informed his narrative of Alexander's reign. Whether or not this source was actually Hieronymus of Cardia, it seems certainly to have been a writer with considerable specialised military knowledge and expertise.[47] Unlike the stylised and rhetorical descriptions of battles in earlier books, Diodorus' narrative of the wars of the Diadochi often provides detailed information on troop strengths, as well as on their dispositions and on tactical and technological innovations. The contrast with Xenophon and the earlier books of Diodorus could not be more marked, and perhaps Hansen is justified in his confidence in Diodorus' accuracy at 18.10.2 and 11.3. Still, if Diodorus' source in book 18 really was Hieronymus, one might wonder how well informed *he* could have been about Athens' military preparations in 323, even if we believe that he would have been as conscientious as possible about finding out.

But if we do not accept these figures as at least approximately right, we do not have any higher quality data with which to work,

---

[46] Hansen 1985, 66–8.
[47] Hornblower 1981, 33–40; Bosworth 2002, 25–6, 169–73, 208–9.

and so we are obliged to make the best of them. If they tell us nothing else, army figures should give us a minimum figure for the number of adult males in the society which deploys that army. However, no society ever sends all its men off to war, so we have to try to work out what proportion of all the men such an army represents. Clearly, this will involve making a number of assumptions, even before the choice of age distribution models is raised. Hansen's approach to these assumptions is thoughtful and detailed, and is worth returning to here.

When dealing with Athenian army figures in this context, we have at least one advantage in that we know that, in principle, every Athenian citizen was obliged to perform military duties in the service of the *polis*. But even at Athens, there must have been a number of men who were exempt from military service, either because they were required for the performance of other duties essential to the running of the city and its institutions, or because they were medically unfit.[48]

In general, the Athenian economy could probably have been left to be run by those *not* required for military duties (women, the old and the young, and some of the metics and slaves), especially as Athenian military operations on the whole did not (and could not at a high level of intensity) take place during the periods in the year when the demand for agricultural labour was at its greatest peaks (principally, although not exclusively, harvest). This was especially true in the fifth century; in the latter part of the fourth century, Philip of Macedon lengthened the campaigning season dramatically. (Demosthenes, in the third *Philippic*, gives a vivid indication of the problems the Athenians encountered in adapting to this new mode of warfare.)[49]

So there were very few Athenian citizens who would have had to be exempted from military service for strictly economic reasons. But some of the political institutions of the democracy needed the physical presence of some Athenians in Athens: Lycurgus 1.37 makes it clear that the *bouleutai*, at least, were exempted from military service. The passage actually describes

---

[48] Hansen 1985, 16–21; Christ 2006, 45–87.
[49] Demosthenes 9.48–52.

how the members of the Council were on this occasion armed and (it is implied) prepared physically to guard the Piraeus. But the context in which this happened was the immediate aftermath of the shattering defeat at Chaeronea in 338. It is admittedly in the speaker's interest to maximise the state of alarm that existed in the city at the time; but it is hard to believe that much exaggeration would have been required, as Athens genuinely had been at the mercy of Philip. Even now, the Council are not being sent out into the field, but down to the Piraeus, in the first instance to deliberate about its security. Even in a crisis of this scale, the councillors were not deployed in the regular army. It is reasonable to infer, then, that throughout the classical period, at least 500 men will have to be added to any army figures on the way to getting a total number of citizen males.[50]

While the councillors are easiest to quantify, and provide the most clear-cut case (in that they seem to have been automatically and unquestionably exempt), there was a wide range of further possible exemptions from military service.[51] Certainty over figures is impossible, especially as no two sets of circumstances will have been the same. But Hansen's estimate of around a thousand men exempted *ex officio* is probably around the right order of magnitude and can be accepted for the sake of argument.

Hansen himself implies that this 'cautious estimate' is a minimum. This may well be right: as Christ points out, Athenian citizens had many reasons to want to avoid military service, and 'almost any exemption could be abused'.[52] On the other hand, it would be possible to argue that the number cannot have been very much, if at all, greater than this. Presumably all the members of the Council would have been equally exempt, and it is hard to see, given that their role was considered important enough to gain them this exemption, how they could have been allowed, even if they wanted to, to go on campaign. With the other groups of people, it is much harder to be so confident. The passage at Demosthenes 59.27 implies that, even if you were technically exempt, there might still be considerable pressure on you to serve with your fellow citizens.

[50] Hansen 1985, 17.
[51] Summarised, with references, by Christ 2006, 53 note 23.
[52] Christ 2006, 54.

Christ is concerned to refute a (widely accepted) viewpoint which emphasises the social conditioning and pressures on citizens that would have encouraged a high level of compliance with conscription. While he presents a generally convincing alternative picture, Athens was, at the level of the individual demes, still a fairly small-scale society where those pressures to conformity might be expected to be strong. (An exception could perhaps be made for an outlier, in terms of size, such as Acharnai; its reputation for being particularly warlike is interesting in this context.) And while a convincing record of military participation was most important for those who wanted to pursue active political careers, any Athenian might be vulnerable to attack on the issue.

As Hansen himself observes, a thousand men is not a huge number, and of these, some will in any case have been exempted on grounds of age. It edges towards being significant only if one is committed to a very small total number of citizens. This is not an unimportant conclusion in itself, however.

More significant must have been the number of men who could not have served on the grounds of (temporary) ill health or (permanent) disability. No society has ever had an adult male population all of whom were physically capable of enduring combat, and the Athenians clearly did not approach the status of an exception. Even if one were inclined to doubt this, there are enough scattered references to disabled Athenian citizens to prove the point.[53] And if the twenty-fourth speech in the Lysianic corpus can be used as evidence for anything, it is firm confirmation that physical disability was not a bar to exercising the rights of a citizen. And, for what it is worth, Aristophanes *Wealth* 716–25 is about the unfortunate blind Neocleides, although we might note that, together with the similar passage in *Ecclesiazusae* (395–406), it hardly gives the impression that a citizen in this condition would have received much respect from his fellows if he tried actively to exercise those rights. None of this helps particularly with the proportion of unfit citizens, though.

As a result, Hansen turns to comparative evidence, drawing on the conscription records of those modern European states that have

---

[53] For example, Plato *Crito* 53a; Thucydides 2.49.7–8.

or had a national service system (which is to say pretty much all of them), which go back in most cases to the nineteenth century. Although there have been wide fluctuations between countries, individual recruiting districts, and from year to year, partly according to the rules that applied (and how they were enforced) and according to the demand for military manpower, Hansen argues that the number of people who *could not* be accepted was fairly constantly in the range of 8 per cent to 15 per cent. And this was for men almost entirely within the age range of 18 to 22. Given that the health status of the population of fourth-century Athens is unlikely to have been all that much better overall than that of the populations of nineteenth-century Europe, and given too that Athenian conscription affected older men between the ages of (probably) 20 and 40 or 50, Hansen argued that probably no more than 80 per cent of the citizen population in the relevant year classes could actually have been fit enough to fight.

Bresson has suggested that the health status of the population of classical Athens could in fact have been significantly better than this.[54] The case is not particularly strong, however. While he is right to observe that the causes of improved longevity and health status in Europe are complex and not straightforwardly related to the Industrial Revolution, there are few positive factors to point to in the ancient Greek world. Bresson emphasises the level of medical knowledge revealed by the Hippocratic corpus, but it is hard to see what actual benefits this would have brought, even to those who had reliable access to such knowledge. The best of the Hippocratic corpus reveals an impressive level of diagnostic skill, but rather less in the way of effective treatments (even if what the corpus reveals about non-Hippocratic medical practitioners is frequently even more alarming). While it is true, as Grmek noted, that there was probably a high level of knowledge and even skill about the treatment of the kinds of traumas inflicted in Greek warfare, the demographic impact of this would surely have been less than the prevalence of conflict in the first place. It would also not have been much help in treating the diseases to which Greek armies would surely have been prey in camps and especially

---

[54] Bresson 2016, 50–6.

the sieges, which were, if anything, an even more prevalent part of wars than open-field battles.[55] Likewise, the concerns of some *poleis* with water supply and (really pretty minimal) waste management, which Bresson also emphasises, need not have been of much real significance for living standards, even if that was the intention of the latter, which is not always clear. Schwartz takes a rather more pessimistic – perhaps even too pessimistic – view of the physical condition of hoplite soldiers.[56]

If we accept Hansen's argument, how we apply it to the army figures we have is still not entirely straightforward. A lot depends on the interpretation of the passages concerned. If the figures are given for the army present at a particular battle, then it would be natural to assume that this excludes men who were unable to serve. The problem then becomes one of determining what proportion of the total available military manpower was deployed for the campaign or battle in question. A minimum figure could be generated without too much difficulty; a force of, say, 6,000 fit men would imply a population in the relevant age groups of around 7,500 (or nearer 8,000 if the Council contained men who would otherwise have been available). But such a figure is obviously of only limited use.

Where we have a figure that claims to represent the whole of Athens' military strength, the problem is different. Even if the figure is credible in itself, it is usually hard to tell definitely whether the figure is to be taken as the number of soldiers who were actually available for operations on a given day or as a 'paper' strength (that is, the number of men were theoretically available, but of whom a portion would have been exempted, unfit, or otherwise unable to serve). And even a 'real' strength might include men who were temporarily disabled or unwell (it might be a theoretical number which simply excluded those who were exempted *ex officio* or from permanent disability) or it might not (it might reflect how many men could be expected actually to turn up, even if they were not always all the same men). Clearly, a range of intermediate positions is possible too. In the end,

---

[55] Grmek 1988, 27–33.
[56] Schwartz 2013, 165–8.

there is no way to tell; we just do not know how the authors of our historical accounts got their numbers, or how precise their sources are likely to have been.

In the end, we have to accept that precision is never possible and that the best we can do is make our assumptions clear and establish the plausible range of any numerical conclusions we draw. Hansen's analysis of the fourth-century evidence led him to conclude that in that period 'the number of citizens living in Attica never dropped below ca. 25,000 and often was ca. 30,000 or perhaps even more'.[57] This still seems a reasonable and fairly secure position, even if some of Hansen's premises are not accepted. What it does not do is tell us anything about the fifth century.

The Fifth Century

Nowhere does Hansen devote much interest to the fifth century, except in so far as it affects his model for the fourth. In terms of historical demography, this seems a curious omission, but it must be driven at least partly by Hansen's predominant interest in political history. The evidence for the fifth century is even less abundant than it is for the fourth, but it is not obviously of lower quality, at least compared to the three items on which Hansen's account, ultimately, depends.[58] Most of this evidence is not considered by Hansen; still the best existing discussion remains that provided by Cynthia Patterson in her account of the circumstances surrounding the passage of the so-called 'Periclean' citizenship law of 451/0.[59]

The relevant material is: (1) the form of the 'Cleisthenic' constitution and its demographic implications; (2) Herodotus' account of Athenian military manpower during the Persian Wars; (3) the so-called 'Decree of Themistocles'; (4) passing indications of the size of Athens' population during the *pentecontaetia*; (5) Thucydides 2.13 and the Athenian armed forces at the start

---

[57] Hansen 1985, 68.
[58] Hansen 1985, 67–8.
[59] C. Patterson 1981, 40–81.

of the Peloponnesian War. I shall take these in roughly chronological order.

1 *The Cleisthenic Constitution*

Lohmann's survey of what he convincingly identified as the deme of Atene shook (though did not everywhere completely undermine) what used to be a firm conviction that the 139 demes that are known for the classical period, and mostly for the fourth century, were all as old as the Cleisthenic reforms themselves. The old view was not an unreasonable assumption, however, and it may still be substantially true. It was based principally on the facts that (1) there is no mention in our sources of a systematic review of the deme system in the classical period (there is nothing to say that any deme was abolished or that new ones were added), and (2) membership in a deme was hereditary, so it would have required quite a major overhaul of the rules to subtract old demes (or even to add new ones, rather than shift them around the tribes). This is not, however, to say that it could not have happened or did not in practice happen. (Adjustment of the bouleutic quotas for each deme to keep them at least roughly in line with the populations of the demes is easier to imagine, at least in theory, although it is also very easy to imagine how this could have been a bone of contention for demes of all sizes.) Atene has generated virtually no evidence of any kind of activity in the sixth century, and it is indeed quite hard to imagine that it was one of the original Cleisthenic demes.[60]

If it really was not, then there must have been at least one constitutional rearrangement in the classical period about which we know nothing (and which must also have been a considerable administrative headache, if nothing else). Speculation about constitutional details need not detain us very long in this context, however. There is still no need to believe that the system with which we are most familiar from the fourth century was not essentially the same as that established by Cleisthenes. Even if the original Cleisthenic system did not include exactly 139 demes,

---

[60] Lohmann 1993.

it probably did include close to that number. In any case, no one would seriously argue that there were fewer than 100 demes.[61] The important point is that *irrespective* of whether any of the rules about membership of the Council were applied at the end of the sixth century, Attica contained a minimum of 100 local communities with a strong enough sense of identity to emerge as demes and persist in the long term, which implies quite a large population at this time. If the rule about serving on the Council no more than twice already applied, then the citizen population would probably already have to have been similar to that of the fourth century. As Patterson observed, though, if Rhodes was right to suggest that originally membership of the *boulē* was restricted to the top three *tele*, then it is unlikely that the restriction to two terms could practically have been enforced at the same time.[62] On the other hand, Athens' military effort in the Persian Wars seems to have been quite closely comparable to what it could manage throughout the fourth century. Gomme's estimate of 35,000 citizens for 480 was probably too high, for many of the reasons that Patterson provided (although her argument about the likely size of the urban population seems to be based on faulty premises). Such evidence as we have, as Patterson observes, in spite of her reluctance to quote a specific figure, is still consistent with a figure of at least 25,000 to 30,000.[63] 'At least' because the figure could be higher, if any of the arguments about the relative cheapness of hoplite warfare in the fourth century have any weight; one would expect the hoplites to have been a smaller fraction of the total citizen population at the beginning of the fifth century than at any subsequent period.

2 *Herodotus and Athenian Military Manpower in the Persian Wars*

Herodotus 9.28 provides the sizes of the forces supplied by the allied Greek cities at the battle of Plataea in 479. Athens is supposed to have sent 8,000 hoplites; it could also be inferred

---

[61] Herodotus 5.69.
[62] C. Patterson 1981, 55–6.
[63] C. Patterson 1981, 68.

that there were about 8,000 light-armed troops from Athens. Gomme reckoned that Herodotus was among the 'incompetent authorities' on army strengths, and it is easy to see why; nonetheless, this figure is not wildly implausible in the way that his figures for the Persian army are.[64] It is notable that Herodotus nowhere provides numbers for the armies at the battle of Marathon. The figures we have for that earlier battle are provided by late sources. Justin (2.9) has 10,000 Athenians, Nepos (*Miltiades* 5) 9,000; both add 1,000 Plataeans. The number for the Plataeans seems fairly clearly to be an exaggeration, or at best the result of some very generous rounding up. The 10,000 figure (whether for Athenians alone or including their allies) may not be far off the mark, but is not authoritative. It could, as How and Wells observe, have been derived from a calculation of 1,000 men to a Cleisthenic tribe; alternatively, it could have been rounded up from Herodotus' Plataea number on the grounds that a self-defence force would be a larger muster than an expeditionary force into a neighbouring area.[65]

3 The 'Decree of Themistocles'

This inscription purports to record provisions made for the evacuation of Attica and the manning of the fleet in the face of Xerxes' invasion in 480.[66] The stone we have may be as late as the third century; presumably it was something very similar to what we have that Aeschines recited in 348.[67] How closely it replicates anything that was actually said or done in 480 is unclear, and rehearsing the arguments here is unlikely to achieve much. For the moment, it is worth considering what the implications are if we assume that the text does preserve at least the content (if not completely the form) of the decisions taken when Athens faced one of its most severe crises. The relevant lines here are 12–35, which deal with the launching and manning of some two hundred ships. Each ship was to have a trierarch, ten marines, four archers,

---

[64] Gomme 1933, 3.
[65] How and Wells 1912, vol. 2, 114, on 6.117. Van Wees 2006, 373–5.
[66] *ML* 23, with Hammond 1982.
[67] Demosthenes 19 (*On the False Embassy*) 303.

an unspecified number of men in the *huperesia* (specialist officers and crew – there need not have been more than a dozen in this instance, but there cannot really have been many fewer than half this number either), and 100 men as rowers, taken from the Athenian citizens and the 'foreigners (*xenoi*) registered with the Polemarch' (that is, the metics, although not called by that name here: it would have been inappropriate to use a term with derogatory implications in an honorific context).[68] The decree makes provision for a crew of about 120 men for each of 200 ships, for a total of 24,000.

There are a number of important things to note. The first is that while it is made explicit that the trierarchs can be no older than 50, and the marines have to be between 20 and 30, no age groups are specified for the rest of the crew. It would be reasonable to infer, however, that (in line with what may have been the normal practice for land armies) they were those aged up to 40 (or 45). In that case, the limit for trierarchs could have been raised to ensure a big enough pool to provide 200 suitable candidates. The decree specifies that they have to own property at Athens and have legitimate children; in practice, one imagines (and hopes, for the sake of the crews) that the criteria for command, whether conceived in terms of social status or military competence, would have been more stringent. The marines are chosen from the physical cream of the military age groups.

The second is that the figure includes both citizens and non-citizens, with no way to tell the relative proportions. Van Wees takes it that the ratio was much the same as he suggests that it was in the hoplite force of 431, or perhaps a little greater in favour of the citizens (and so roughly a sixth of the crew, 20 of the 120 in each ship, might have been metics).[69] This is not implausible in itself, although it might be challenged on two grounds. Van Wees may have understated the number of metic hoplites available in

[68] See below, 137, on the metics. The roles identified in Pseudo-Xenophon 1.2 – helmsman, rowing master, bow officer, pentecontarch (apparently effectively the purser), and shipwright (and perhaps a flute player, as in *IG* ii² 1951) – would seem to be an irreducible minimum for the *huperesia* even for a short campaign – but there may also have been specialist gangs of deckhands to work the ships under sail.
[69] Van Wees 2004, 243.

65

431. On the other hand, it would not be unreasonable to suggest that, whatever the origins of the metics, their numbers may have been substantially larger, in both absolute and relative terms, near the end of the *pentecontaetia* compared to its beginning.[70]

Third, the evidence we have throughout the classical period seems to suggest that a trireme's normal crew complement was around 200, of whom 170 were oarsmen.[71] Granted that in an emergency some shorthandedness in the deck crews could probably be accepted, still there seem to be 60 or 70 rowers missing. Were the ships for the Salamis campaign sent out undermanned, in order to get as many hulls in the water as possible? Assuming for the moment that they were not, the missing rowers have to be accounted for.[72] The simplest explanation is that they were slaves. Graham showed that there is no reason to doubt that the Athenians made regular use of slave oarsmen in their ships throughout the fifth century.[73] At a time of acute military crisis, all available manpower would surely have been deployed. The large-scale adoption of chattel slavery in sixth-century Athens is widely accepted.[74] It is also possible that the Athenians, even if they did not suffer from the same level of anxiety that the Spartans displayed, would have wanted to keep their slaves of military age where they could keep an eye on them when they went out *en masse* to fight for the survival of their *polis*, rather than leaving them with their women and children in Troezen.

It is important to recall in this context the later mobilisation of slave manpower for the Arginusae campaign.[75] This was exceptional, and is therefore prominent in our literary sources, but that does not mean that it was unprecedented, or that the large-scale use of slaves for the Salamis campaign was unlikely or impossible. The two situations were similar in that Athens desperately needed naval crew if it were to survive. What was different in the latter

---

[70] See 120–138 in Chapter 4. The origins of metic status are a potentially vexed issue: see Watson 2010.

[71] Morrison, Coates, and Rankov 2000, 111.

[72] See 43–44 above on responses to Wallinga's undermanning argument.

[73] Graham 1992, 1998.

[74] Garlan 1988, 37–40; Fisher 1993, 15–20; Morris 2002, 31–41; Patterson 2007, 155–7; Rihll 2011, 48.

[75] Xen. *Hell.* 1.6.24; Hellanicus *FGrH* 323a F 25.

case was that the slaves had to be promised not just manumission but enfranchisement to secure their loyalty. No such reward (and not even explicit recognition in the Themistocles decree) was provided for the slaves in 480 – but perhaps it did not have to be. The slaves were rowing in ships which all had crews with a clear majority of free men in them; the latter could collectively wield a large enough stick that no carrot was necessary.

4 *During the* Pentecontaetia

Between the Athenian musters for the Persian Wars and her military strength on the eve of the Peloponnesian War, there is little useful direct evidence. The clearest and most explicit piece of information here is a reference to one of the grain distributions. In Philochorus fr. 119, it is claimed that in 445/4 Athens received a gift of grain from Egypt (of 30,000 *medimnoi*; Plutarch *Pericles* 37.3 has 40,000 *medimnoi*), which was distributed between a maximum of 19,000 citizens. It has not generally been thought that this represents a credible figure for the total number of citizens, since it seems far too low.[76] The number of recipients has more usually been taken to represent some (unknowable) proportion of the whole citizen body, which is as compatible with the text as the assumption that it was all the citizens. The other indications that we have of Athens' population in the middle of the fifth century suggest that it was positively awash with citizen manpower. The (rather enigmatic) explanation provided for the Periclean citizenship law of 451/0 given by the Aristotelian *Athenaion Politeia* (26.4) is the large number of citizens. In her treatment of that law, Patterson argued persuasively that the ambitious scope of Athenian military operations in the 450s (as we know about them, if only partially, from Thucydides) also corresponds with an abundance of citizens, perhaps as many as there were in 431. (For Patterson, at the time she was writing, that would mean at least 40,000 or so, and possibly as many as 50,000; although she was rightly sceptical about Gomme's population

---

[76] Gomme 1933, 16–17; Hansen 1985, 45–7.

estimates, she did not mount a thorough challenge to his figures and seems still to have had them in mind.)[77]

5 *Thucydides 2.13: Athens at the Start of the Peloponnesian War*

Thucydides famously reports that, soon after the Peloponnesian War started, Pericles made a speech to the Athenians to reassure them of their chances of victory, pointing out the unmatched scale of their resources. Towards the end of the speech there is a passage which, if it can be taken seriously, is of unparalleled importance for our subject:

And he [Pericles] said that there were 13,000 hoplites, apart from the ones who were in the forts or who manned the city defences, of whom there were 16,000. For there were this many men on garrison duty at the start of the war, whenever the enemy invaded; they were drawn from the oldest and youngest men, and from the metics – as many of them as were hoplites ... He pointed out that there were 1,200 cavalry, including the mounted archers, and 1,600 infantry archers; and that there were 300 seaworthy triremes.

Unlike any of the authorities (if that is the right word) on whom Hansen had to rely for the fourth century, Thucydides was a contemporary observer of events in Athens at the outset of the Peloponnesian War. It is beyond dispute that he was also an intelligent one. It might be possible to doubt whether Pericles actually ever made a speech quite like the one that is reported in 2.13. But it surely cannot strain our credulity too far to believe that Thucydides, who would, within a few years of the events he is describing here, be a general in command of a crucial theatre of operations, might have a reasonably accurate impression of the scale of Athens' military resources. Many of the objections that could be levelled at almost every other army figure we have for classical Greece cannot be applied to this passage. It is hardly surprising that Gomme started his detailed account of the population of Athens here.

In spite of this, Hansen was rather pessimistic about the prospects for using it as a source of demographic data.[78] In part, this

[77] Patterson 1981, 68.
[78] Hansen 1981.

may have been due to the fact that it is an isolated datum in the fifth century. There is nothing with which to compare Thucydides' testimony here, except Diodorus 12.40.4, but that may ultimately be derived from Thucydides too. On the other hand, it is worth noting that in Hansen's account of the fourth century, Diodorus 18. 10–11 is considered 'detailed and reliable' and given considerable weight, even though it is similarly isolated.[79]

But Hansen also had specific difficulties with the text itself. Many scholars from Beloch onwards have had difficulty with the fact that Thucydides makes the reserve force guarding the walls – 16,000 men – bigger than the field army of 13,000 hoplites.[80] Hansen noted the variety of responses to this problem (although it should be noted that the 'problem' only exists if one is unhappy with the idea of a very substantial metic population in 431).[81] Given that there is precious little other evidence for the number of metics resident in Attica, it seems at least possible that the problem lies rather with modern preconceptions rather than with Thucydides' text. But Hansen suggested that all previous attempts to interpret the passage were flawed, as they rested on two untested assumptions. The first assumption is that the 16,000 comprise *all* the oldest and youngest and metic hoplites; especially as regards the oldest and youngest, Thucydides provides us with a paper strength that can be interpreted as a population figure rather than an army figure. The second assumption is that the oldest and youngest comprise only citizens *of hoplite census*.[82]

Unsurprisingly, Hansen questioned both these assumptions. Concerning the first one he has a fair point: ἀπό τε τῶν

---

[79] Hansen 1985, 43.
[80] Beloch 1886, 60–6; Jones 1957, 162.
[81] See also Figueira 1991, 201–17; French 1993. Both Figueira and French start from the position that the 16,000 figure is implausible as Thucydides presents it, mainly because of the implication of a large number of metic hoplites. Both justify their scepticism partly on the grounds that this large force has left little trace in the military narrative of the war. Figueira accounts for the extra hoplites by appealing to forces from elsewhere in the empire (in his account, nearly half of them would have come from 'colonies and satellite communities' 216); French, less plausibly, denies that the 16,000 were all hoplites at all. Figueira however also provides some excellent arguments to explain why it would have been difficult to deploy a large force of metic hoplites in the field, as opposed to behind static defences, which would help to explain why they do not appear more prominently in the military narrative.
[82] Hansen 1981, 19–20.

πρεσβυτάτων καὶ τῶν νεωτάτων, καὶ μετοίκων ὅσοι ὁπλῖται ἦσαν does indeed imply that the 16,000 were recruited from the oldest, the youngest, and the metic hoplites. *Pace* Gomme, the 16,000 does seem to have to be taken as an effective strength rather than a paper strength.[83]

But having made this point, Hansen is plunged into extreme pessimism about the value of the figure:

So the 16,000 constitute an army force recruited from the oldest and youngest and the metic hoplites, and it is impossible, on the basis of Thucydides' information, to say anything about population figures. The total population of oldest and youngest and metic hoplites may amount to say, 20,000 or perhaps even to 25,000. We do not know and any attempt to make calculations is doomed from the start.[84]

Taken in isolation, this is rather hard to understand, as Hansen is elsewhere perfectly happy to try to convert army figures into population figures. Why this particular army figure is so intractable is not clear until he comes to the second assumption, that the oldest and youngest comprise only citizens of hoplite status.

Hansen argues that this is not what Thucydides actually says. He starts by observing that in 2.13.7, the omission of the article before μετοίκων shows that ὅσοι ὁπλῖται ἦσαν refers back only to μετοίκων and not to τῶν πρεσβυτάτων καὶ τῶν νεωτάτων. In this he is surely right. It can also be accepted that

when Thucydides emphasises that only metic hoplites served in the defence army and not all metics between 20 and 49, he probably indicates some kind of opposition between the metics, on the one hand, and the oldest and youngest, on the other.[85]

But is it true that, as Hansen claims, 'if the whole group of "oldest, youngest, and metics" comprised hoplites only, it would be odd to mention in connection with the metics only that they were hoplites'? Surely the natural way to read Thucydides at this point is that the 16,000 included only hoplites, and that the point of Thucydides' qualification of the metics as ὅσοι ὁπλῖται ἦσαν is first that only hoplites are being counted, and second that there

---

[83] Gomme 1956, 36.
[84] Hansen 1981, 20–1.
[85] Hansen 1981, 21.

were plenty of metics who did not or could not serve as hoplites. Hansen's point might be better made if Thucydides had omitted these three words.

Hansen's argument about 2.13.6 is similarly hard to accept. He claims that it is unwarranted to read ἄνευ τῶν ἐν τοῖς φρουρίοις καὶ τῶν παρ'ἔπαλξιν as meaning 'apart from the *hoplites* in the forts and on the walls', and that instead 2.13.6 should be read '13,000 hoplites apart from the forces manning the forts and the walls *viz.* 16,000'. I think that it is important to quote this passage in full in Greek, as Hansen does not:

ὁπλίτας δὲ τρισχιλίους καὶ μυρίους εἶναι ἄνευ τῶν ἐν τοῖς φρουρίοις καὶ τῶν παρ'ἔπαλξιν ἑξακισχιλίων καὶ μυρίων.

When the start of the sentence is seen, it seems clear to me that the natural way to take τῶν (especially given the prominent placing of ὁπλίτας) is that it refers to the hoplites and not some more general 'forces'; Hansen's rendering is not impossible, to be sure, but it seems to be rather unlikely, and to be straining the Greek.

Hansen claims some support from looking at who the men ἐν τοῖς φρουρίοις were. He finds that at least some of them were light-armed troops and not hoplites.[86] This is certainly true, but it does not suffice to make his point. It is also clear from Thucydides' narrative that light-armed troops made up an important part of Athenian field armies too; but apart from the 1,600 archers, there is no mention of them at all in 2.13. Hansen complains that the 'traditional interpretation' of 2.13 leaves no room for the oldest and youngest of the *thetes* or for the poor metics. Again, this is true, but it could be observed that this is not surprising given Thucydides' attitude throughout his work to non-hoplite forces,[87] and that it is even less surprising when one considers that nowhere in 2.13, whether one takes the 'traditional' interpretation or Hansen's, does it give any numbers for the *thetes* or non-hoplite metics of active military age. True, some of them were presumably manning the triremes, but there must have been thousands, too, serving as light-armed troops on land.

---

[86] Hansen 1981, 21.
[87] Hunt 1998, 132–8; Van Wees 2004, 61–5.

Hansen is right to stress that the 16,000 is an army figure and not a population figure. The absence of the Athenians and metics who discharged their military obligations as light-armed troops or in the fleet is indeed a problem. Hansen's arguments regarding the absence of a single centralised hoplite *katalogos* can stand.[88] But he fails to dismiss the 'traditional' reading of the 16,000 men as referring only to hoplites, and as a result his pessimism about the value of the figure for demographic purposes seems to be unjustified. If the number of men who had hoplite equipment in the primary military age groups is known, then the numbers of oldest and youngest hoplites can be estimated, given a plausible model for age distribution. The remainder of the 16,000 can be assumed to be metic hoplites, presumably of all adult ages.[89]

There seems, in short, to be no compelling reason why we should not, like Gomme, take Thucydides 2.13.6–8 as representing valuable evidence for the population of Athens in 431. Furthermore, I think that the approach taken by Hansen to the army figures of the fourth century (and especially those in book 18 of Diodorus) can fruitfully be applied to this text.

Using Thucydides 2.13

First, a number of assumptions have to be made about Thucydides 2.13. Whatever model of age distribution is adopted, the issue of exactly who the 'oldest and youngest' were is going to be important; only after this has been settled can the other figures be assessed.

It is conventionally assumed that the 'youngest' were those aged 18 and 19. The basis for this assumption is that these were the age classes who participated in the ephebeia described in the Aristotelian *Athenaion Politeia* 42. The ephebeia as it is described here dates only from 335/4 – it was one of the measures that was taken in response to the defeat of Chaeronea in 338. It is possible that the compulsory training described by Pseudo-Aristotle was based on an existing practice of deploying young men in garrison

---

[88] Hansen 1981, 24–9; Van Wees 2011, 109–10.

[89] Hansen was not alone in finding the 16,000 figure problematic, especially because of the implication of a large number of metics: see note 84 above, and also 123–138 below.

roles. The assumption seems to be sensible, even if certainty eludes us. The possibility cannot be ruled out that the 'youngest' also included younger men of 16 and 17 (although probably not all of them).

The question of the 'oldest' is more problematic. Again, the conventional assumption has been that they were men aged 50 to 59.[90] A passage in Lycurgus' *Against Leocrates* (39–40) is the clearest piece of evidence for this, although the date (330 BC) is relatively late.

Jones insisted that there was no fixed upper limit for field service, and that instead the call-up was adjusted according to the needs of the situation. He took the Chaeronea levy, to which Lycurgus indirectly refers, as an extreme emergency measure. Certainly, Lycurgus seems to be suggesting that the fact that the defence of the city rested entirely with those aged over 50 was a mark of the desperate nature of the situation. For the Thermopylae campaign of 347, and for the Lamian War, the levy seems to have been restricted to those under 40.[91] Jones read Thucydides 2.13 as implying that home defence was a higher priority than offensive operations, and that this in turn implied that in this particular case a larger proportion of manpower would have been allotted to the former than the latter, and so the oldest were more likely to have been those aged 40 or more.

Against this, there is the battle of Delium in 424, fought by an Athenian army of 7,000 hoplites, which is generally supposed to have included at least one man over 40 – Socrates, who should have been about 45 at this time. But even if we could be sure that Socrates really did fight in this battle, it cannot straightforwardly be inferred from this that the field army was regularly composed of those aged up to 50. It is possible that the age limit was raised for the Delium campaign to help compensate for the heavy manpower losses suffered during the 'plague' – apart from those who died, many who contracted the disease and survived were, according to Thucydides, permanently disabled in ways that would have compromised their fitness for military service. Alternatively, there is

[90] Gomme 1933, 5, for example.
[91] Aeschines 2.133 for Thermopylae; Jones 1957, 164, observes that some manuscripts have 30, not 40.

some evidence of levies including men up to the age precisely of 45, and not 50. Then again, it is not impossible that the age limits were not strictly adhered to. As Rhodes suggested, it is not hard to imagine a situation where men over the theoretical age limit would volunteer and that no one would take much notice.[92]

It is true that the number of Athenian hoplites at Delium (7,000) seems rather low for what is supposed to be a *pandemei* force. Plague losses can account for a great deal, but it might be thought unlikely that any epidemic could do this much damage. The problem, moreover, is exacerbated by the fact that it is unclear exactly what the significance of the term *pandemei* is and exactly how literally it should be taken. (Clearly, it cannot really mean everyone in the demos, but instead 'everyone who was, under a certain set of conditions, available'.) In the end, we have to accept that we just do not know how Athenian armies were levied in a lot of cases, especially in the fifth century. The system based completely on age classes seems to have been introduced in the period 386–366, but clearly the pre-existing system of lists drawn up by the generals had some differentiation by age.[93] It is also possible that sizeable Athenian forces that Thucydides has not told us about could have been committed elsewhere at the time.[94]

The result of all of this is that it remains unclear exactly which age groups constituted the youngest, the oldest and the main field force. Fortunately, the range of plausible alternatives is limited. But whichever age groups are represented by the 13,000 hoplite figure (for example), we still need to determine what proportion of those age groups is included in that figure. There is no easy way to establish whether the figures Thucydides gives at 2.13 are paper strengths or real ones. The context of the speech might suggest the former – Pericles would presumably not be underestimating Athens' strength here, and the figure does seem quite high. Then again, the force that invades Megara is supposed actually to have comprised 10,000 citizen hoplites at a time when another 3,000 were still dug in around Potidaea; so perhaps at the beginning of

[92] Rhodes 1988, 274.
[93] Christ 2001; Van Wees 2004, 102–4.
[94] Van Wees 2006, 343–5.

the war the Athenian generals really were confident of having 13,000 hoplites to command if they needed them.

Still, unless the Athenians of the fifth century BC were uniquely healthy, it does not seem unreasonable to assume that around 10 per cent of the men in active military age groups would have been permanently unfit.[95] Edwards stressed that quite an extreme level of disability would be required to gain exemption from military service.[96] She rightly observed that even a crippled man could play a non-combatant military role (although how many such roles existed at this time is open to question), but this does not affect the current argument. Furthermore, while a fair proportion of men with congenital disabilities may have been able to fight, the near-constant state of warfare at Athens must have produced a fair number of men who had been disabled in combat. A limp might not be too much of a disadvantage in a hoplite battle (so long as the hoplite in question was on the side that won), but the complete loss of use of a limb would have made fighting impossible – and the capacity of ancient weapons to produce fearful wounds should not be forgotten. What one thinks about this will, of course, be affected by the view one takes of hoplite battle; a wide variety of views is collected in Kagan and Viggiano's edited volume *Men of Bronze*.[97] Our hoplite with a limp might have been less disadvantaged in one of the phalanxes imagined by Hanson than in the looser and more flexible formations suggested by Van Wees. In the same volume, Adam Schwartz, while generally an enthusiast for a Hansonian interpretation, takes a dim view of the physical prowess of typical classical hoplites, which, if correct, might have made it harder for long-term or permanent injuries to be 'carried'.[98]

It is worth recalling what this passage does not tell us. There are no figures for those citizens (or indeed metics) who did not or could not afford to (not necessarily the same things) serve as hoplites or cavalry, but instead fought in the fleet or as light-armed troops on land. Thucydides himself seems to have had little

---

[95] Hansen 1988, 25; Rhodes 1988, 274.
[96] Edwards 1996, 90.
[97] Kagan and Viggiano 2013.
[98] Schwartz 2013.

information about the numbers of these kinds of people. Thucydides 3.87 provides the most obvious example of his ignorance, but 2.31 is relevant again for its vagueness about the numbers of *psiloi*.

For the moment, we should do what we can with the hoplite numbers. For all kinds of reasons, precision will elude us. The best that can be hoped for is that we can establish the parameters for a plausible range of figures, and then, perhaps, think about the implications of choosing different figures within that range.

The first step is to turn to the models of age distribution discussed in Chapter 2, so that population figures can be derived from the army figures. The relevant data are presented in Table 3.1. Starting with a 'high' figure, if the field army of about 14,000 men represented 85 per cent of the men aged 20 to 39, then the total number of men in these age groups would have been about 16,500. These models imply that the total number of males in the population would have been around 50,000 to 55,000. In turn, 29,000 to 34,000 would have been over the age of 18 and so full citizens. The 'oldest and youngest' would have numbered between 10,000 and 12,500, implying about 3,500 to 6,000 metic hoplites in total. In other words, beyond the 3,000 metic hoplites who are known to have participated in the Megarid campaign, there would have been at most another 3,000, and perhaps only a handful more.

On the other hand, if that figure of 14,000 represented all the men with hoplite equipment between the ages of 20 and 49, then they would reflect a total male population of 33,000 to 35,000 individuals, and maybe 19,000 to 22,000 citizens. The 'oldest and youngest' would number about 3,500 to 4,000. There would therefore have been about 12,000 hoplite-equipped metics.

So far, we have only been considering the portion of the population that was able to fight as cavalry or hoplites, and for which Thucydides gives us tolerably detailed figures. We still have the problem of the rest of the citizens. One line of approach would be to assume that normally these men would discharge their military obligations in the fleet. This requires the further assumption that the bulk of the light troops who went out in support of the hoplite army would have been metics, mercenaries, and/or slaves. Many of them could have been the (generally) slave attendants of the

3.1 Comparison of age distribution of males in the citizen population in different demographic models

Age range	Hansen's chosen model[*]	Model based on Woods' South Europe high-mortality table[**]	'Hybrid' model, using Coale–Demeny Model West[***]
'Youngest': 18 to 19	3.85	3.58	4.06
20 to 39	31.44	29.51	32.21
20 to 49	41.77	40.03	42.08
All adult men liable to conscription: 20 to 59	48.62	48.21	48.20
'Oldest': 40 to 59	17.18	18.70	15.99
'Oldest': 50 to 59	6.85	8.18	6.13
0 to 17	42.53	39.31	43.83
'Oldest and youngest' where 'oldest' are 40+	21.03	22.42	20.26
'Oldest and youngest' where 'oldest' are 50+	10.70	11.76	10.19
'Citizens': all males aged 18+	57.47	60.69	56.17

The figures are percentages of the total male population.
[*] from Coale and Demeny
[**] with $e^0 = 30$, growth rate 0.5 per cent pa
[***] males, mortality levels 8 (age 15) and 2 (for ages over 15); growth rate 0.5 per cent pa

hoplites themselves, who could easily have performed auxiliary combat roles.[99] There is no direct evidence for the normal ages of service for Athenians in the fleet. It seems reasonable to assume, however, that in practice they were roughly the same age groups as for land-based service, and that front-line crews were drawn from men aged 20 to 39 or 49 (depending on circumstances and the need for manpower).

After the army figures at 2.13, Thucydides tells us that in 431 the Athenians had no fewer than 300 triremes in a seaworthy condition. How many of these could actually be manned is, however, another matter, although we do sometimes get an indication of the size of Athenian fleets that were actually deployed. The big problem to face is that, at the time of the Peloponnesian War, Athenian warships were not crewed exclusively by Athenian citizens. Thucydides tells us (at 8.73.5) that the crack crew of the state galley *Paralos* was made up entirely of citizens, with the obvious implication that the other crews in the fleet were not (with the probable exception of *Salaminia*). Metics served both as rowers and as deck crew, but so too did non-resident foreigners from the allied cities, and slaves. There is also some potential for a confusing blurring of boundaries with the metics and allied rowers. Was a metic still a metic if he was away from Athens for a period of several months? The implication of Nicias' speech in Sicily would be that the answer is 'yes', but it is rather harder to understand how this would have worked in practice.[100] It is hardly surprising that our sources are almost completely silent on the relative proportions of these different crew elements, which in any case probably changed over time and according to circumstances. The question of how younger and older men who did not fight as cavalry or hoplites discharged their military obligations to the *polis* is presumably what led Hansen to lump them in with the garrison troops. There seems no reason, however, not to assume that they would act as a kind of reserve of naval manpower, or that they acted as a light-armed equivalent to the oldest and youngest hoplites.

[99] Hunt 1998.
[100] Thuc. 7.61–4, especially 63.

Nonetheless, a significant number of citizens must have served as trireme crewmen. That so many citizens performed this vital military role was a factor intimately connected with the nature and extent of Athenian democracy in the eyes of contemporary observers.[101] Furthermore, Thucydides has Pericles claim (at 1.143) that, even without foreign recruits, the Athenians together with their metics would be able to outmatch their enemies at sea. This comes partly as a 'response' to the Corinthians' claim at 1.121 that the Athenians' power was 'bought' (ὠνητή, usually translated as 'mercenary' or 'consisting of mercenaries') rather than 'their own' (οἰκεία). In a sense, of course, the whole fleet was 'bought', in that everyone, including citizen crewmen, was paid, in partial distinction from the hoplite field army, which was theoretically more self-supporting and self-financing, or at least had traditionally been so.[102] However, the comparison with 'bought' (ὠνητή) makes it clear that Thucydides' Corinthians really are suggesting that the bulk of Athens' navy was comprised of foreign mercenaries. This comes in a speech with a particular persuasive intent and is not likely to be a statement of straightforward historical fact. But as Hornblower notes in his commentary, it is unlikely that Thucydides would have Pericles accept a small degree of truth in the Corinthian claim if it were wholly groundless.[103]

At 1.142.7, later in the same speech, Pericles seems to imply, by referring to ὑμεῖς ('you'), that the fleet is in fact mainly crewed by citizens. At 3.16, the Athenians actually man 100 ships with citizens and metics, and only citizens from the *pentacosiomedimnoi* and the *hippeis* were excluded from the call-up. This cannot, however, have been a typical situation, as usually a field army could be deployed at the same time as a fleet, and tension between the two manpower requirements seems not generally to have been a major problem. Morrison, Coates, and Rankov argue that trireme oarsmen were too specialised and too valuable to be used as infantry; the other side of this coin is that those who lacked training, practice, and expertise would not have been much use

---

[101] Most obviously (for the fourth century) in Aristotle *Politics* 1304a, 20ff., but also Pseudo-Xenophon's *Athenaion Politeia* 1.2; 1.20; Aristophanes *Knights* 541–610.
[102] Whitehead 1977, 86; Pritchett 1971, 3–29.
[103] Hornblower 1991, 198–9.

on the rowing benches. They quote an interesting example of a rule-proving exception in 428, when

Athenian naval resources were fully stretched, with 200 triereis at sea in home waters, another force raiding the Peloponnese and some ships also probably in northern waters, as well as 40 ships sent to Lesbos to avert a threatened revolt. It is therefore no wonder that when reinforcements had to be sent to Lesbos they included 1,000 hoplites who also served as oarsmen. Thucydides here (3.18.4) uses the word *auteretai*, which he had used before only of the Greeks at Troy. In Homeric conditions such a thing was normal, but it was highly abnormal in the fifth century.[104]

The fact that the Athenians, with their metics, could still, with an effort, crew 100 ships in the immediate aftermath of the plague is only of pretty limited use. Trying to get figures for active Athenian fleets out of Thucydides is not easy, and certainly harder than Morrison, Coates, and Rankov imply. The rather troublesome passage at 3.17 is most easily read as confirming that at the beginning of the war the Athenians had 250 ships on station. The problem is that this is rather hard to reconcile with 2.93.4, where Attica and the 'home waters' seem not to be protected by a fleet. Rhodes observes that the largest number of ships deployed at a time that we are sure of is at least 218 (in 413).[105] In the absence of much firm evidence, it seems about right to assume an actual operational fleet of the order of 200 ships at the beginning of the war.

We could assume that there were only 30 citizens on board an 'Athenian' trireme. This number is largely, although not completely, arbitrary as a realistic minimum figure for the number of citizens on board an 'Athenian' trireme; it would be the equivalent of the deck crew, officers, and marines. This would still mean 6,000 men in total. Again, this is an 'army' figure (and one obtained by even more dubious means than the land army figures) that needs to be converted into a population figure by the same means as before. Again, we have to make assumptions about both the age ranges involved and about the pattern of age distribution. Since 6,000 is likely to be a minimum figure, it seems most appropriate to treat it as such and to take it as representing men drawn from the 20 to 49

[104] Morrison, Coates, and Rankov 2000, 115.
[105] Rhodes 1988, 275; with the note, 209, on 24.2 for the calculation of this figure from references throughout the Sicilian Expedition.

age range. If all the men in this age range were fit and available, this would require us to add a notional figure of about 14,000 males of all ages to the totals above. If only 80 per cent of the men in this age range were able to serve in this capacity, then the figure would be closer to 18,000.

It is important to remember, though, that as with the army figures, the fewer citizens there were in the fleet, the greater the requirement for non-citizen manpower would have been, as a further 34,000 men (whether slaves, metics, or mercenaries) would have been required, in addition to the metic hoplites and various non-citizen light troops. The important conclusion to be drawn is that if citizen numbers are pushed down as far as they will go, then the non-citizen numbers have to come up to compensate. From a purely military point of view, the significance of this kind of picture is that non-citizens would have been in many ways the mainstay of the Athenian armed forces, not only guaranteeing the security of the Athens–Piraeus fortress but providing the backbone (and more) of the crews for the fleet which formed the basis of Athens' offensive potential. For the current discussion, it is more important to observe that this also means that the total population of Attica cannot be pushed below a certain level, whatever arguments are made about the numbers of citizens.

Strauss took a different approach to fleet numbers, using Thucydides 1.143.1 as a starting point.[106] Pericles must surely here be implying a minimum of 60 ships crewed fully by citizens and metics. Strauss suggested that two-thirds of these could have been citizens. More conservatively, we could assume that the fraction was only a half, to derive a minimum figure – in which case we again arrive at a figure of 6,000 citizens in the fleet, and only 6,000 metics would have been required in addition – but also a huge number of allied/mercenary rowers in the actual fleets that Athens deployed throughout the war.

On the other hand, Thucydides here could be taken as implying a fleet of around 150 vessels, with a two-thirds complement of citizens, implying 20,000 citizen crewmen (and 10,000 more metics). If they were only a fit, trained, and experienced

---

[106] Strauss 1986, 71–3.

80 per cent of the available 20- to 39-year-olds, the number of 'citizen' males of all ages that this would imply would be up around the 80,000 mark. Even if they only represented say 90 per cent of all the 20- to 49-year-olds (which is perhaps more plausible, as the implication would be that this was pretty much all of Athens' available trained manpower in the kind of hypothetical emergency being envisaged by Pericles), it would still mean something over 50,000 males in total.

Choosing between these kinds of hypothetical figures is, of course, impossible on the basis of the evidence of Thucydides alone. However, they become more interesting in the light of the argument that Hansen provided about the citizen population in 431. In his 1988 article, Hansen was not really interested in what Thucydides had to say for its own sake. Instead, he was trying to show that his account of the fourth-century citizen population was not weakened by any reading of Thucydides. Drawing on and expanding Strauss' enumeration of Athenian casualties in the Peloponnesian War, Hansen argued that there must have been at least 60,000 citizens at the outbreak of the war, since only a population this size could have withstood the elevated mortality of the war years and still had a minimum 25,000 men to allow for the normal constitutional operation of the democracy after the overthrow of the Thirty. The detail of this argument need not detain us here (see Chapter 5). Two observations can be made here. The first, briefly, is that it is often overlooked that Hansen explicitly claims that this figure is a minimum – a still larger figure might be possible. The second is that, if it is roughly right, then the figures of Thucydides 2.13 are not only compatible with it, but become rather more interesting.

For the sake of argument, we could assume that it is right, and look at the consequences for our earlier interpretations of the hoplite figures in Thucydides. On the former, higher estimate of the population, there were about 29,000 to 34,000 citizens in the 'hoplite' group. There would then have been roughly another 30,000 citizens who contributed to the city in other ways. These in turn would imply a further total male population of roughly 49,000 to 54,000 individuals, of whom around 15,000 to 17,000 would be of military age (20 to 39 years old), of whom in turn about 12,000 to 15,000 would be fit and available for service, the equivalent of 60 to 75 full trireme crews. On the other hand, if there were only 19,000 to 22,000 citizens in the 'hoplite' group, as in the latter, more conservative interpretation of Thucydides, then there would have been about 40,000 more citizens without hoplite equipment. In turn, this would imply 66,000 to 71,000 males in total, of whom 25,000 to 30,000 would have been militarily active 20- to 49-year-olds. These men would have been sufficient on their own to crew well over 100 triremes, and perhaps as many as 150.

Both of these interpretations are compatible with the figures given in Thucydides. The text itself cannot help us any further to decide between them. However, we have, I think, made some progress. An inescapable conclusion is that the citizen population at the beginning of the Peloponnesian War really was very large – probably at least twice as large as it was either in the fourth century or during the Persian Wars at the start of the fifth century. Accounting for changes of this scale will be the subject of Chapter 5; the implications and impact of those changes will be for later chapters. The bare numbers themselves are also important when seen in their context. This includes aggregate levels of consumption, but a key issue will be the distribution of wealth within the citizen population. This is an area where other evidence can be brought to bear, and that wider context might help us to decide which interpretation of Thucydides 2.13 is more likely to resemble reality.[107]

Conclusion

There seems no compelling reason not to accept Hansen's main conclusion about the fourth century – that there were, most of the time, around 30,000 citizens resident in Attica – even if it is possible to take issue with some of the arguments supporting this figure. The approach taken by Hansen can also profitably be extended to the evidence for the fifth century, even though

---

[107] Van Wees' discussions of Thuc. 2.13 will be covered later for this reason, as they are substantially concerned with the proportion of the total citizen population which was represented by the hoplites, and use the 60,000 figure in Hansen 1988 as a starting point.

Hansen himself denied that as a possibility. That fifth-century evidence does not turn out to be much more problematic than the fourth-century material. At the time of the Persian invasion, the citizen population was probably about 30,000 strong (implying a figure of roughly 120,000 inhabitants, including women and children). At the outbreak of the Peloponnesian War, however, Thucydides' account strongly implies that there were many more citizens. Working back from the fourth century, Hansen suggested that at the start of the war there must have been at least 60,000 citizens (and a total of roughly 250,000 inhabitants). Such a figure is compatible with Thucydides' account, but so would be a still larger total. These are important conclusions, but there is work still to do. The metics, or at least some of them, have appeared already in Thucydides; in Chapter 4, we shall look further at the size of the non-citizen population. Similarly, we already have some crude indications of the scale of the change in the size of the citizen population over the course of the classical period; after looking at the non-citizen population, we shall be able to consider in more detail not only the changes in the size of the whole population, but changes in its structures.

Archaeology and the Historical Demography of Classical Athens

The most obvious of archaeological evidence that can be brought to bear directly on questions of population is that generated by surface survey. Since its enthusiastic adoption by archaeologists working in the Mediterranean a few decades ago, this form of archaeological investigation has provided us with vastly more information than we had previously about the landscapes of antiquity and the people who inhabited them. The optimism of early practitioners about the demographic potential of survey data has to a certain extent receded, but the implications of this kind of evidence for assessing population size and density, and comparisons across time and space, are of potentially great importance and continue to be debated.[108]

---

[108] Alcock 1993; Sbonias 2000; Alcock and Cherry 2004; Osborne 2004; Forsdyke 2006.

Intensive field survey campaigns have not covered very much of Attica; nor, given that urban development has covered most of the areas that one would want to survey (and which would have been susceptible to this kind of investigation), is this likely to change in the future. There are only two real exceptions: the Skourta plain survey, and Lohmann's study of Atene.[109] Unfortunately, the usefulness of each is limited in the present context. Neither can reasonably be taken as typical of the region. Atene only developed in response to a very specific set of economic circumstances, which is intrinsically both interesting and important, but does not make it suitable as a basis for generalising about Attica.[110] The Skourta plain is, if anything, even more marginal: as well as being an upland pasture, again quite untypical of the dominant landscapes of Attica, it was a border territory constantly contested between Athens and Boeotia. Survey data from other Greek cities can provide some comparative context for what was happening in Attica, but their results cannot be taken as predictive for this region. If the danger of Athenocentrism is that we may wrongly generalise from Athens to other Greek cities, then we have to accept that we cannot always generalise from a wider Greek experience to Athens.

Such a cavalier response will not do, however. Although intensive surface survey data may not be available for Attica, still the area has been subject to intense archaeological excavation, and we are not completely in the dark about the landscapes of Attica 'beyond the Acropolis' (and the agora).[111] In fact, this leads to problems in itself, in that the vast mass of available data is hard to synthesise meaningfully, and the rapid pace of development and consequently equally rapid generation of new archaeological data has had inevitable effects on the pace of publication by the Archaeological Service. While most of this investigation has not proceeded according to any kind of directed research agenda, sheer volume can count for something even if a sample's quality is not directly (or even at all) correlated to its size. Research-led

---

[109] Skourta: Munn and Munn 1989, 1990. Atene: Lohmann 1991, 1993, with Osborne 1997.
[110] Compare Moreno 2007, 72–3.
[111] Runnels and Van Andel, 1987.

archaeological survey is not free from biases in the collection of data either, and in principle it should be possible if not to correct them then at least to take them into account.[112]

The real problem, both with survey data and with what we have for Attica, is in interpreting the relationship between the archaeological data and the size of the population in antiquity. It seems entirely reasonable to think that the larger the population, the more sites they will occupy and the greater the traces of their occupation. In general terms, this can even often be true. In the case of Athens, the large volumes of data from the end of the archaic period to the end of the classical period compared both to earlier and later periods surely do correspond to a large and densely settled population. In itself, however, this does not tell us much that we would not be likely to infer from the literary record. Both survey data and the kind of patchy material we have for classical Attica can be revealing about population trends at the level of periods of hundreds of years. They are much less good at revealing short-term fluctuations at the scale of human lifetimes, which can be much more dramatic, and are often of vital interest to historians. Such trends are also easiest to establish in relative terms. More classical than archaic or Hellenistic sites in a region might reasonably be taken to imply a larger population in the classical period. It is much harder to use the same evidence to establish absolute population numbers or even to provide a more quantitative aspect to the relative picture – how much bigger was the classical population?[113]

There are a number of problems here, which in the context of survey data have been discussed by Osborne, and in terms of what we have in Attica by Oliver (focusing specifically on the difference between the fourth and third centuries BC).[114] The first is that the dating of much archaeological data is not fine enough for us to be confident about tracking detailed change at the timescales that are interesting to historians. Clearly, stratigraphic excavations can and do provide very fine dates for events, both relatively and

---

[112] Moreno 2007, 37–76, is illustrative of the potential for synthesis in at least one area in Attica.

[113] Sbonias 1999; Bintliff and Sbonias 1999.

[114] Osborne 2004; Oliver 2007, 100–110.

(sometimes) absolutely. One potential problem for historians here is that this dating can be too fine to be really helpful. A skilled excavator may be able to distinguish different bucketsful in a single fill and establish their relative order of deposition, providing a relative chronology of (say) a single morning's work. While this may help interpretation of a particular area of a site and is an impressive piece of technical skill, it is unlikely to be of much wider significance. While this is an extreme case, it is almost as hard to generalise from detailed excavations of a small number of farmhouses (such as we have for Attica). This is not to deny that having secure chronologies for some sites (such as the agora of Athens, or the theatre of Dionysus) would not be helpful for some historical questions, nor that more excavation of residential sites might well help shed light on some demographic and wider economic issues. Many sites in Attica can be dated to either the fifth or the fourth centuries (or can firmly be said to have been occupied throughout both); many more, though, can be dated no more accurately than 'classical'. This is of limited use for those interested in the possibility of change during the classical period, even if such sites contribute to the general impression of the classical period as one of high population. As Sbonias concludes:

Concerning archaeology and survey data it seems almost impossible to follow these short-term population fluctuations and see how they relate to phenomena such as famines and agricultural production, wars or diseases. It seems also difficult to investigate the way these short-term fluctuations inter-relate with general social and economic variables in the local trajectory to initiate or affect long-term trends.[115]

The second problem is that archaeological data are often good at showing 'activity' in rural areas, but it is often unclear that increased activity in the countryside is straightforwardly linked to increased total population. Again, it is not unreasonable to see an increase in deposition of material, or apparent density of settlement, as indicating increased intensification of agricultural production (at least where there is no suggestion that levels of pottery supply are at issue, or where the greater visibility of one period's ceramics over another's is affecting archaeological recovery

[115] Sbonias 1999, 16.

rates). However, there can be more than one reason for intensification of production: external food supplies may have become less desirable or available, or there may be greater demands on producers for taxation or tribute; on the other hand, the emergence or expansion of a market for produce may more benignly have a similar effect.[116] The social or economic context could also be undergoing more radical change; I shall argue later that increased intensification of production in fourth-century Attica could be explained partly by a decrease in population (see Chapter 6).

Perhaps most problematic of all is Osborne's observation that the survey data from mainland Greece and the Aegean islands suggest that fluctuations in rural settlement will often have been quite trivial in their implications for total population size compared to the numbers of people living in towns. If this held for Attica too, then the paucity of (published) excavations of urban residential areas, and especially in the Athens–Piraeus complex, may be a bigger handicap than the absence of intensive survey data for the lost agricultural plains.[117]

This does not mean that we can afford to ignore the archaeological evidence; clearly, any interpretation will have to be at least consistent with it. Nor does it mean that archaeological data will not have more impact on the debate in future; in the long term, there is every reason to anticipate progress in answering interesting and relevant questions from environmental archaeology. But for now our discussion of the total size of the population will have to start with well-travelled paths through the written sources as enumerated by Hansen, and, as far as the literary sources go, essentially as they were available to Beloch and Gomme.

[116] Osborne 2004, 170–1.
[117] Osborne 2004; Hansen 2006a, 15–25, 35–63.

CHAPTER 4

POPULATION SIZE 2: NON-CITIZENS

The number of non-citizens – metics and slaves – in Athens has always been controversial and recognised as problematic. We have even less evidence to go on than we do for the citizens, and definitive answers will remain elusive. The situation is further complicated by the fact that estimates of metic and slave numbers cannot be separated from those of citizen numbers, nor entirely from other debates about the nature of Athenian economy and society. In the absence of much direct attestation for their numbers, we are forced instead to consider what roles they might have played, or their numbers in relative terms to those of the citizens. In the latter case, the danger of circularity arises, as an important reason for wanting to know their numbers is precisely to shed light on the ratios of free to unfree and citizen to non-citizen. As it turns out, moreover, the metics and slaves themselves can be hard to disentangle not just from the citizens (as the Old Oligarch complained) but from each other.[1] Few deny that manumitted slaves became metics; no one would deny that at least some of them did so.

Rachel Zelnick-Abramovitz falls into the former camp, suggesting that only those freedmen who were fully manumitted – whom she argues were those termed 'exeleutheroi', as opposed to the 'apeleutheroi', who remained in a state of dependence on and subjugation to their masters – became metics.[2] Her argument fails to convince for two reasons. In the first place, the distinction between exeleutheroi and apeleutheroi does not seem to be as consistent or clear as she maintains. In the second, and more

---

[1] [Xen.] *Ath. Pol.* 1.10.
[2] Zelnick-Abramovitz 2005. See also Meyer 2010.

seriously, the argument requires that metic status really be in at least some minimal sense a privileged one. Whitehead's demonstration that there was nothing positive or honorific about being identified as a metic remains more convincing; rather, it was a clear definition of the obligations of a resident non-citizen in Athens in his or her dealings with citizens.[3] For practical purposes, however, this may not be important. Even Zelnick-Abramovitz would not deny that the exeleutheroi were metics, and her apeleutheroi would have been very hard to distinguish from slaves. Once it is accepted that the boundary between slave and metic was porous and, *pace* Whitehead, that metic status did carry at least a tinge of servility in citizen eyes (132–138 below) then there is relatively little to be gained from yet more definitional squabbling.[4]

The conclusion of Sargent, whose treatment remains the best full-length attempt to get to grips with classical Athenian slave numbers, is hard to fault: 'the number of slaves employed ... varied considerably at different periods during the fifth and fourth centuries before Christ, and stood in direct relation to the size of the free population and the general economic conditions'.[5] However, not only do we have only a precarious grip on the size of the free population, but the 'general economic conditions' are what we are trying to elucidate by starting from the size of the total population.

Slaves

The number of slaves in Athens has attracted more attention and controversy than that of the metics. While this has not obviously brought definitive answers any closer, at least the terms of the debate have become clearer. It will be easier, therefore, to start with this part of the non-citizen population. The direct literary evidence is scanty and can be summarised very briefly.

There are only two total figures surviving from antiquity, both of which we have already met in the discussion of citizen numbers in Chapter 3. First, there is the passage from Ctesicles in

---

[3] Whitehead 1977, 69–97.
[4] Whitehead 1977, 114–16.
[5] Sargent 1924, 126.

Athenaeus 272c, where it is claimed that in the late fourth century there were 21,000 Athenians, 10,000 metics, and 400,000 *oiketai*. Whatever one makes of the figures for citizens and metics, it is now generally accepted that the figure of 400,000 for slaves is simply too high to be credible as an accurate figure.[6] The arguments go back to Hume. The *oiketai* figure could be salvaged by translating it as 'household members'. That in itself is not an obviously implausible suggestion. In the first place, however, that does not make it any more informative about the number of slaves. In the second place, the fact that it is plausible need not make us believe that Demetrius' census-takers could actually (even if they had wanted to) have reached an accurate figure for the total population of Attica at the time. Even Van Wees, who has recently argued that the number deserves to be taken seriously, concedes that it is 'uncertain' whether the number can be taken as accurate, and that it seems 'unfeasibly high'.[7]

The figure provided by Hyperides fr. 29, is barely, if at all, more believable. After the crushing defeat of Chaeronea, the orator proposed conscripting 'the 150,000 or more slaves from the silver mines and from the rest of the countryside'. At least it is tolerably clear here that only adult males are being counted, but the total figure is still very high – indeed it implies a total figure (including female slaves and males who were not suitable for military service) of the same magnitude as Ctesicles'.

What these passages tell us, if they accurately reflect fourth-century Athenian views at all (not necessarily a foregone conclusion), is that there was a belief, at least in the later part of the century, that the free residents of Attica were hugely outnumbered by the unfree. This is an important observation in itself, but it is of limited help to us here.

The only figure from the fifth century is provided by Thucydides at 7.27.5, where he claims that more than 20,000 slaves fled from Attica during the Decelean War. Perhaps just because it is in Thucydides, this passage has sometimes been taken very seriously.[8] Although I have argued that Thucydides'

---

[6] Hume 1752, 220–6; Sallares 1991, 54.
[7] Van Wees 2011, 111, 112. See 41 above.
[8] Sargent 1924, 87–8; De Ste Croix 1981, 506.

numbers at 2.13 and 3.87 should be treated with respect, it is much more difficult to be as confident about this figure. In the first place, by this stage in the war, Thucydides had been in exile for some years, and can no longer be considered a first-hand observer of what was going on in Attica. In the second, even if he had been on the spot, it is hard to see how he, or anyone else, could possibly have known how many slaves ran away or were captured by Athens' enemies during the course of the war. The vagueness that comes over him when he talks about the numbers of poorer citizens is hardly likely to have been lifted when it came to non-citizens. It seems unlikely too that the garrison at Decelea kept detailed records of the numbers of slaves that passed through their hands one way or another – or even that all the slaves lost to the Athenians actually ended up in the fort at all. The 20,000 figure should be treated in a similar manner to the figures of 20,000 or 30,000 given in literary sources for the size of the citizen population – as a conventional 'big number' that means nothing more precise than 'lots'. Having said which, it may be of some relevance that this is the number that Thucydides – who did after all have some idea of the size of the citizen population, and was in a position to judge the relative proportion of the slave and free populations – actually chose to represent 'lots'. There is also some interest in asking who these slaves were, or rather how they were employed, and this is a question to which I return below.

Given how few data there are, it is hardly surprising, then, that there is wide variation in the estimates for slave numbers provided by modern historians. The most minimal view was famously articulated by Jones, who argued for a total number of slaves in Attica of around 20,000 to 30,000.[9] At the other end of the scale, Gomme suggested a total number of slaves in 431 of 115,000.[10] Most other estimates have fallen between Jones' and Gomme's positions. Sargent concluded that there were perhaps 70,000 to 100,000 slaves in the period when 'the slave population reached its greatest expansion', that is 'in the fifth century, after

---

[9] Jones 1957, 10–20.
[10] Gomme 1933, 20–3, with table 1 at 26. There appears to be a discrepancy of 5,000 between the text and the figures in the table.

the Persian Wars, and before the disasters of the Peloponnesian War'.[11] Rhodes has suggested a round figure of 100,000.[12] At the lower end of the scale, Hanson followed Jones and suggested 20,000 to 30,000.[13] Scheidel, in an article concentrating on the importance of women's labour in Greek households, and so rhetorically disposed to play down the importance of slaves, suggested that 30,000 to 50,000 should be considered a maximum. Jameson again responded that a figure of 50,000 is more likely to have been a minimum.[14] Hansen suggested a moderate-to-high range of 66,000 to 93,000.[15] Wood, while concerned to play down as far as possible the importance of slaves in agriculture, is less concerned about global figures. In fact, she argues that even if Gomme's high estimate were allowed to stand, the number of agricultural slaves would still be very small.[16] In his general account of Greek slavery, Fisher avoids committing himself to any numbers in his own voice (reasonably enough in what is essentially a textbook), but implies support for a moderate maximalism. More recently, Bissa was happy to follow Hansen, and Moreno to follow Sargent.[17]

It is worth noting that in his 'conservative' estimate of the population in 431, Moreno adopts Sargent's higher maximum number of slaves of 97,000 (higher of two: the other one is derived from Beloch's estimate of the free population, which entailed smaller figures for slaves engaged in household service). This in turn was based on Meyer's estimate of the size of the free population.[18] This figure included 700 to 1,000 'slaves owned by the state', 29,000 to 30,000 'employed in household service', 10,000 to 12,000 'employed in agriculture'; 15,000 to 20,000 'employed in mining'; 28,000 to 30,000 'employed in other industry', and 9,000 to 10,000 'children under nine years of age'.

---

[11] Sargent 1924, 126–7; for the fourth century, she reckoned 60,000 to 70,000 was more likely.

[12] Rhodes 1992, 83.

[13] Hanson 1992a.

[14] Scheidel 1995; Jameson 2002, a modification of the views expressed in Jameson 1977–8.

[15] Hansen 1988, 10–12.

[16] Wood 1983, 43–4.

[17] Bissa 2009, 172; Moreno 2007, 29–30.

[18] Moreno 2007, 29–30; Sargent 1924, 126.

Although Moreno's comment that Sargent's 'methodology of pro-portionality and of differentiation between individual sectors of ownership (public, household, agriculture, mining and other industry) is ... sound' is fair enough, it is less obvious that it 'yields conservative results, useful in achieving minimum esti-mates of population and consumption'.

Moreno has committed himself earlier in his account to the traditional picture of Greek (and by extension Attic) agriculture defended by Isager and Skydsgaard; presumably this makes him sympathetic to the relatively small fraction of Sargent's total represented by 'slaves employed in agriculture'. Sargent's account remains valuable; it is thorough, sober, and sensible. Moreno's evident admiration for Meyer is not at all unjustified. Nonetheless, the Sargent–Meyer model is reflective of the times in which it was produced, and of the modernising orthodoxy that prevailed (and which Meyer himself had, of course, done so much to establish). That there were 30,000 slaves in domestic service, and another 30,000 in 'other industry' would not now necessarily appear to be 'conservative' estimates. In the case of 'other industry', one might wonder what these industries were, and whether they were as fully dominated by slaves to the extent implied by such a figure. The most impressive remaining products of imperial Athens, its painted pottery and its monumental buildings, were each probably the work of a few hundreds of men at a time, and the majority were not slaves. As for the 'domestics', this figure would be most easily explained by fairly deep penetration through the citizen group of slave-ownership – and one would expect many of them to have been engaged at least some of the time in some kind of agricultural labour, in what would have been quite ordinary farmers' house-holds. It is also possible that views about the indispensability of domestic servants were rather different in the early twentieth century from those after the Second World War. The figure for mining slaves here is not especially low, although it is not at the top of the range of modern estimates. Peter Acton has argued for quite large numbers of slaves involved in manufacturing, but is reluctant (understandably) to suggest definitive total numbers.[19]

---

[19] Acton 2014, 288.

The 'representative' figures he deploys in his appendix are derived from existing scholarship, including Sargent.[20]

In the absence of good direct evidence, all of these arguments depend on the same two basic approaches. In the first place, there are inferences about the extent of slave-ownership in the citizen population, based on what the literary sources seem to think is normal. In the second there are attempts to look at the tasks in which slaves were certainly employed in classical Athens, and to try to work out how many slaves it would have taken to carry out those tasks.[21] While some progress has been made with variations on the second approach since Sargent, it is important to note that while she ended up with quite high (maximum) estimates, Jones developed his extreme minimalist position by arguing that there were really very few places where we can be sure that significant numbers of slaves were employed.

The overriding impression given by the literary evidence, however, is that slave-ownership was normal and widespread, if not universal, among the whole citizen body, and so the natural inference is that the slave population was indeed large. Beyond the very large totals given by the Hyperides and Ctesicles passages, the usual assumption in oratory and comedy seems to be that most citizens could routinely be expected to own at least one slave. Most clearly, there is Lysias 5.5, delivered in the aftermath of the restoration of democracy:

This trial should not, I think, be a private matter for these men alone, but a common concern for everyone in the city. For it is not just these men who own slaves, but everyone else too: slaves who, when they consider the fate of these men, will no longer think about what service they could do for their masters to gain their freedom, but rather about what false allegations they could make about them.

Todd's comment in his commentary is worth noting: 'it is extremely dangerous to draw demographic conclusions from a remark like this, not least because Lysias is seeking to magnify the argument from social consequences by generalising the threat'.[22]

---

[20] Acton 2014, 299–317.
[21] Acton 2014, 299–317, presents both approaches. He is only interested in manufacturing workers, but slaves are prominent in his account.
[22] Todd 2007, 396.

We might compare Lysias 24.6: 'My trade, at which I can now only work with difficulty, can only help a little, and I cannot yet acquire someone to take it over from me.' The implication here is that even the most destitute of citizens expected and aimed to be able to buy slaves to assist them in their work. The problem with this particular (and rather inept) speech is that it may well not have been delivered in an actual case, and also may not accurately reflect the views of ordinary Athenian citizens.[23] On the other hand, it strengthens the impression that at least some people in fourth-century Athens thought that slave-ownership was very widespread.

Likewise, Aristophanes gives us a consistent picture of men who are apparently to be taken as 'ordinary' citizens – men like Dikaiopolis in *Acharnians* and Chremylus in *Wealth* – who possess not one but several slaves.

In detail, this kind of evidence is open to attack, and Jones exploited the openings with some vehemence:

A man for whom Lysias wrote a little speech does indeed roundly assert that everyone has slaves; but he is trying to convince the jury that it is contrary to public policy to encourage slaves to inform against their masters. In comedy domestic slaves appear when dramatically convenient, even in the poorest households, but this evidence is suspect: comedy was written after all by well-to-do authors, and slaves provided a variety of stock comic turns.[24]

While admitting that 'slaves were employed in many capacities – as domestic servants, as clerks and agents in commerce and banking, in agriculture, and in industry and mining' and that 'all well-to-do Athenian families had several servants, and no doubt wealthy men kept large households of a dozen or more' – Jones also contended that 'the domestic servant probably did not go very far down the social scale'. The point about the well-to-do authors of comedy is potentially a telling one, but Jones seems to have overstated the strength of his case: such a consistent picture cannot just be explained away in the terms he uses. Still, reference to the direct literary evidence alone is clearly going to remain indecisive. Most estimates, and certainly the more generous ones, rely on the

---

[23] Reeve 1968.
[24] Jones 1957, especially 11–13.

identification of the *roles* that slaves played in classical Athens. The principal areas of slave employment that need discussion are public slaves, agriculture, warfare, mining and other industry, and 'domestic' slaves.[25]

Two of these categories are relatively unproblematic. The *polis* of Athens clearly owned a certain number of slaves who performed a variety of functions. While we surely only hear about some of them in the sources, there are unlikely to be huge numbers of which we neither know anything nor can reasonably infer the existence. Estimates here are all in the hundreds (the largest single body may have been the Scythian archers of the fifth century), with about 1,000 being a plausible round estimate for the total. In the mines, estimates for the numbers of men employed at periods of peak production vary from 11,000 to 30,000. The lower estimate is that of Conophagos, whose detailed and knowledgeable account has strong claims to be taken seriously. His argument centres on the physical remains of the Laurion district, but it is also entirely compatible with such written evidence as we have. His total compares interestingly with what Xenophon recommends in the *Poroi* at 4.23–4; although what Xenophon goes on to say implies that he believed that far larger holdings existed in the fifth century. Still, the figures that Xenophon provides at 4.14–15 for the (presumably unusually large) holdings of Nicias, Hipponicus, and Philemonides, if we can have any confidence in them at all, seem to be at least consistent with a total labour force that only just gets into five figures at times of particularly intensive exploitation.[26]

The other categories are much harder to get to grips with, not least because they are less clearly defined. Public slaves and mining slaves only had one job. A slave owned by a private household might perform a range of tasks according to the needs of that household and the time of year. In a household with a small farm, a single slave might help in the fields at times of peak demand for labour, but at others might perform general domestic duties and/or be employed in petty manufacture or retail to

---

[25] Compare Rihll 2011.
[26] Conophagos 1980. Rihll 2001 on the logistical implications of this number.

supplement the household's cash income; a male slave might attend his master when the latter went to war, whether as hoplite or as rower. In wealthier households, there would undoubtedly have been at least some greater specification of slave tasks (such as the overseers referred to by Xenophon in the *Oikonomikos*, and perhaps also nurses for childcare tasks) and, defining 'household' more widely, the workshops owned by the wealthy contained slaves who were engaged permanently in the relevant artisanal activities.[27] We can, however, at least make a start at quantification. As with the citizens, even if there is no possibility of reaching absolutely firm numbers, it is worth establishing the limits of the possible (or at least the plausible), and the exercise itself can generate some interest by making us confront our assumptions.

With 'other industry' (possibly something of a misnomer, since the silver mines and the dockyards were perhaps the only sectors of the Athenian economy that can meaningfully be said to have been industrialised), there is a limit to what we can say at present. The most familiar and enduring physical remains of classical Athens – its monumental architecture and its painted pottery – were certainly in part the products of slave labour. But both probably only required the work of at most a few hundreds of men at a time, the majority of whom were free men in any case.[28] Clearly, there were some quite large manufacturing businesses, each employing dozens of slaves, but it is very difficult to know how many there were beyond the ones we hear about.[29] The workshops belonging to Demosthenes' father and to Polemarchus are not referred to as if they were utterly exceptional, but they also clearly belonged to some of the very wealthiest men in Athens, and ones who may in fact have been unusual in their focus on manufacture rather than agriculture. How many more workshops were there on this kind of scale? And how many more that were smaller, like the perfumery we hear about in Hyperides 3? To supply the needs of a city the size of Athens, not to mention the other sizeable towns of Attica, there must have

---

[27] Acton 2014, especially 281–8: at 282, Acton appears to endorse a maximalist position.

[28] Hannestad 1988; *IG* I³ 475.

[29] Lysias 12.19; Aeschines 1.97; Demosthenes 27.9, 36.11.

been very many people making all kinds of goods.[30] But how many of them, and how many were slaves, is virtually impossible to establish with more precision than 'thousands'.

With the central concerns of *polis* existence – warfare and agriculture – there is, however, some more scope for assessing the scale of the contribution of slaves.

Slaves at War

The military employment of slaves gave even Jones slightly more pause than their ubiquity in comedy and oratory. A central piece of evidence is Thucydides 3.17.4, which implies that every Athenian hoplite would normally expect to take a slave attendant on campaign with him. Gomme observed that this could be used to argue for a male slave for every citizen and metic over the age of 20 in the 'hoplite and cavalry classes' – although he also considered a figure of around 35,000 adult male slaves derived on this basis as very much a maximum for male 'domestics'.[31] He suggested a slightly higher maximum for the female slaves in domestic service – a number essentially plucked out of the air, with the justification that there 'may' have been more women than men slaves in this role (his note 3). On the basis of Thucydides 7.27.3–5, Gomme inferred (implicitly assuming that the 20,000 figure was genuine and accurate, and taking a very literal reading of Thucydides' text) that 'something like 40,000 to 50,000 slaves were engaged in 'industry' (excluding mining), for a total maximum slave population in 431 of c. 115,000.[32] The impression of every hoplite and cavalryman having his own slave is reinforced by Thucydides 7.75, where their absence from the defeated Athenian army at Syracuse is a measure of the wretched state of that force. These followers are variously referred to as *akolouthoi, skeuophoroi,* and *huperetai.* As Hunt notes, there was not always any clear distinction between these terms.[33]

---

[30] This is the 'demand' side of Acton's appendix (2014: 311–17).

[31] Gomme 1933, 21.

[32] Gomme 1933, 26, table 1. Note that there is a slight discrepancy between the text on 21 and this table for the number of male domestic slaves.

[33] Hunt 1998, 167 note 7; Welwei 1974, 58–62.

The sceptical Jones, however, noted that while 'those hoplites who owned suitable slaves certainly used them for this purpose ... there is no evidence that every hoplite's attendant was his own slave'.[34] This is perhaps fair enough, although as long as we are only concerned with global figures, it is not a major problem. As Jones went on, 'the high rate of the state allowance [according to Thucydides, one drachma per hoplite, plus another drachma for his attendant], on the contrary, is only explicable on the assumption that many hoplites would have to hire a man for the purpose'.[35]

This is a more problematic claim. A lot depends in fact on *why* the hoplites (and cavalrymen) themselves were given state support at this relatively high rate. If it was simply to enable them to procure provisions (at presumably inflated campaign prices in the siege camp), then their own slaves will have needed to have been fed as well. If, as could be suggested for the pay provided for dikasts, it was meant to compensate ordinary citizens for the loss of produce or earnings while they were away from their farms and workshops, then they would surely also need to have been compensated for the diversion of the labour of their slave assistants. It is not therefore obviously true that the 'only' explanation for the drachma a day paid for each attendant was to enable the hiring of that man.

Jones goes on, as if to strengthen his point, that 'Thucydides' inclusion of the baggage carriers with the light-armed among the Athenian casualties at Delium implies that they were citizens'.[36] It does not, unless one presupposes that the *psiloi* were all citizens, which there seems no good reason to do. In fact, one might instead argue that the Greek actually serves to separate both the light-armed and the baggage carriers from the 'Athenians', who are presumably the citizens: they are not specifically hoplites and cavalry only.[37]

It is undoubtedly true, however, that not all of the attendants, baggage carriers, and so on of an Athenian army on campaign

---

[34] Jones 1957, 12.

[35] Jones 1957, 12–13. See 124–125 below for the suggestion that perhaps a rental market for slaves may not have existed away from the mining industry.

[36] Jones 1957, 13; Thuc. 4.101.2

[37] ἀπέθανον δὲ Βοιωτῶν μὲν ἐν τῇ μάχῃ ὀλίγῳ ἐλάσσους πεντακοσίων, Ἀθηναίων δὲ ὀλίγῳ ἐλάσσους χιλίων καὶ Ἱπποκράτης ὁ στρατηγός, ψιλῶν δὲ καὶ σκεοφόρων πολὺς ἀριθμός.

were slaves, or even non-citizens. There is one clear exception: the story in Isaeus 5.11 (*On the estate of Dicaeogenes*). Here it is alleged by the speaker that one Cephisidotus was sent off on campaign to act as a servant to his uncle Harmodius by his other uncle Dicaeogenes. There are a number of points that can be made about this passage, apart from the fact that it provides one instance of a man of citizen birth being employed as an *akolouthos*. It is not entirely clear how old Cephisidotus was at the time, and so he may not have been formally enrolled as a citizen. In the first place, as Van Wees has observed, it is interesting that the attendants of Athenian hoplites seem to have been expected to maintain certain standards of dress: Cephisidotus is chastised for his shabby appearance when he reports for duty.[38] But it is also worth noting that Cephisidotus is sent out *ant' akolouthou*, that is, 'in place' of an attendant, not 'to be' an attendant. The whole point of the story is to paint Dicaeogenes as an absolute blackguard who has utterly failed in his duties to his kinsman. Sending Cephisidotus as an attendant is proof of his *hubris* and *miaria* – extremely strong words – especially because he was receiving a healthy income at the time from an inherited estate. The mention of his income implies that he was acting meanly. Whether this was because he was refusing to risk one of his own slaves, or that some of these funds should have been used to hire an appropriate attendant, is unclear, but not important here. Since Cephisidotus was apparently dishonoured by being despatched to fulfil this duty for one of his relations, it seems unlikely that another *citizen* would have done the job for a stranger in exchange for pay.[39] It is perhaps worth mentioning, as Van Wees is clearly aware but does not make quite explicit, the case of Cephisidotus is a powerful reason for really believing that the 'Homeric' attendants of a warrior, themselves freeborn young men, sometimes of high status, were not a feature of the classical period. This incident also took place during the rather straitened circumstances of the Corinthian war; it might not be wise to try to use it as evidence for what happened

[38] Van Wees 2004, 68–9.
[39] Jameson 1992, 141 note 41. A similar kind of rule-proving exception in Xenophon's *Anabasis* is discussed by Hunt 1998, 168–9.

in the more prosperous Athens of the 430s and 420s, or later in the fourth century.

Jones, however, held that:

> more significant than these uncertain inferences is a remark by Demosthenes, who, castigating the harshness with which Androtion and Timocrates collected the arrears of war tax, pictures them 'removing doors and seizing blankets and distraining on a servant girl if anyone employed one' [Dem. 24.197]. Now the payers of war tax can be estimated to have numbered only about 6,000 out of a population of 21,000. If not all of them had a domestic servant, one may hazard that under a quarter of the population enjoyed that luxury.[40]

The argument for the 6,000 figure is essentially that there were 100 war tax symmories (on the basis of Cleidemus *FGH* 3.323, fr. 8; according to Demosthenes 14.14, there were only 20 trierarchic symmories, so the symmories to which Cleidemus refers must be the *eisphora* symmories) and that there were the same number of men (60) in the *eisphora* symmories as there were in the trierarchic ones (Demosthenes 14.16–17: the trierarchic symmories are supposed to have been modelled on those for the *eisphora*.)

The domestic servants to which Jones is referring here are all female; strictly speaking, this evidence is not relevant to the question of how many households had male slaves available to accompany their citizen members to war. Again, it is not immediately apparent that the situation that Demosthenes describes, in the 350s, need be reflective of the situation in Athens at other times, (say, 70 or 80 years previously), even if it were safe to take it at face value.

Jones' scepticism alone gives us little reason to doubt that the size of Athens' field army (13,000 hoplites, 1,000-odd cavalry) at least should make us think in terms of a similar number of slave attendants – or somewhere between 10,000 and 15,000 reasonably able-bodied male slaves – as a minimum starting figure. When not required on campaign, these men could have been employed in a variety of occupations, according to those of their masters. Since hoplite-based military operations took place principally in the slack periods of the agricultural year, those who could most easily be spared may have been those who normally worked in the fields,

[40] Jones 1957, 28–9.

as well as those who were domestic attendants. Skilled craftsmen were probably more likely to be left behind to continue a more profitable activity.

Van Wees, however, has provided a possible reason for doubting the validity of this picture. He has argued that the hoplites to whom Thucydides refers in 2.13 were not, as is usually assumed, all (or mostly) members of the *zeugitai* property class.[41] In Van Wees' model of the citizen population, the *zeugitai* were (relatively) wealthy and part of a relatively small elite within Athenian society, rather than the more moderately well-off part of the broad mass of the citizens. (That is, he sees them as more aligned with the *hippeis* and *pentacosiomedimnoi* than with the *thetes*.) Only the *zeugitai*, he suggests, were liable to be conscripted to fight as hoplites; while some (even many) of the *thetes* might have had the necessary minimum equipment to fight in a phalanx at need, they would not necessarily be expected to. The relevance of this in the current context is that only the *zeugitai* hoplites would routinely have had slave attendants. The support of these attendants would have allowed them to operate for longer periods at greater distances from home. Van Wees notes that the hoplite forces deployed for relatively distant operations from Athens were much smaller than Thucydides' totals in 2.13; the incursion into the Megarid, in this light, would have been exceptional in mobilising the whole active hoplite force – and we should not assume that every hoplite in this expedition, of short duration and close to Attica, *would* actually have been attended by a slave. If Van Wees is right, then our minimum figure for able-bodied male slaves would have to be roughly halved. The strength of the argument depends on Van Wees' picture of the distribution of wealth within the Athenian citizen body; as such, I shall defer full discussion until later. For the moment, we can accept that Van Wees presents an argument for minimising the number of able-bodied male slaves. That argument, however, could not bring the figure below about 5,000 or 6,000 at any time, given the scale of deployable hoplite forces apparently available to Athens.

Although slaves provided a vital part of the logistical support of the hoplite army, this was, of course, not the full extent of their

---

[41] Van Wees 2001.

military role. Particularly important for Athens was their use in the manpower-hungry trireme fleet. Again, we run up against the problems of establishing the exact composition of trireme crews and of estimating the total numbers of such crews. However, it is clear that slaves were employed in significant number in Athenian fleets, as they were in all the navies involved in the Peloponnesian War.[42]

Morrison, Coates, and Rankov suggest that 'slave oarsmen were unusual in Athenian ships at this time, but they are sometimes to be found and they were not always lacking in skill. When the Athenians were hard pressed to relieve Conon at Mytilene in 406, they promised freedom to the slaves who served in the ships they sent. Such an incident clearly indicates that their service in the fleet was unusual.'[43] This argument was well dealt with by Peter Hunt.[44] The situation at Arginusae was certainly unusual, but there is nothing to indicate that it was the recruitment of slaves into the fleet that was unusual. The desperation of the situation explains why the slaves were promised their freedom, which seems best explained as a mechanism for retaining the loyalty of these slaves and keeping them in the Athenian fleet in rather trying circumstances.

The evidence is far from abundant, but what there is suggests that in round figures about a third of Athenian trireme crews were made up of slaves, whether they were the attendants of the marines and officers, or rowing alongside their masters, or provided in some other way. *IG* i^3 1032 (ex ii^2 1951) implies a proportion of between 20 per cent and 40 per cent.[45] If the 'missing' crew from the Themistocles decree really were slaves, then they would have made up about a third of the crews too.

Since the Athenians at the start of the Peloponnesian War (and during most of it) seem routinely to have been able to deploy fleets of around 200 vessels, this would imply around another 13,000 or

---

[42] Van Wees 2004, 211–30; Jordan 2003, most recently arguing for between 50 and 60 (state-owned) slaves for a typical crew, and 2000, especially 92–3; Cohen 2000, 18; Hunt 1998, 122–43; Graham 1998, 1992.

[43] Morrison, Coates, and Rankov 2000, 118.

[44] Hunt 1998, 87–95.

[45] Hunt 1998, 88, with Laing 1965, 93.

so able-bodied adult male slaves added to the total for that period. Since they were presumably mostly skilled crewmen, they would have been less clearly available for other tasks, even when there were not active hostilities in progress. Likewise, because of the lack of obvious conflict between the manpower demands for the fleet and for the land forces, these men should be assumed to have been separate from the attendants of the hoplite army. Just as with the citizens, consideration of Athens' military potential does allow us to say *something* about the minimum number of slaves in Athens. At the least, even bearing in mind the implications of Van Wees' arguments about hoplites and wealth distribution, for 431 we must think in terms of 20,000 able-bodied adult males to add to the 12,000 or so employed by the *polis* and in the mines. This gives us the *total* figure suggested by Jones, even before we take into account any female slaves (who clearly did exist), or those male slaves who either were not needed by or were too valuable to their masters (by virtue of specialised skills) to take on campaign. Extreme minimalist views of the number of slaves in Athens cannot be accepted, on this basis.

Slavery in Athenian Agriculture

The role of slaves in Athenian agriculture has been a more intensely controversial issue. Even by his standards, Jones was particularly dismissive at this point, claiming that 'in agriculture, we hear little of slaves'.[46] His argument turned almost entirely on Androtion and Timocrates' seizure of slave-girls and what he took to be their consequent absence from the households even of many of those who were liable for the *eisphora*. Although his extreme picture has won few adherents, the idea that slave labour was only of importance to the Athenian elite as far as agriculture was concerned has been much more vigorously defended. On the kind of 'minimalist' model advocated by, in particular, Wood and Sallares, for the majority of Athenian farmers, any extra labour demanded by the household would have come almost entirely from neighbours or from hired workers. In opposition to

[46] Jones 1957, 13.

this view, it has been argued by 'maximalists' that slaves were more commonly used – that not only did all members of the *eisphora*-paying 'class' own slaves, but also very many poorer citizens, most or even all of the 'hoplite' class, or even some of the '*thetes*'.[47]

It is worth observing in passing, following Fisher, that even a 'maximalist' view does not hold that slave-owning enabled 'ordinary Athenians to become men of leisure, able to devote all their lives to politics or leisure, nor that the limited amounts of payment offered for jury service, political office-holding, or military service would release them from the need for hard manual work'.[48] Finding anyone who would seriously hold such a view now is difficult. This was a position that was already the subject of attack from Sargent. Wood was also concerned to dispel this image, but the positions she was attacking were not always quite those occupied by the people she cast as her opponents.[49]

The literary evidence is simply insufficient to resolve the issue. On the one side, we have Jones claiming that there is little direct indication of slave employment in agriculture, and similar views more recently developed by Wood. On the other, there are those who, like Garlan and De Ste Croix,[50] suggest that much literary evidence presupposes the widespread existence of agricultural slavery and assumes that the original audiences in classical Athens would have been intimately familiar with it. And this is indeed a major problem for an extreme minimalist position like that held by Jones – the overall picture consistently given by the literary evidence really is that there were quite a lot of slaves in Attica. The key question then becomes what they were doing, as one strategy that could be adopted by the advocates of a minimalist position on slaves in *agriculture* is that there were, or could have been, lots of slaves but, except on the estates of the rich, they were all doing something else.[51] This is essentially the line taken by

---

[47] Fisher 2001, 40–2, for a fuller summary and the categorisation of 'minimalists' and 'maximalists'.

[48] Fisher 2001, 42.

[49] Wood 1988.

[50] Garlan 1988, 64; De Ste Croix 1981, 505–6.

[51] A point on which the 'minimalist' Sallares and the 'maximalist' De Ste Croix were agreed; Sallares 1991, 54.

Wood, although how far she adopted this position simply for the sake of argument is not clear.[52]

The key attempt to argue for the widespread use of slaves in Athenian agriculture was advanced by Michael Jameson.[53] Influenced in part by Ester Boserup, he argued that as the population of Attica increased while the available land remained the same, farmers would have been obliged to pursue strategies of intensified production.[54] With the available technological base, all such strategies would have depended on increased inputs of labour. While yields per unit area could be increased, however, this would have come at the expense of (either or both of) the ideal of *autarkeia* (a restraint on the extent to which specialisation of production for a market could be adopted), or 'the periodic leisure for social functions the Greek valued'.[55] These undesirable consequences for the ordinary Athenian citizen could be avoided (or at least mitigated) by the employment of slave labour. This is an important point.

The picture presented by Jameson of increased population leading to agricultural intensification (broadly defined) is in many ways a compelling one. The picture that is emerging about the size of the total population undercuts to an extent one of the key objections to Jameson's argument presented in Wood's critique, that 'Jameson's propositions about demographic growth and intensification turn out to be rather vague and indeterminate'.[56]

It is also, I think, an unfair exaggeration to argue, as Wood does, that Jameson's 'whole case turns on the proposition that "slave-holding enabled the Athenian to be a participant in a democracy"'. That would be a potentially serious objection, but in fact it does not so turn, or at the very least need not. It is worth considering here the observations of Scheidel; that citizens had other calls on their time is not irrelevant to the scale of use of slave labour.[57] To a large degree, the argument for intensification turns instead on

[52] Wood 1988.
[53] Initially, Jameson 1977–8; but restated and partially modified in Jameson 1992, 1994, 2002.
[54] Boserup 1965.
[55] Jameson 1977–8, 129.
[56] Wood 1988, 52–3.
[57] Scheidel 2008.

the proposition that without intensifying production 'the Athenian' would have had great difficulty just in surviving.[58] At the very least, there would have been severe pressures (positive and negative) on him to intensify production. The logic of Jameson's argument is not nearly as weak as Wood contended.

It is true that the use of chattel slavery was not the only option available for those who wanted to intensify production on their land (or just wanted to employ extra labour). It is clearly the case that waged, free labour was employed on Athenian farms, and this is a point that Wood makes very well.[59] It is also true that wage labour and slavery are not the only two (and mutually exclusive) forms of labour available, whether to the elite or to ordinary citizens. However, Wood does not deal with the sheer ubiquity of slaves, even those engaged (at least some of the time) in agriculture, as it is presented in the literary texts. Trying to explain them away in terms of 'linguistic and conceptual ambiguity' is insufficient, not least because the existence of such ambiguity is in fact itself questionable.[60]

Here we should return briefly to Thucydides 7.27.5. The *number* he gives of 20,000 has, as we have seen, no claim to be taken at all seriously. What may be more interesting is what the slaves he is referring to did before they were lost to the Athenians. The natural reading of the passage as a whole is that Thucydides is stressing the Athenians' loss of control over their *chora* – which seems, first and foremost, to be the countryside as a place of agricultural production. The slaves who 'deserted' are mentioned along with the flocks and the yoke animals. The silver mines are not explicitly mentioned here, in spite of attempts to argue that many, if not most of the slaves must have come from there.[61]

This is not altogether surprising. Laurion is after all quite a long way away from Decelea, and the Athenian cavalry, at least, were maintaining a posture of active defence. In spite of Wood's derision, De Ste Croix was surely right when he observed that slaves

---

[58] Moreno 2007, 37–76.

[59] Wood 1988, 70–2.

[60] Wood 1988, 46–51; Jameson 2002, 168, provides a response to the claim of ambiguity in references to agricultural labour.

[61] Recently Patterson 2007, 160; *Poroi* 4.114–5 is cited in a footnote, but its immediate relevance to this context is unclear.

who worked in agriculture would have had more opportunities for escape.[62]

That mining slaves had more to gain by escaping, since those slaves who ended up in Decelea were sold on to new Boeotian masters, is not a strong argument. The *Hellenica Oxyrhynchia* (London 17.3) implies that many in fact were captured, not deserters. Thucydides also does not quite say that the slaves who deserted did so to Decelea. The implication of his claim is that the fort caused the Athenians to lose control over their countryside, and that as a result they were unable to prevent escapes – and not necessarily that it provided a refuge for escaped slaves in the way that, for example, the Athenian *epiteichismos* at Pylos had for Spartan helots. Peloponnesian League troops would presumably have been as happy to round up deserters as to capture slaves who were not trying to escape. In any case, it is not necessary to assume that even slaves who did choose to run away to Decelea knew what fate awaited them. Not all escapes need have been carefully thought out or well pre-pared. Furthermore, for many slaves, just removing themselves from an active war zone may have been sufficient incentive for an escape.

The reference to *cheirotechnai* is not decisive proof that large numbers of miners were among the escapers. Miners could indeed be *cheirotechnai*, but so could all kinds of other craftsmen and artisans. It may well be too much to assume that they were specialist agricultural workers such as vine dressers. Rather than 'specialist' agricultural workers, the Greek would surely allow them just to be 'skilled' at various aspects of farming. Success in farming is not, after all, just a matter of common sense and hard work, even if Xenophon's Ischomachus might want us to think so.[63] But in spite of what Wood asserts, if they were not specialist agricultural workers, this is not as damaging to Jameson's position as she allows the reader to infer. Precisely part of his point about intensification in the wide sense (which for Jameson includes diversification of household activity) was that slaves could be

---

[62] De Ste Croix 1981, 506; Wood 1988, 67–8. It may be worth noting in passing that the mines are not mentioned at all in Thuc. 7.27 or, incidentally in the summary of Athenian resources at 2.13. The only time that the mines are mentioned as being (potentially) vulnerable to a fort at Decelea is in the voice of Alcibiades at 6.91.7.

[63] Xen. *Oec.* 15–21.

turned to other productive work in a diversified and commercialised economy.[64] As Wood observes:

> the slave population of the *chora* would certainly have included mineworkers and domestic servants, as well as the skilled craftsmen who laboured in the villages and small townships scattered throughout Attica. (It is, after all, important to remember that 'urban' craftsmen cannot have been confined to the city of Athens.)[65]

This is entirely true, but the crucial issue is who owned these slaves. If they were part of small citizen households, the fact that they were not primarily (or even at all) agricultural workers is rather beside the point.

Another approach that tried to get away from the exiguous direct evidence for the number and location of slaves in Attic agriculture was taken by Osborne. Osborne worked indirectly to assess the degree to which slaves would have *had* to have been exploited by the elite.[66] He started by assuming that something like 50,000 ha of land in Attica each year would have been under cereal cultivation (about 20 per cent of the total land area). On the basis of his earlier suggestions about patterns of landholding, he reckoned that about a quarter to a third of this land was owned by the 2,000 richest families, which would have meant something like 15,000 ha being cultivated by the richest 3,000 citizens.[67] The remaining 35,000 ha would have been divided among the remaining citizens – around 25,000 of them in the fourth century.

One of the periods of the agricultural year when labour is most in demand is harvest. By using the comparative data collected by Halstead and Jones,[68] Osborne suggested that getting in the harvest from the small estates belonging to the bulk of the Athenian citizens (the 25,000) would have required the labour of something like 35,000 people. The harvest from the comparatively large estates of the rich would have required the labour of 15,000.

---

[64] This is a point made more explicitly in Jameson 2002.
[65] Wood 1988, 68.
[66] Osborne 1995.
[67] Osborne 1991. All the figures are debatable in detail – see 207–210 below – but there is nothing obviously implausible about them which would prevent them being accepted for the sake of the argument.
[68] Halstead and Jones 1989.

What this suggests is that there really was a need for a considerable amount of extra labour beyond the family on the estates of the rich – at least at times of peak activity. But there does not *obviously*, on Osborne's model, seem to have been such a need on the farms of the more 'typical' Athenian farm. In fact, Osborne notes that 'on a family farm the labour available varies considerably at different stages of the family's own history, depending on the amount of female and juvenile labour available, a variation emphasized by the normally late age of male marriage'.[69]

---

[69] Osborne 1995, 33, with a reference to Gallant 1991, 11–33, 60–112. It is certainly true that, as Gallant argues, there will be times in the life cycle of a household when the amount of labour available will be small relative to the number of dependents present, and that in these circumstances the purchase of a slave might well be attractive if there is the cash available to pay for one. That 'if' is quite a big one, but here again the provision of *misthos* in cash and the generally diversified, commercialised, and monetised nature of the economy of classical Athens might make it smaller than elsewhere in Greece, especially combined with the pressures towards intensification of production within households. On the other hand, there will be times when households have lots of labour available to them – if the children are teenagers or adults, and the parents are still alive, or when a couple has just married and have no dependants, for example. In Attica there were tens of thousands of households at all stages of the household life cycle. Those which were short of labour were probably matched in number by those which were overflowing with it. These households did not exist in isolation – indeed, another potentially unusual aspect of Attica was the wealth and strength of local and wider social networks that existed there, many of which were based on various forms of reciprocity. There seems no reason in principle why labour-rich households could not have provided labour to those which were labour-poor, without any recourse to slaves. In fact, this must surely have happened, but there were dangers for both parties to such a strategy if the labourers provided were of citizen birth. The household providing the labour could be seen to be creating a reciprocal obligation on the household that received the labour; on the other hand, the actual labourers might be in danger of appearing to be subservient to the household for which they were working. However, the delicacy of the situation may help to make sense of a passage in Xenophon which has appeared rather baffling to modern readers. This is the story of Eutheros' conversation with Socrates in *Memorabilia* 2.8. In the aftermath of the Peloponnesian War, Eutheros was reduced to manual labour to make his living. This can only be a temporary expedient, as he is no longer a young man. Socrates suggests that he instead seek employment as a farm bailiff, but Eutheros retorts that he does not want to be a slave. Socrates then goes on to try to persuade him that such a job would not in fact be any worse than any other kind of work. The point that concerns Socrates – whether being a bailiff is actually servile – is not at issue here. What modern readers have had more difficulty with is why Eutheros does not perceive his *existing* employment as slavish – and clearly he does not. Part of the reason may be that by providing labour for another household he can (at least in his own mind) be considered to be in the superior position in social terms, whatever the economic reality. That is, he is not dependent on that household but doing them a favour. Taking up a position as a bailiff, a permanent employee, would remove that possibility. Wood 1988, 69, is right to observe that the logic of the story is that many citizens actually did act as bailiffs – but she goes too far in saying that it says nothing about the existence of slave bailiffs. A job that was characteristically performed by citizens surely could not be

Osborne's argument is ingenious and stimulating, but it is supposed to apply directly to the situation in the fourth century. The picture must have been different in the fifth – although to what extent and in what ways, we have yet to establish. However, one possibility must be that the 'structural necessity' for extra labour in the households of the rich was even greater in the years leading up to the Peloponnesian War, as more land will have been concentrated in the hands of those households.

The effect on poorer households is harder to judge, but a couple of points have to be made. One is that we have a kind of parallel here with the exploitation of livestock. Slaves in the household would indeed have been extra mouths to feed, but there were social benefits aside from the economic implications. Further, employing extra agricultural labour was not the *only* way of pursuing an intensification strategy for small householders. In addition to craft production, slaves could be taken along to row in the fleet (with the master pocketing the pay). As plots of land became smaller, the *need* for extra labour at times when the household's native resources were, for whatever reason, depleted would have become all the more intense. Slavery was not the only option for plugging the gaps, but it did provide some unique advantages.[70]

This is consistent with the picture painted by Scheidel, who has developed another interesting line of argument about the place of slaves in classical Athens by placing them in a comparative economic context with their counterparts in the Roman empire.[71] Scheidel observes that the suggestions made in the past by Jones and Duncan-Jones about the low cost of slaves in Attica seem to be borne out by more exhaustive surveys of evidence than they had been able to carry out. Slave labour in classical Athens really does seem to have been cheap when reckoned in terms of 'wheat equivalent' in relation to daily wages for free hired labourers and grain prices, compared to

---

considered slavish. Quite possibly many bailiffs were metics, but that would not necessarily suffice to remove the taint of servility from the role (see 136–142 below).

[70] On the last point, see especially Jameson 2002. Forsdyke 2006 emphasises that 'intensification' is not a single activity.

[71] Scheidel 2005, 2008.

those in Roman Egypt and elsewhere in the empire under the principate.[72] He goes on to note:

It must have paid to buy slaves instead of relying on hired labor … High real wages indicate labor scarcity. Imported slaves were both cheaper and more dependable than free wage-laborers. In this environment it may even have been profitable to keep slaves simply to hire them out.[73] This creates an apparent paradox. If slave labor was so competitive and readily available, why didn't demand increase until slave prices rose to less inviting levels and the value of free labor fell? I suspect that slave markets may have been limited in scope. Greek states that relied on more archaic forms of bondage had lower incentives to bid for slaves, and even within the 'slave society' *poleis* of central Greece, only a limited proportion of the population would control sufficient resources to invest in chattel slaves. In conjunction with abundant supplies from many different regions, these factors may have stabilized slave prices at relatively low levels.[74]

This passage illustrates well just how complex some of the problems of interpretation are here. Scheidel's basic point is that slaves were cheap in Athens. At a superficial level, this should mean that slave-ownership could have extended quite a long way down the economic hierarchy in Athens, as those citizens who had a need or desire for slave labour should have been able to acquire it without too much difficulty. This is, again, consistent with the general impression given by the literary texts.

However, things are unlikely to have been that simple. Scheidel's identification of his 'paradox' is only the beginning of the difficulties. Granted his premises, his attempts to resolve the paradox make sense and are surely part of whatever story we end

---

[72] Scheidel's argument, which he deliberately and explicitly weakens for rhetorical purposes by making assumptions that are as unfavourable as possible to his case, is potentially made even stronger if the volume-based units of measurement used for grain in classical Athens really were as light as the Grain Tax Law seems to imply – i.e., if an Attic *medimnos* of wheat really only weighed about 33 kg rather than the 40 kg that Scheidel assumes. In the former case, the 180 drachma cost of a typical slave would only have bought about 1–1.2 tonnes of wheat, as opposed to the 1.2–1.4 tonnes that Scheidel uses. On the other hand, such a reconstruction also makes the real price of wheat in Athens higher than Scheidel thinks.

[73] Of course, this is precisely what Xenophon tells us that Nicias and other wealthy Athenians of the late fifth century did in providing labour for the silver mines. This was a special case, however. Work below the surface in the mining industry was, as far as we can tell and unsurprisingly, exclusively carried out by slaves; and probably a lot of the work done on the surface was also done by slaves. Where the possibility of hiring free workers was effectively zero, a very particular form of 'labour scarcity' would result.

[74] Scheidel 2005, 14–15.

up telling. Abundance of supply would have helped to keep slave prices suppressed, and there is rarely any indication of any shortage of slaves for the Athenian market. The endemic warfare of the classical period would have generated huge numbers of slaves just within the Greek world; significant Athenian military victories would have dumped hundreds and occasionally thousands onto the market overnight, quite apart from the sources that existed outside Greece, even if those sources are not always as easy to identify as we might wish.[75]

Even in Athens, however, the outright purchase of a slave was not a trivial transaction: 180 drachmas was a substantial sum of cash, more than a labourer's annual wages if we assume a rate of about three obols per day and a substantial number of wage-free days in a year. Once bought, a slave could amortise himself or herself relatively quickly if they could bring in as much as two or three obols in profit every day, although the investment would not be without risk, as slaves could and clearly sometimes did abscond. Whether a typical citizen would routinely expect to have access to a couple of hundred drachmas in cash is still open to question. Sources of credit existed, but it may be significant that where we have a clear instance in the sources of a loan being made for the purpose of purchasing slaves, the rate of interest seems punitive.[76] Abundant supply and restricted demand would have kept prices low, but penetration of slave-ownership in the citizen body would still have been shallow if the cash was usually not available.

There is another paradox lurking behind the one pointed out by Scheidel. Slaves were cheap in relation to free labour, which was expensive. The latter observation should be surprising; although population levels fluctuated in Athens, the *polis* was densely populated throughout the classical period. As Scheidel points out, Athens should have had a 'thick' labour market, where free

---

[75] Occasions which saw large-scale enslavements (and which are recorded in literary sources) are collected and conveniently tabulated in Pritchett 1991, 226ff. For obvious reasons, the capture of whole cities and enslavement of populations was more a feature of the fifth than the fourth century, although in the latter, some unfortunate ship crews did find themselves enslaved. See also Lewis 2016.

[76] Lycurgus, *Against Leocrates* 23. Acton 2014 very much minimises the obstacles to acquiring a slave.

labour was cheap. In such circumstances, there would be little chance of slaves playing a significant role in the agricultural sector – and this was indeed the case in Roman Egypt. In Athens, however, as Scheidel points out, real wages seem to have been high. Scheidel's explanation for this centres on the 'commitments' to which free labourers were subject and which constrained their availability. By this he means not just the requirements of participation in Athenian civic and social life, but the ideological constraints that made it difficult for a citizen to be seen to be subordinated to another citizen.

What further complicates this picture is that it is not clear that real wages really were all that high throughout the classical period. Such evidence as we have is suggestive, but it is far from conclusive. Scheidel cites Loomis' 'exhaustive' survey to suggest that '1 drachma appears to have been a common [daily] wage for civilians and soldiers in the fifth century BC. Unskilled workers at the Erechtheion received 1–1.5 drachmas per day, skilled employees 1.25–2.5 drachmas.'[77] In a note (37), Scheidel goes on:

If a deliberately matter-of-fact list in comedy is to be trusted, 3 drachmas was a credible outlay to rent a cook for a day, while 1 drachma paid for a waiter (Men. *Asp.* 216–35); at the very least, these wages are consistent with the documentary evidence. This also suggests that state wages need not have been wildly out of sync with wages in the private sector. The strong presence of slaves among the Erechtheion builders also speaks against the assumption that wages associated with the project were abnormally high. The fact that Athenian citizens could apparently get by on 3 obols a day if they had to (M. M. Markle, 'Jury pay and Assembly pay at Athens', in Cartledge and Harvey, eds, 1985, 265–97, at 276–81) is consistent with this scenario of high (i.e., significantly higher than mere subsistence) real wages.

The Erechtheum builders' wages are undoubtedly important. However, it is worth noting that the relevant inscriptions do not tell us what Scheidel says that they do. Scheidel's figures (1–1.5 drachmas per day for unskilled workers, 1.25–2.5 drachmas per day for skilled workers) are not from the Erechtheum accounts but from the Eleusis accounts of the 320s. The Erechtheum workers seem almost all to have been paid one drachma per day,

[77] Scheidel 2005, 11–12.

although in some cases exactly for what period of time or for what task they were being paid is unclear.[78] Given that Scheidel is at this point claiming to be talking about the fifth century, the relevance of Menander is not all that apparent, unless we already have some reason to think that real wages did not change over the course of a century. On the other hand, if Scheidel was meaning to talk about Eleusis and the fourth century all along, then a consistent picture does emerge of wage levels and labour prices – for the late fourth century. This is in itself a valid point, but the evidence for slave prices is mainly from earlier periods. It comes from Xenophon and Demosthenes (including the cases about the latter's inheritance, which must have taken place around 363 BC), and from the public auctions of the property of the Hermokopidai, which were much closer in time to the Erechtheum accounts. Whichever way we look at the evidence, Scheidel's case has a problem with a lack of contemporary data to compare – unless, again, we assume that nothing of importance changed over the course of the classical period. This is possible, of course, but it probably needs to be demonstrated rather than being taken as a premise.

The problem with the fifth century is that there is almost no evidence for wages outside the public sector, so it is virtually impossible to tell how far the private sector was 'in sync' with it (although to be fair there is no particular reason why it should *not* have been). There does not seem to be any particular reason to accept Scheidel's comment that 'the strong presence of slaves among the Erechtheion builders ... speaks against the assumption that wages associated with the project were abnormally high'. As Loomis points out, there are reasons for thinking that the Erechtheum accounts actually do record a quite abnormal

---

[78] Loomis actually concludes that the one drachma per day rate apparently attested for the construction of the Erechtheum is exceptional, or at least exceptionally egalitarian – and, for a time when soldiers and sailors were receiving only three obols per day, unusually high. He is at something of a loss to explain, concluding (reasonably enough), 'at our distance, and with our relatively meagre evidence, we cannot always understand why the Athenians made the judgements that they did on questions of social value and comparability' (238). He goes on, 'but the mere asking of these questions does clarify the initial question about a standard wage: there is *no* evidence of a standard wage that applied to all workers in all fields' (238–9). Loomis has an axe to grind here, but while it does not contradict Scheidel's first point, it is worth bearing in mind that we have very little useful wage data for the fifth century in general.

situation. Even if this were not the case, Scheidel's claim seems to be a non sequitur, unless he believes that the slaves were able to keep the entirety of their wages. An equally plausible assumption would be that the sums would be pocketed by the slaves' masters, who would then have had every incentive to bring their slaves along if the wages had been abnormally high.

The most important part of his argument however is the claim that a wage of three obols a day was sufficient to support a citizen. Here he is on safer ground, although it is worth noting that if the implication of the Grain Tax Law for the weight of a *medimnos* of wheat is right, then not only would slaves have been cheaper in terms of wheat equivalent but the value of wages would have been reduced. Markle's calculations, on which Scheidel relies here, do assume a daily ration of 1.2 *choinikes* of barley. This was very much a maximum, as this would have provided nearly 100 per cent of a 'very active' male's daily calorie requirements as calculated by the FAO.[79] As Moreno points out, a lighter *medimnos* would bring the 'daily ration' down into the realms of a likelier number of calories.[80] Still, it would cost the best part of two obols for a family of four to buy the barley they needed. We need not accept Markle's claim that 'the other kinds of food in Athens were so cheap that they are hardly worth reckoning' – on his terms, it would cost two-and-a-half obols to provide very basic rations in barley, a very little olive oil, and some wine for that family of four.[81] If the normal daily wage was actually three obols rather than one drachma (as Markle assumed), then wages would not have been significantly above subsistence after all – and perhaps Scheidel's paradox can be made to disappear.

Markle assumed that one drachma per day was a normal wage in the fifth century. It is worth reflecting that even if the Erechtheum accounts are after all reflective of wages in general, by 409 the labour market in Athens had been significantly 'thinned'; the situation earlier in the fifth century could well have been rather different.

We shall return to some of these issues later on. For now, it is enough to observe that whatever we make of Scheidel's

[79] Markle 1985.
[80] Moreno 2007, 32.
[81] Markle 1985, 280.

observations, they could be used to suggest that slaves perhaps did not, after all, play a huge role in agriculture. If slaves were cheap and remained so, then that suggests that the market was constricted (as Scheidel points out) and demand was not sufficient to drive their price up. If they were not in fact as cheap as Scheidel suggested, then real wages were not as high, and it would have been easier to hire free labour (probably including, although by no means limited to, citizens).

Isager and Skydsgaard's argument against the widespread employment of slaves in agriculture was that at times of peak demand hired labourers could be employed. As we saw, Wood made the point well that hired wage labour clearly did exist in classical Attica. Against this, there is Scheidel's argument that, at least for those elite families about whom Osborne was talking, it may well have been more cost effective to buy slaves. True, the additional labour would only have been needed in the fields during some parts of the year, but for the rest of the year the slaves could be put to productive use in other ways. From an elite perspective, they could have helped with the generation of the cash they needed both to meet their obligations to the *polis* and to maintain their status and lifestyle. For poorer (but not destitute) Athenians, such a slave would help provide the economic flexibility that was stressed by Jameson and Halstead. For moderately well-off Athenians – that is, those who had their own farms and/or work-shops, however small – the low cost of slaves would have been a good thing, especially if it was being held down mainly by an abundance of supply. For the very poorest citizens, whose only real asset was their labour, it may have been a rather different story.

The number of slaves in Athens is then connected to the size of the citizen population, but the correlation is not a straightforward one. The key issue that emerges, beyond the implausibility of extreme minimalist views like that of Jones, is not so much one of the absolute size of the citizen population, but of how wealth was distributed within that population; and here overall size, while important, is not the only determining factor.

Before moving on, however, it is worth making one final observation. All the scholars mentioned so far have assumed that there was a straightforward choice between employing slave labour and free hired labour when work needed to be done. At least for Jones and Scheidel, it was a short and unproblematic step from there to assuming that slaves could themselves be hired out for profit by their owners. This might be right, but slave labour and free labour cannot always be directly substituted for each other. One set of differences between free and slave labour was discussed by Scheidel, as he sought to investigate the impact of the differences in incentives required by a slave and free labour force on the kinds of work for which they have been employed.[82] The situation one would intuitively expect, and which does apply to a certain extent, is one where free labourers are provided with positive incentives to work hard, whereas slaves are constrained with negative, pain-based incentives. In turn, one would expect this to lead to a situation where slaves are used for unskilled labour, but not for tasks that require attention to detail and care about the outcome, and that are harder to supervise. In practice, the situation is much more complicated, as slaves were clearly used for high-skilled labour in antiquity. One crucial factor is the desire of slave-owners to gain the benefit of investments made in the human capital represented by their workers. The turnover of workers in a skilled workforce is much easier to control if those workers are slaves rather than free men who can choose to go to another employer. However, while Scheidel is right to stress owners' investments in the intangible human capital of a skilled slave workforce, it is important to recall that slaves represented a more basic form of capital invest-ment too, and that this could have affected their roles in the labour markets of the classical world.

It is well known that rental markets for animal power (provided by bullocks, for example) often fail in the developing world today.[83] While it may appear to be adding insult to injury to compare slaves to draught or plough animals, there is, potentially, an important similarity. One important reason that the rental mar-kets in animals fail seems to be that owners are concerned that the

---

[82] Scheidel 2008.
[83] Hayami 2001, 413.

renters will overwork and abuse the animals to extract the max-imum output from them in the short term, as they have no interest in the long-term health of the animal. Similar concerns could have existed on the part of slave-owners, constraining the existence of a rental market in slave labour and further complicating the inter-action of slaves with the labour market. It may be significant that one place where we are sure that there was a rental market in slaves was the silver mines. This industry provided a special case, as there seems to be no doubt that the slaves must have been brutally constrained and no one (among the owners or renters) had much concern for the long-term prospects of the slaves, as there were none. Again, there was little or no competition with free workers for this kind of work. The peculiar circumstances of the mining industry cannot be used as a guide for the rest of the economy, where there may have been no, or only weak, rental markets for slave labour. If this were the case, then it would be a further step to resolving Scheidel's paradox.

Metics

The metics – free, but non-citizen residents of Attica – constitute the third and last significant portion of the population that we need to discuss. They present some of the same sorts of problems for us as do the slaves. There is very little in the way of direct evidence for their numbers. Such evidence as we do have suggests that they were, throughout the classical period, present in substantial num-bers, but going beyond this observation is much more difficult. Although their numbers were of some interest in antiquity, just because of their ubiquity – and what seems to have been their general reliability – the Athenians seem for much of the time just to have taken them for granted. From our perspective, it is difficult, if not impossible, to get to grips with the question of their numbers separately from that of the number of citizens. To make matters worse, the relationship between the number of metics and the number of citizens is potentially more complex than the relation-ship between the number of slaves and the number of citizens. It is also important to raise the question of what the metics actually did in classical Athens, just as Jones did with the slaves – even if that question is not a straightforward one to answer at all definitively.[84]

In other ways, however, the metics seem to be a rather less troublesome category of people for us to understand. The definition of a metic in Athens was, in at least some senses, pretty clearcut – a metic was someone who was subject to a particular tax, the *metoikion*. The people who had to pay this tax were non-Athenians who were resident in Attica for some period that was extended beyond a certain minimum – usually, and plausibly, taken to be 30 days. The situation in classical Athens should in fact be especially clear, and not just for the familiar reason that we are much better informed about metics in Athens than we are about their counterparts in other Greek *poleis*. Athens also presents a clear case because under the democracy (or at the very latest from 451/0 BC onwards), where there was no property qualification for what amounted to full citizenship, we can be sure that almost everyone who was not either a citizen (or a citizen's direct kin) on the one hand, or a slave on the other, was going to be a metic. The only exceptions would be visitors who were merely passing through.[85] This is obviously not the case in those other cities where there were other non-citizen but free groups in the population. The clearest example is provided by Sparta with its *perioikoi*, but the overwhelming majority of other *poleis* would have fallen into this category too.

Furthermore, we know, as surely as we know anything about classical Athens, that metics were, and were sometimes explicitly recognised as being, essential to the continued well-being and even existence of the city. This importance is clearest in the operation and maintenance of the fleet (as Pseudo-Xenophon makes explicit, but which we could reasonably infer in any case

[84] I have discussed several of the issues in this section from a slightly different perspective in Akrigg 2015.

[85] Whitehead 1977, 6–20. It is Watson who argues that in fact this relatively strict definition of metic status, and the clear tripartite division of the permanent population of classical Athens, was an artefact of the Periclean citizenship law of 451/0. In Watson's account, in the first half of the fifth century, this clear distinction between who was a metic and who was a citizen did not exist, with the former term meaning only something like 'immigrant' in a non-technical sense. The background to Watson's claim and the argument he develops to support it are both, to a large degree, demographic. See below and in Chapter 5.

on consideration of the logistical realities), but we also find metics playing important roles in land warfare and involved in almost every sector of Athenian economic and intellectual life.

Finally, and not least importantly, there is the fact that we are very well informed about some individual metics. These are figures as familiar to us as any Athenian citizen, and have done as much as any of them to shape our picture of classical Athens: Aristotle can be and is cited for almost every subject in Greek history, and the speeches of Lysias – quite apart from providing many students' first extended encounters with genuine Attic prose – are central to our understanding of early fourth-century Athenian society.

This clarity and familiarity, however, comes with a cost, which is that we are often blinded to or complacent about the metics and their roles. Full-length treatments of the Athenian metics have tended to concentrate either on the legal status of metics and their relationships with the formal institutions of the Athenian *polis* or with what Whitehead famously discussed as the 'ideology' of the metics – which is, of course, the ideology constructed by the Athenians about the metics, not one constructed by the metics themselves. While these are, undeniably, important issues, further points of interest emerge from consideration of what may seem to be the more basic question of how many metics there actually were in Athens to make them so important. This question in turn should inspire us to wonder from where these non-Athenians were coming to live in Athens. Exactly as with the slaves, we should also ask what they were doing: unlike the slaves, however, they had at least some choice about where they did it, and so there is also a question about what it was that made them stay.

We can start with the 'how many' question. Again, the best evidence we have, just as with the slave population, gives us only an impression of the size of the metic population. Having said that, the indications are that it was quite large, and a significant fraction of the size of the citizen population. The only explicit numbers we have are those given by Thucydides (in the passages in book two previously discussed, which deal with the metic hoplites alone), and Ctesicles (the figures reported, including one for the metics, for Demetrius of Phaleron's census).

An attempt to get to grips with the numbers question is complicated by the reluctance of some scholars to accept that there really might have been very large numbers of them, both in absolute terms and relative to the size of the citizen population. This reluctance is well illustrated by Whitehead, who in his fundamental and influential treatment of the Athenian metics, relegates discussion of their numbers to little more than a page.[86]

Whitehead was willing to accept the figure Ctesicles gave for Demetrius of Phaleron's census – that is, 10,000 metics compared to 21,000 citizens (and of course the 400,000 slaves) – but seemed less prepared to accept the implications of Thucydides 2.13, although his reasons are not clear. Whitehead cites Clerc's arguments simply to show (what he considers to be) their obvious weakness:

Using general demographic statistics (while admitting their fallibility) Clerc (1893) calculated that c. 11,750 of the 16,000 reserve hoplites were metics; he then estimated metic '*thetes*' (i.e., *psiloi* and those in the fleet) at least this figure, thus arriving at a total of c. 24,000 metics under arms; and the margin of error in this arbitrary figure was then compounded fourfold in an estimate of a total metic population of 96,000, as against 120,000 citizens (i.e., a 4:5 ratio, though this was immediately undercut by his final contention – unsupported – that there were half as many metics as citizens). I pick out Clerc's reasoning only *exempli gratia*, but certainly his high figures have won no adherents. Something has gone seriously wrong here.[87]

It is not unreasonable, I think, to focus on Whitehead's own reasoning *exempli gratia* here, given the influence of his account. It is implicit, of course, that what has gone wrong is in Clerc's argument, rather than in the opinions of those who are not his adherents. Clerc's numbers, while speculative, are however perhaps not quite as obviously silly as Whitehead suggests. The 11,750 figure, as we shall see, seems to be an entirely reasonable inference from Thucydides – although not the only possible one. The suggestion that metics should be half the number of citizens does, of course, contradict the results of Clerc's calculations, but to be fair to him it is what is implied by Demetrius'

---

[86] Whitehead 1977, 97–8.
[87] Whitehead 1977, 98.

census, which suggests at least that this is what was believed in Athens at the end of the fourth century.[88]

Gomme suggested a figure of just under 30,000 in 431, and this is the 'consensus' figure alluded to by Whitehead.[89] Rhodes, in the *CAH* suggested about 50,000;[90] Implicit in Duncan-Jones' approach is a figure nearer 100,000, which actually reaches a similar conclusion about Thucydides to Clerc's.[91]

Clearly we do need to look at Thucydides 2.13 again, but in the light of the discussion in Chapter 3. If, in our interpretation of the figure given there for the main hoplite army of 13,000, we make assumptions that minimise the number of citizens, then that does seem to imply a figure of 10,000 to 12,000 metic hoplites. Such minimising assumptions – that the 13,000 figure is actually a population figure for all the men with hoplite equipment between the ages of 20 and 50 – would mean that relatively few of the 16,000 figure for hoplites on guard duty could have been citizens, and so the number of metic hoplites that is implied is really very large.

If, however, we make a different (and perhaps more plausible) set of assumptions about the 13,000 figure – that it is meant to be a realistic army figure, and it represents a narrower range of age groups – then there might only have been 3,000 to 6,000 metic hoplites. We could further assume that, as seems likely, Hansen was right to argue that there must have been a total of at least 60,000 citizens in 431. In that case, if we minimise the number of citizen hoplites, then we seem to be required to accept that Athens was overflowing with citizen manpower in groups other than the hoplites. But if we were to make these other, different assumptions, then the hoplites would have made up a much larger proportion of the citizen population. But the assumptions which are less minimising about citizen hoplites should in turn imply that there was a smaller supply of citizens to row in the fleet.

---

[88] See also Van Wees 2011, who suggests that the 'metics' here include those former citizens who fell short of the property qualification for citizenship under Demetrius' regime, and that the number of non-Athenian residents was closer to a sixth than a third of the free population.

[89] Whitehead 1977, 108 note 183.

[90] Rhodes 1992, 83.

[91] Clerc 1893, 367–80; Duncan-Jones 1980. See also Thür 1989.

Now, there is a consistent assumption in the contemporary sources that the metics were crucial in some way for the fleet. Their importance is made explicit by the Old Oligarch, who claims (at 1.12) that Athens 'needs the metics because of the multitude of their skills and because of the fleet'. Unfortunately the reason for this importance is left frustratingly vague. If we assume that more citizens were fighting on land, there was (at least potentially) greater scope for that metic contribution to be a quantitative one, with the metics filling many places on the rowing benches of manpower-intensive triremes. But if we return for a moment to the minimising assumptions about citizen hoplite numbers, the metic contribution to rowing manpower might not have been so great; in this case, the crucial contribution could have been qualitative, with the metics providing not rowing muscle but more specialised technical skills. Which of these situations is more plausible – whether the contribution of the metics was important quantitatively or qualitatively – will therefore depend partly on what we end up concluding about the citizen population (including the distribution of wealth within it, and how much of a socio-economic elite the hoplites constituted), but also on what kind of people we think the metics were. Putting this issue this way does perhaps overemphasise the distinction, since it is entirely possible that the metics were important in both respects. It is, however, important to emphasise that there *is* a distinction. Were all the metics like Polemarchus, at ease among the wealthiest Athenians, or were they mainly poorer men? We shall turn to this question in a moment, but it is also worth returning briefly to the question of what the ratio of citizens to metics was.

As we have seen, the results of Demetrius of Phaleron's census imply that there were roughly two citizens to every metic (at a time when there was a property qualification for citizenship, as there had not been earlier in the classical period). But even if we want to trust these figures, the situation may not have been quite so straightforward as that suggests. For example, Hansen takes the 21,000 citizens to be essentially an army figure. That is not unlikely in itself, and it is possible that the figure for metics was an army figure too. However, it is easier to imagine that the number of metics was simply derived from the amount of the *metoikion* tax that was collected in a year. In fact, the metics, because of this tax, were probably the one part of the population whose numbers could at least roughly be quantified in antiquity – even if the figure was probably too low, as presumably there was a significant degree of evasion of the tax; however, in terms of assessing the ratio of citizen to metic, this probably does not matter all that much, as military service was clearly evaded too.[92] In that case, the number of metics would actually represent a population figure, albeit a rather odd one, as it would include not just all the adult males but single adult females too. On that basis, Hansen ended up suggesting about 40,000 non-citizen long-term residents in total, at a time when the number of people in citizen families would have been in the range of roughly 100,000 to 120,000, giving a ratio between two-and-a-half and three to one.[93]

It is worth considering briefly if there was a similar pattern in the 430s. If there was, a figure of 60,000 citizens might be taken to imply a population of 20,000 to 30,000 (adult) metics. On their own, the army figures provided by Thucydides, while they do not rule out such a figure, would also be consistent with a population of 10,000 to 15,000 metics. That is a similar absolute number to that of Demetrius' census, but one smaller relative to the size of the citizen population, with a ratio of citizens to metics of between four and six to one.[94] Again, deciding whether either the absolute numbers or the relative numbers of metics changed between 431 and 312 requires us to think about what kind of people the metics were, and what they were doing in Athens.

There is still a widespread, and not inherently unreasonable, assumption that the bulk of the metics were people like Lysias and Polemarchus, even if most of them were not nearly as successful or as wealthy. Because metics could not own land, then surely, this line of reasoning goes, they must have been making their living by other means than agriculture. Therefore, they should mainly have been working in trade and manufacture. This is fair enough as far as it goes, but this is not as far as it might appear. Being unable to own land does not prevent one from farming. Farmland could be

---

[92] Christ 2006, 45–87.
[93] Hansen 1988, 10–11.
[94] Van Wees 2004, 241–3.

(and at least sometimes was) rented by metics, and it was also possible to work for people who needed additional labour, at least at times of peak labour demand like harvest.[95] It is also worth remembering that some of the views that remain common about metic employment were formed first in a period when it was more widely believed that citizens would have despised *any* employment in trade and manufacture, and that therefore these fields would have been left more or less completely to non-citizens. While this picture may not be wholly misleading, it is nonetheless clear that citizens were engaged in the full range of non-agricultural economic activities, and at all levels.

This last point is accepted now almost as a truism, but it bears repeating explicitly – because the usual explanation for the presence of large numbers of metics in classical Athens is that they were drawn there by the opportunities provided by a large urban centre and major port. There must be some truth in this, and it is part of the way to explain the presence of men like Lysias and Aristotle. On the other hand, it might reasonably be asked how many opportunities there really were for non-Athenians of lesser means and/or talents, given that they would have had to compete, on generally unfavourable terms, with the citizens, who were themselves present in numbers far too large to be supported by agriculture alone. The large number of metics was not inevitable; urban centres do not attract economic migrants, or grow in size generally, just because they are urban. Something has positively to attract voluntary migrants: rural poverty and landlessness can act as 'push' factors (where they are present), but for a given urban centre the 'pull' factors have also to be explained. If the migration is economically motivated, then there has to be something for those migrants to do; otherwise, they tend to migrate elsewhere (or just go back where they came from, when the city proves not to be what they had hoped for).[96] James Watson has suggested that Athens' political stability was a factor in encouraging immigration.[97] There were extensive periods in the fifth and fourth centuries when Athens genuinely appeared politically stable, and

---

[95] Metics in agriculture: Lysias 7.10; Osborne 1988, 289–90; Papazarkadas 2011, 323–5.
[96] On rural–urban migration, see Ray 1998, especially 372–9.
[97] Watson 2010, 262 note 24.

this may well be relevant: it is easy to imagine that this played into Cephalus' calculations, for example. On the other hand, Athens was not always predictably stable, and may have looked a bit different to those without the benefit of hindsight. If this was a factor, then the way in which the Athenians were able to take the loyalty of the metics for granted becomes even more surprising (more on this below). If stability was what they were after, then one would expect them to have left when that stability was threatened, as it was on many occasions.

One source of those opportunities was provided by the fleet. Even if Athens' warships were not necessarily all built in the Piraeus itself (since it may have been more practical to build them in the areas where both timber and the skills to work it were abundant), there would have been a market for specialist labour in the shipyards and military harbours for maintenance, as well as a need for trireme crews. Bissa suggests that the difficulties of transporting ship-building timber would have led to most of Athens' warships being built outside Attica. These difficulties were real, but they may not have been insurmountable: although the convenience of building near sources of supply was recognised, local resources could often be overwhelmed by demand, and so later wooden navies were often obliged to look far afield for their raw materials.[98] We might expect non-citizens to play an important role here anyway, but the Old Oligarch's comment compels us to consider it. Neither demand is easy to quantify (as we have seen in the case of ship crews); comparative data (from later and better documented times and places where large wooden fleets were operated) might be some help with assessing at least the likely scale of the demand.

One obvious source of a comparison is another city-state with a maritime empire dependent on a substantial galley fleet, and about which we are reasonably well informed: the republic of Venice, especially in the fifteenth to seventeenth centuries. In that period, the republic's naval strength was concentrated in a fleet of galleys not so very different from those of classical Athens.

---

[98] Bissa 2009, 117–40.

The basis of the fleet, as the name implies, was the *galia sotil* or ordinary galley, the very distant descendant of the classical warship via the *dromones* of the Byzantine fleet: early fifteenth-century examples tended to be about 38 metres long, with a beam of just over 5 metres (very similar in fact to the reconstructed *Olympias*, which is slightly shorter and beamier). Later galleys were built rather longer (41 m) but with the same beam: the addition of heavy cannon armament at the prow with a counterweight at the stern contributed to a significant increase in displacement but also to the increase in length. Before the battle of Lepanto in 1571, the ships were overwhelmingly rowed at three levels, like Athenian triremes. A shift to the alternative system, where three men pulled a single oar, took place in the Venetian navy only in the decade after the battle, when crews were increasingly dominated by convicts chained to the oars. There were 25 to 30 rowing benches each side, with three men to a bench (allowing for 150 to 180 oarsmen). The important difference was in armament: Venetian galleys (and their contemporaries in other navies) did not carry the heavy bronze rams at the water line of their ancient counterparts. Their projecting prow spurs were metal-tipped, but were meant to function as boarding bridges rather than weapons in their own right.[99]

The home base of the fleet of these vessels, Venice's Arsenale, was a centre for both production and maintenance. In the 1560s, when in the face of imminent threat the Arsenale was at its busiest, the number of men employed there seems to have fluctuated between a minimum of around 1,000 and an 'emergency' peak of around 3,000, with 2,000 being fairly typical. At this time the republic aimed to maintain a reserve of 100 seaworthy galleys, while it actually deployed fleets in the order of 40 to 60 ships.[100]

These are smaller resources than those maintained by Athens at the height of its power, of course, when hundreds of galleys were not only available but might actually be sent out in very large numbers. In the fourth century, however, the number of Athenian galleys manned and at sea was also likely to be around 40 to 60,

---

[99] Alertz 1995.
[100] Lane 1973, 362.

even though there were still hundreds of hulls on hand.[101] Presumably Athens would not have needed significantly fewer shipyard workers than Venice to maintain a fleet of similar size: probably a figure of about 2,000 men in the fourth century would not be too far off. The figure in the fifth century would certainly have been higher, although it is difficult to tell how much; as with later dockyards, the number of men employed would have varied according to need.

There are two possibly relevant factors to bear in mind here. First, Venetian galleys seem not to have had such long service lives as their Athenian predecessors, only lasting about 10 years as opposed to the 20 of the latter. They were however considered at the time to be of good quality (although this may not have been a straightforward reflection of reality). Second, the hull-first method of constructing ancient galleys would have made them harder to maintain than later vessels that were built frame first. Very many of the men employed in the Arsenale were caulkers, whose work was necessary to keep vessels seaworthy throughout their service lives. Older vessels (and those captured from the enemy) would have required a great deal of work to keep (or make) them seaworthy. Because of the labour demand generated by maintenance (which could have taken place within the Piraeus' ship sheds), the question of where new ships were built may not be so important for our current purposes, where it is the overall size of the establishment we are interested in, not the specification of the tasks undertaken there.

At times when Athens regularly sent a hundred or even more ships to sea, perhaps a figure of 4,000 or 5,000 men would not be excessively high. This kind of figure would have made the naval shipyards of the Piraeus a very large centre of industry indeed – about which our relative ignorance is therefore all the more frustrating. To provide a little more context, in the seventeenth century, the English Royal Dockyard at Chatham never employed more than 1,000 men, even at moments of extreme crisis, and usually fewer.[102] In their eighteenth-century heydays,

---

[101] Cawkwell 1984, 335.
[102] MacDougall 1987, 30–1; 41.

the Chatham, Portsmouth, and Plymouth dockyards each employed about 2,000 men, of whom about a third were engaged in clerical activities.[103] In this context, it is also well worth noting that in the earlier period a great deal of the work in English dockyards was seasonal. Much the same may have been true at the Piraeus, with the migration it induced being 'circular' in many cases.

Chatham was, of course, in many ways a quite different kind of establishment from the Piraeus; uniquely for an English royal dockyard, however, it acquired some specialised facilities for galley operations, including a dry dock built in 1571.[104] The later history of the dockyard also illustrates what should be obvious (but in fact is not always to ancient historians): that a naval dockyard may not always also be a naval base.[105] Chatham's increasing unsuitability as one of the latter led to its replacement in that role over the course of the eighteenth century by Portsmouth and Plymouth. Although these ports on the south coast also had ship-building facilities, this was not their main focus, which instead was on the maintenance of operational fleets. However, this in turn meant that they had spare building capacity, which was taken up in emergencies when new ships were needed in a hurry. It may not be too far-fetched to imagine that the Piraeus worked in similar fashion, so that although some ships were built there, most new Athenian triremes need not have been – except in exceptional circumstances, such as the construction of the fleet that fought at Arginusae.

Not everyone in the dockyard could have been a metic. We should expect that both citizens and slaves worked there too: even in the fifth century, we can hardly believe that more than 2,000 metics could have found regular employment in the naval yards. Beyond this, though, how much scope really was there for men of limited means to make a living in classical Athens? Clearly there were not 10,000 Lysiases, each living off the proceeds of substantial armaments workshops. The city provided a large potential market of consumers, but presumably it was possible to

---

[103] MacDougall 1987, 55; 2012, 54.
[104] MacDougall 2012, 13.
[105] MacDougall 2012, 71–2.

make money selling things to the Athenians without having to live with them, let alone having to fight for them. And what would have forced the metics to stay in times of war and hardship, as during the Peloponnesian War? Armaments manufacturers and food merchants would have had fairly strong financial incentives (at least while there was money to pay for their goods), but again, how many metics can these activities explain, given that citizens were clearly involved here too? Have we been too influenced by later examples of the pull exerted by cities over migrant workers? Athens was not in every way like imperial Rome; nor was it necessarily like cities in the modern industrial and industrialising worlds.[106]

At this point, it is worth coming back to the fact that at least some metics were not voluntary immigrants, but instead were freed slaves. This is generally accepted, but its potential significance has not always been fully appreciated. It is, for example, a surprising feature of Whitehead's study that although he was determined to debunk what he saw as a prevailing orthodoxy that being a metic at Athens was in some sense a privileged status (an idea which, in spite of the strength and cogency of Whitehead's arguments, has proved remarkably resilient),[107] he was almost as determined to deny that metics as a body were tinged with the negative connotations of servility. Whitehead rightly pointed out that having the status of 'metic' was not inconsistent with retaining one's status as a citizen of another *polis* (although he also rightly observes that after too prolonged a stay in Attica, and after the first generation, it may have become harder actually to get one's entitlement recognised at home). There is no reason to doubt

---

[106] Hin 2013, 210–57, on migration and republican Rome, arguing persuasively that there are problems with using the (relatively well documented) case of early modern London as a comparative model for Rome (250–4); the broader point is that sweeping and generalising assumptions will not always be helpful: every city has its own story. See especially 212–18, which include important general observations. Hin rightly emphasises the complexity of migration and its demographic effects. In particular, it can be difficult to separate, and to evaluate the relative importance of, the 'push' and 'pull' factors that motivate migration (elite literary sources, then as now, often tend to emphasise the 'pulls'). Hin (217) quotes Seneca to this effect, but the same is true implicitly in the Old Oligarch and explicitly in Xenophon's *Poroi*.

[107] For metic status as privileged, see for example Cohen 2000; Zelnick-Abramovitz 2005; Acton 2014, 279.

that there must have been many metics who fell into this category. But that still does not affect the extent to which the term 'metic' was in fact associated with servility, and so in my view Whitehead underplayed the number of metics who were freedmen and women.

Whitehead must be right when he says:

although freedmen were subsumed juristically under the *metoikia* they seem in fact to have been perceived as a distinct sub-group by the ordinary observer: in saying 'the metic or the freedman' the Old Oligarch is confounding the legal pedantry of official status-classifications with the illogical pedantry of common sense.[108]

I would, however, question whether the Old Oligarch can really be cited as an 'ordinary observer'. The evidence of his problematic text can cut both ways on this issue. Slaves, metics, and freedmen are lumped together (and apparently equally reviled) by this author as much as they are distinguished. The text does not seem necessarily to support Whitehead's claim that 'the inclusion does not appear to have been felt to characterise or contaminate the whole class'.[109]

The crucial point, I think, is one that is not quite explicitly addressed by Whitehead. He notes that the *metoikion* 'was ... unique in Athens in being not merely a direct tax but a poll-tax, levied on the person rather than his (or her) property of activities',[110] but he does not address the obvious implication that this in itself made metics look closer to slaves than to citizens. The tax was unique precisely because it was unthinkable to impose such a levy on citizens. It is also highly suggestive that (as Whitehead does note) the punishment for failing to pay the *metoikion* was enslavement. Whitehead goes on to consider the extent to which the tax was a financial burden. How much of a burden it was must have depended on individual circumstances: for the poorest metics, it could not have been trivial.[111] But to consider the tax only in this way is, surely, to miss precisely the ideological point.

---

[108] Whitehead 1977, 116.
[109] Whitehead 1977, 116.
[110] Whitehead 1977, 75–6.
[111] Acton 2014, 279–81, for possible consequences.

That metics were subject to (and to a large extent defined by) the payment of a tax not on their property but on their bodies would on its own have made them vulnerable to identification with slaves. Even more strikingly, however, they were (theoretically) liable to torture in judicial settings. The need for a *prostates*, whatever their precise role, also smacks of servility. It is further worth noting that the passage (Lysias 31.9) where this is explicitly sneered at concerns an Athenian citizen who was a metic in another city.[112] The role of the metic women in the Panathenaic procession can hardly have been seen as anything other than servile.[113] These surely served to align them, at least in the official view of the Athenian *polis*, much more closely with slaves than with citizens.

Whitehead was, of course, absolutely right to point out that metics rarely if ever described themselves as metics (and the city in certain contexts avoided the word too), preferring to use patronymics and city ethnics, except when they were able to describe themselves as *isoteleis*. Whitehead's response to his own observation is curiously half-hearted, however. On the use of city ethnics, he wonders briefly whether describing oneself as, for example, 'Samios' (not a neutral claim in fourth-century Athens, of course) entails a realistic claim to citizen status in one's home city. His conclusion is essentially 'why not?' On the preference for the use of *isoteles* as an identifier, he notes that it shows how keen metics were to show that their adoptive city was honouring them. It strikes me that there are alternative ways to read this pattern. If 'metic' did carry a tinge of servility, then an assertion of citizen status somewhere (irrespective of whether or not it was justified) would be one way to counter it. Being *isoteles*, however, was a matter of public record in Athens itself, and was a status that could only be achieved by someone who was wealthy enough to have done significant service to the city; it could have lifted a metic unmistakably out of the ranks of those who were subject to suspiciously servile obligations and treatment.

If we take many of the metics to have been freedmen and -women, then many of them, still largely dependent on their former

---

[112] Whitehead 1977, 46.
[113] Parker 2005, 258, with note 25.

masters, will have had few realistic alternatives to remaining in Athens, even in the midst of plague and military defeat. This might have reduced the numbers who left (although it is also obviously true that many metics who could have left did not – again, Lysias is a familiar but not necessarily typical example). From the perspective of military history, it might also influence how we interpret the significance of Thucydides' mentions of metic troops when he seems so interested in the Spartans' use of freed slaves (like Brasidas' *neodamodeis*).

Whitehead also observes that there was a well-developed vocabulary of abuse in servile terms for those who wanted to employ it, whereas no one is ever explicitly denigrated by being called a metic. This is true, but it need not be as decisive as Whitehead thinks – if metic status was linked to servility, then it would be at least as effective, and probably more so, to label an opponent straightforwardly as a slave rather than labelling them as a bit like a slave. After all, we know so much about this servile vocabulary of abuse precisely because it is frequently directed at citizens.

Whitehead thinks that where metics are referred to as such, there is in fact a certain amount of sympathy and even affection for them. This, I think, is entirely in the eye of the beholder. The two key passages for him are Thucydides 1.143.1–2:

Suppose, again, that they lay hands on the treasures at Olympia and Delphi, and tempt our mercenary sailors with the offer of higher pay, there might be serious danger, if we and our metics embarking alone were not still a match for them. But we are a match for them: and, best of all, our pilots are taken from our own citizens, while no sailors are to be found so good or so numerous as ours in all the rest of Hellas. None of our mercenaries will choose to fight on their side for the sake of a few days' high pay, when he will not only be an exile, but will incur greater danger, and will have less hope of victory. (Jowett's translation, as quoted by Whitehead)

and Aristophanes *Acharnians* 507–8:

This time we are alone, ready hulled; for I reckon that the metics are the bran of the *astoi*. (Whitehead's translation)

Thucydides has Pericles acknowledge the necessity of the metics, along with a breezy assumption that they are absolutely reliable.

In the Aristophanes passage, which, as Whitehead puts it, characterises the metics as the citizens' 'inescapable (if nutritionally inferior) companions', Whitehead sees sympathy; the patronising element to which he also refers seems rather more apparent. Nothing in these passages, even if we were to accept that there is something favourable, necessarily makes implausible the idea that the metics were considered, as a body, to be somewhat servile. Whitehead takes them as 'perhaps elevat[ing], if only momentarily, the social status of the freedman *qua* metic, as perceived by the citizen'. However, some moral qualities and standards of behaviour could perfectly well be expected of, or at least recognised in, slaves.

The clearest message from these texts seems actually to be the *inseparability* from the citizens. This would make more sense if the metics were substantially composed of freedmen and -women than if they were economic migrants. Freedpersons had no other homes to go to in hard times, and clearly owed continuing obligations to their former masters.

Xenophon's well-known discussion of the metics in *Poroi* 2 is consistent with this picture. It is often taken to confirm the view that the majority of metics were economic migrants. This is because Xenophon suggests a variety of possible methods for enticing this kind of immigrant, to the economic benefit of Athens. Austin and Vidal-Naquet suggested in this context that there may really have been a distinction between a fifth-century metic population that was made up mainly of immigrants from other Greek cities (and who might settle permanently, and be more easily assimilated) and a fourth-century one that was more 'barbarian' and, partly for that reason, more transitory, and unassimilated even when they chose to remain.[114] Miller, however, presented reasons for doubting this – for example, the existence of a 'Little Phrygia' in Athens in Thucydides 2.22.2, and the introduction of new cults in the fifth century.[115] However, it is important to note that nowhere does Xenophon actually claim that there were few metics in contemporary (mid-fourth-century)

---

[114] Austin and Vidal-Naquet 1977, 104.
[115] Miller 1997, 84.

Athens. Rather, he seems to think that the problem is that there are not enough of the *right kind* of metics. Those that are in Athens (and fighting alongside the Athenians) are 'Lydians, Phrygians, Syrians, and all kinds of other barbarians',[116] of whom there seems to be no shortage. The named peoples are, of course, some of those that provided Athens with many of its slaves. Clearly the wealthier economic migrant-type metics (including, albeit not exclusively, those of Greek origin) could and did leave Athens when they saw no particular advantage in staying, or indeed they could choose to stay at home, or go elsewhere in the first place. It would, surely, be extremely odd if these were the sort of men of whose loyalty the Athenians could be so complacently sure.

Instead, we must see at least two quite distinct types of metics. In the first place, there was a relatively small elite of wealthy men, many of whom were probably citizens of other Greek cities who could take advantage of the opportunities offered by Athens, but whose first loyalty might not always be to Athens. In the second place, there would have been a much larger, but to us less visible, number of freed slaves. A few of the latter (such as former banking slaves) might be wealthy, but the majority would have been a good deal poorer; alienated from their natal communities and still with ties of dependency to their former masters, they would have been short of alternative places to go.

If there is any truth to this suggestion, it has implications for how we think about the structure of the metic population. The usual assumption that metics were economic migrants tends to encourage a further assumption that they would mostly therefore have been young (and mainly single) men – so that, for example, the thousands of metic hoplites in Thucydides have not usually been taken to imply necessarily similar numbers of women or of dependent children.[117] But if many metics were freedmen, they would have had every incentive to marry, even if their choice of partners was restricted, and to have children.

---

[116] Xen. *Poroi* 2.3.
[117] Starting with Gomme 1933, and rarely challenged, but see note 106 above on the danger of making this assumption in the case of Rome.

Moreover, the proportion of women in the *metoikia* may have been rather higher than is usually assumed. In all slave societies where it is possible to tell, women tend to be manumitted at a higher rate than men. The reasons are as obvious as they are depressing. Women are generally more likely to be employed in domestic household situations which lead to manumission more often than employment in distant farms (or silver mines); in paternalistic societies, the continued dependence of a freedwoman on her master is easier to assure; and prostitution is often the most common way to earn the money to buy one's freedom.[118]

Freedmen and -women appear to be a good source of some of the thousands of individuals on whose continued presence the Athenians seemed absolutely able to rely in the fifth century. However, we know very little about rates of manumission in the fifth century. It *need* not in fact have been practised very much at all. Labour was cheap and the economy was expanding rapidly; for most of the period, Attica was militarily secure, and most of the time there was relatively little disunity in the citizen slave-owning group (part of the 460s and the oligarchic episodes towards the end of the century notwithstanding). These are not the circumstances where one would necessarily expect high rates of manumission. On the other hand, a low rate of manumission in a large population of slaves could still produce a sizeable number of freedmen in absolute terms. This might, therefore, incline us towards stability in the absolute size of the metic population, with change over time being seen in the number of metics relative to the number of citizens. At which point, it is time to turn to the issue of population change more generally if we are to make any progress.

[118] Wrenhaven 2009.

CHAPTER 5

POPULATION CHANGES

Introduction: Long-Term Stability, Short-Term Fluctuation

Chapters 3 and 4 have been mainly concerned with looking at what are at best snapshots of the size of the population of classical Athens. Here we turn to what was happening in between those snapshots, and try to assess and account for the scale of change in the population. The emphasis will remain on size, but the principal issues of structure will also be raised. Most of the discussion will centre on the fifth century. It was in this period that the most dramatic changes took place. Both the reality and the scale of these changes are the source of considerable controversy. Change in the population of classical Athens, whether in size or in structure, has not, however, directly provoked a great deal of discussion among ancient historians in the past (archaic Athens is another story). In part, this is another unintended effect of the dominance of Hansen's *Demography and Democracy*, and of political history, in the field. Although Hansen presents a slightly more nuanced picture in his conclusion to the book, his account of the fourth-century citizen population is still easily summarised, and is a fairly static one.[1] When we look at the changes in the size and structure of the population of Athens, it seems particularly unfortunate that the attention of scholars has focused on the fourth century. The fifth century, by contrast, was a period of colossal and rapid demographic change, but these changes have received relatively little serious attention.[2]

This is not meant as a criticism of Hansen, or of political historians. For an institutional history of the Athenian democracy in the period when we know it best, a picture of a basically

---

[1] Hansen 1985, 65–9.
[2] The main exceptions being Patterson 1981 and Watson 2010.

139

stationary population lends clarity; it may well also be tolerably accurate for much of the fourth century. It is also, however, a consequence of the emphasis in recent work on the very slow pace of increases in pre-industrial human populations over the long term. It is generally accepted that sustained long-term growth could have a large aggregate effect: few people would deny that there were more people in the Greek world of 300 than there were in 800 (and it is now widely accepted that there would have been *many* more; the actual estimates vary, partly according to what is counted as 'Greek').[3] More attention has been given to the early part of this period than to the middle or the end, however, and the emphasis on the long term has obscured the fact that we are sometimes interested in a very small part of Greece that could in the short term have behaved in a quite different manner.[4]

If we take the admittedly rather impressionistic figures from Chapter 3 at face value, they imply two striking changes over the course of the fifth century: first, a huge *increase* in the apparent size of the citizen population from the end of the Persian Wars to the beginning of the Peloponnesian War; and second, an equally dramatic and even more rapid *decrease* in the remaining decades of the century. Much of this chapter will be devoted to arguing that these changes really were as dramatic as they seem. The most important issues to emerge in the fourth century are easily resolved by comparison, consisting of what seems to have been a sustained recovery from the low point that was reached at the very end of the Peloponnesian War.

The fifth century, by contrast, presents some greater challenges. This was clearly a period of much greater and faster change than anything seen in the fourth century, but as we have seen, it has received relatively little attention. Hansen's work is still important and fundamental. Although most of his attention was on the fourth century, his 1988 piece, which we have already encountered, makes an important contribution to understanding the scale of Athens' losses during the Peloponnesian War, even if he was not particularly concerned with looking at its consequences.[5] Hansen

---

[3] Hansen 2006, 1–34; Ober 2015, 74, 85.

[4] Interest in the long term: Scheidel 2003; Morris 2013; Ober 2015, 71–100.

[5] Hansen 1988.

here drew on Barry Strauss' book *Athens After the Peloponnesian War.* Strauss based an important part of his interpretation of early fourth-century factional politics on the manpower losses Athens suffered during the Peloponnesian War, and it was this analysis that was put to use and expanded by Hansen.[6]

Patterson's discussion of the Periclean citizenship law takes centre place when we look back earlier in the fifth century. But because she was interested in the immediate context of the law, Patterson did not need or want to carry her demographic interest beyond 431. Patterson was aware of the weaknesses of earlier accounts (especially those of Gomme and Jones) and was, understandably, reluctant to commit herself to explicit numbers. She did, however, think that it was possible at least to think in relative terms about the citizen population that was her main concern at the time.[7]

Thus all three scholars were only really interested in the citizens, and Strauss alone was interested in the changes experienced by Athens during the Peloponnesian War for their own sake – and even then only for quite a narrow set of political implications. In this chapter, then, I shall present a brief summary of the major changes in the size and of the population throughout the classical period. Where it is possible, I shall point out some of the implications for the structure of the population too, and attempt to give appropriate attention to the non-citizens. The previous chapters have shown how difficult it is to put precise figures on the size of the population at any given moment during the classical period. Nonetheless, Patterson's observation that it is both possible and worthwhile to think in relative terms still holds.[8] Thus, while it is easiest to phrase the discussion in numerical terms, no great certainty can be claimed for any of the figures here.

Population Growth in the Fifth Century

Once again, any discussion really has to start from the number of citizens. When it comes to the size of the citizen population in the

---

[6] Strauss 1986.

[7] Patterson 1981, 40–71. See also Watson 2010, who is interested in metics but starts from Patterson and from consideration of citizen numbers.

[8] Patterson 1981, 4, 71.

fifth century, the closest things we have to fixed points are still the relatively detailed indications we have of Athenian military musters, first for the Persian Wars and then later at the outbreak of the Peloponnesian War. Beyond this, we have only the even vaguer intimations that are provided, first, by the apparent logic of the Cleisthenic constitution, and second, by the abridged accounts we have of Athenian imperial and military activity throughout the century. Along with the latter are the (also often vague) reports of the casualties suffered by the Athenians.[9]

The figures for the Persian War musters (9,000 to 10,000 hoplites at Marathon in 490; 180 triremes crewed at Salamis in 480; and 8,000 hoplites at Plataea in 479) seem to be quite closely comparable to the maximum levels of military effort that Athens was able to make in the fourth century.[10] If it is true that the Cleisthenic system really did not undergo much in the way of substantial organisational change during the fifth century (the reforms associated with Ephialtes being apparently concerned more with the distribution of powers), then the normal operation of the institutions of democracy (and especially the Council of 500) would also have required a similar number of citizens, then as later. In very general terms, and on the assumption that in broad terms Hansen's arguments about the fourth century should be accepted, it seems likely that the citizen population of Athens in the first couple of decades of the fifth century also numbered around 30,000.

Turning to the other end of the *pentecontaetia*, Hansen argued in his 1988 article that there must have been at least 60,000 citizens in 431. His starting point was the conclusion he had already reached in *Demography and Democracy*: that at no period during the fourth century do there seem to have been significantly fewer than 30,000 citizens in Attica, with the possible exception that in the years immediately after the Peloponnesian War there might have been as few as 25,000.[11] Drawing on Strauss' account, Hansen observed that the narratives of the war provided by Thucydides and Xenophon suggest that the Athenians suffered very high casualties throughout the war. For these casualties to have been sustained without,

---

[9] Patterson 1981, 46–65, provides a useful summary.
[10] See Chapter 3.
[11] Hansen 1988, 26; Hansen 1985, 68.

apparently, any need to compromise the rules governing recruitment to the Council or the operation of the assembly, he argued, there must have been a very much larger number of citizens at the start of the war than had previously been accepted.[12] The usual figures quoted in previous scholarship were Gomme's of 43,000 or 47,000, sometimes rounded up to 50,000.[13] Hansen instead suggested that the *minimum* that was compatible with the known level of wartime casualties and the size of the post-war population was 60,000. The point that Hansen needed to make was that a population of this size was at least *compatible* with Thucydides' summary of Athens' pre-war resources. As we saw earlier, Hansen had already decided that Thucydides was of no positive help for Athenian historical demography. Crudely put, his aim in this piece was to demonstrate that even if Thucydides *were* to be taken seriously and at face value, his account could not be used by anyone else to argue against Hansen's account of the fourth century.

So Hansen had his eye on the fourth century even when he was discussing the fifth. His discussion of the casualties suffered by the Athenians during the war is nonetheless important, and we shall return to it later. His argument about 431 has also generally been accepted (although the fact that he thought 60,000 was a minimum figure for the citizen population at that time is usually down-played); the discussion in Chapter 3 provides no reason to reject it. Such a figure is also consistent with an interpretation of Thucydides that counts forwards rather than backwards. On the basis of plausible assumptions about Athenian military manpower and Thucydides' report, we might think that of those 60,000 citizens perhaps half would have been from families rich enough to afford hoplite equipment. It would be possible to accept that the total number of citizens was as high as 70,000, in which case Athens would have been able not only to run a substantial fleet with her citizens and metics but to provide a sizeable force of light troops for the land forces at the same time; or alternatively, to sustain a higher rate of exemption or absenteeism from military service than we allowed. This might also mean that, even on these

---

[12] Hansen 1988.
[13] Gomme 1933, 1959.

figures, 'hoplite' citizens would only have been about 40 per cent of the total, as Van Wees has suggested.[14]

So, although there were probably only 30,000 citizens in around 480, 50 years later there seem to have been at least 60,000. If this really was the case, then this represented a period of *very* rapid population growth. That doubling of the adult population would, as Robert Sallares observed, have involved an annual rate of increase of about 1.4 per cent. Sallares was concerned to point out that such a rate of increase was well within the bounds of possibility for a human population, contrary to the claims of 'several Greek historians [who] have asserted, on the basis of inappropriate parallels from early modern Europe which had a fundamentally different demographic system in any case, that only rather slow population growth (less than 1 per cent) was possible in human populations in the past'. He did not pursue the consequences of this very far, as he was most interested in Athens when it was in the 'demographic mainstream'; the imperial Athens of the fifth century was untypical of the Greek world whose ecology he sought to describe. However, in asserting the possibility of annual growth rates of well over 1 per cent, he raised an issue of central importance.[15]

It is interesting to note that Sallares got the 60,000 figure for 431 directly from Hansen, but went on in his own discussion to suggest a figure for the 450s of about 50,000.[16] This is not obviously implausible, but his source for that figure was Patterson's discussion of the Athenian citizen population at the time of the Periclean citizenship law. Patterson was, however, wary of hard figures and was not committing herself to this number. She could not have anticipated Hansen's argument about 431, and the 50,000 figure instead looks back to Gomme. Patterson's point was not that the citizen population was about 50,000 strong in the 450s and would keep growing, but that it had by the 450s already attained the size it would have in 431.[17] That is, the logic of Patterson's argument is that

---

[14] Van Wees 2004, 241–3; 2006, 381–2.
[15] Sallares 1991, 50–107; the quotation is from 95.
[16] Sallares 1991, 95.
[17] A point that is lost in Watson's thoughtful discussion (which uses the figures from both Patterson and Hansen), although it only strengthens the case he is making. See 2010, 262, including his table 1.

the citizen population doubled not in 50 years, but in only 25 or 30. This would imply a growth rate of well over 2 per cent per annum.

Sallares' point was that a figure of 1.4 per cent per annum would not make Athens look at all exceptional. However, even a figure of nearly 3 per cent, needed for a doubling in a quarter century, could not, according to Sallares' account, be ruled out, as he had argued that such figures can be paralleled in pre-industrial human populations: 'there is no good *a priori* argument for supposing that the Athenian population was physically incapable of achieving rates of natural increase of the order of 2–3 per cent per annum during that period.' (The period in question at this point of Sallares' discussion is the eighth century BC.)[18] Most scholarship on the historical demography of the ancient world has continued to emphasise that pre-industrial human populations had very low potential for sustained growth.[19] For ancient Greece, the case was made in some detail by Scheidel in his frequently cited 2003 article in *JHS*, and he repeated the point with wider application in the *CEH*.[20] As Sallares observed, however, appreciation by Greek historians of the basic point goes back further than this. The clearest illustration lies in the relatively low rates of growth that were selected by Hansen (and by others) for their models of the age structure of the Athenian citizen population.[21] Scheidel was not concerned with Sallares' arguments for the fifth century as such, but his challenge to Sallares' picture of the eighth century is important. An important part of Scheidel's criticism of Sallares is the latter's selection of comparative evidence, which is essentially the same for both the eighth and the fifth centuries. This in itself is unsurprising, as Sallares' point was about the limits of what is humanly possible, and so effectively a timeless one.

Clearly, it is undeniable that pre-industrial human populations increased in size only very slowly over the long term. Furthermore, anything we say about what seems to have been happening in Athens, even over the relatively short course of the classical period, does nothing to alter this. From the early fifth

---

[18] Sallares 1991, 87.
[19] Bresson 2016, 49–64, presents a more nuanced view, however.
[20] Scheidel 2003, 2007.
[21] Hansen 1985; Rhodes 1988, 271, provides a summary of other views to this point.

century to the middle of the fourth century there was little net change: even if the population was sometimes much bigger, this did not last. Our knowledge of the size of the citizen population depends on what we know about the scale of Athens' military resources and about the operation of the city's political institutions. By both measures, early fifth-century Athens and late fourth-century Athens are broadly comparable. Militarily, at both these periods, the city had a few thousand hoplites and could, at a pinch, man around a couple of hundred warships. If those resources could be mobilised effectively, this was sufficient to make the city a powerful force in southern and central Greece but not enough for decisive unilateral action on the wider stage of the Mediterranean world. The basic political institutions of the democracy – the demes and tribes into which the citizens were divided, and the assembly, council, and courts through which they worked – seem to have been of similar scale and to have worked in essentially the same ways and with similar levels of participation. Whether we are talking about the 480s or the 330s, the best interpretations of the evidence suggest that there were about 30,000 citizens. The number of non-citizens is more problematic, but it would be difficult to argue for wildly different numbers of slaves or metics in one period compared to the other, even if the technical sense of 'metic' really is a post-480 development.

The picture painted by the archaeological evidence is also fairly consistent across the classical period, revealing a landscape that was densely settled and worked throughout the fifth and fourth centuries. That is, of course, not to say that there were no changes: in particular, the urban development of the Piraeus is a spectacular example of a permanent change in settlement in Attica.[22] Still, the harbour town did not flourish in later times as it did in the classical period. There is nothing here to suggest that that 'mean long-term growth rate deviated significantly from a range of between perhaps 0.25 and 0.45 per cent per year', just as Scheidel argues; indeed, the actual net rate could well have been closer to zero.[23] Classical Attica was, surely, significantly more densely occupied than

[22] Hoepfner and Schwandner 1994, 22–50; Garland 2001, 7–100.
[23] Scheidel 2003, 123.

archaic Attica, but also more so than later Hellenistic and Roman Attica. When an even longer perspective is adopted, the picture remains the same: the population, even in this small corner of the Greek world, showed little or no tendency to increase. The demography of Attica only changed really significantly in this respect in the nineteenth century, when Athens became the focus of striking changes as the capital of independent Hellas.[24]

However, while the long-term picture is unproblematic, very low 'mean long-term growth rates' clearly do not have to imply that actual annual growth rates could never have exceeded these levels. This issue has been discussed most thoroughly in the context of archaic Greece, and especially the eighth century. In the final quarter of the twentieth century, a number of scholars suggested that it was possible that during this period Greece (and specifically Attica) could have experienced a period or periods of explosively fast population growth, and that this could provide a crucial part (at least) of the explanation of the apparently major changes that were taking place in the Greek world at the time. Scheidel's 2003 *JHS* piece was a reaction against some of these arguments. Scheidel's argument is careful and generally convincing (and the article as a whole ranges much more widely than this), but once again it is important to appreciate the *limits* to the implications of what is said. While over the course of the classical period as a whole there was at best only very slow growth in the size of the population of Attica, within that period we do after all have what seems to have been a period of very rapid growth. If growth of the pace claimed above (a doubling of the citizen population in a maximum of 50 years) for fifth-century Athens is wildly implausible or even impossible, then something has clearly gone wrong, either with our sources or with our interpretation of them. This would include the extent to which we attribute the increase in the citizen body to immigration by and naturalisation of foreigners. There must have been some, especially before the Periclean citizenship law. Assessing its scale, however, requires that we have a clear view about the plausible limits to 'natural' population growth within the already-existing citizen population,

---

[24] Gallant 2001, 75–115; 2015, 187–91.

about what motivated the immigrants, and about what positive evidence there is for such immigration.

Scheidel's article was an intervention in a long-running debate. Archaeologists had been quicker than ancient historians to employ population as an explanatory factor for wider changes in society (partly as a result of early optimism about the potential for field survey results to inform us about population sizes and trends). In the late 1970s and early 1980s, Snodgrass pointed out that the number of burials in Attica increased very markedly between about 780 and 720, and suggested that the increase in burials was more or less directly reflective of an increase in population that ran at an annual rate of some 3–4 per cent.[25] It was this model that Ian Morris famously criticised in his *Burial and Ancient Society*.[26] Morris argued that the changes in the number of burials were in fact better explained as changes in social structure and commemorative practices, which in turn led to changes in the visibility (and hence recovery rate) of burials in the archaeological record. Although it was not central to his argument, Morris also pointed out that a 4 per cent per annum rate of increase in a population was rather 'improbable'.[27] It was partly in response to this observation that Sallares chose to argue that, while certainly not typical, such a high rate of increase was not completely impossible.

The details of Sallares' argument about the eighth century are not directly relevant here.[28] As Scheidel noted, Sallares' interpretation was overcomplicated by his argument about the breakdown of an age-class system in early Archaic Athens (although it is only fair to say that this was an important issue to address at the time of its publication). What matters instead is the way in which Scheidel went about refuting the notion of an eighth-century population explosion as posited by Sallares (and a little later by Tandy).[29] Scheidel pointed out that:

[25] Snodgrass, 1977, 10–14; 1983, 169–71.
[26] Morris 1987.
[27] Morris 1987, 72.
[28] Sallares 1991, 86–90.
[29] Tandy 1997, 19–58.

two separate issues are at stake: (1) whether judging by comparative evidence, short-term growth rates of 2–4 per cent per year are possible in principle, and (2) whether the mortuary record may be taken to reflect any such increases.[30]

The former is clearly what concerns us here. The latter is of interest for the eighth century, because the burial data are the only available potential source of quantifiable demographic data. This is not the case for the fifth century. This is fortunate for us, because Scheidel's (entirely justified) conclusion on this issue was that 'attempts to derive demographic growth *rates* from burial data are irremediably flawed and must be abandoned'.[31]

The plausibility of high growth rates in the short term, however, is obviously crucial; and, in the absence of direct evidence, comparative data are all we have to go on. If such growth rates are not in fact plausible, then the consequences for most interpretations of fifth-century Athens (including the one being developed here) would be severe. We would be forced to conclude that the population in 431 was not as big as Thucydides' account makes it look, or that it was *already* a good deal bigger at the beginning of the fifth century than we thought, or that very large numbers of immigrants to fifth-century Athens were fully enfranchised, presumably before 451/0 and the passage of the citizenship law (as suggested by Watson, although it was the implausibility of claims made about such large-scale enfranchisements that prompted Sallares' comments in the first place).[32] There was surely some immigration and some successful integration. However, if the citizen population had been 30,000 in 480, and if 'natural' increase could *only* have been 0.5 per cent per year, then by 450 the citizen population could have increased by such means to about 35,000. If the total citizen population were 50,000 to 60,000 by this stage, then at least 30 per cent to 40 per cent would *have* to have been such recent immigrants. If this really were the case, it would surely have profound consequences for our understanding of Athenian citizenship (and the history both of Athenian democracy and of the Athenian empire).[33]

---

[30] Scheidel 2003, 127.
[31] Scheidel 2003, 131.
[32] Sallares 1991, 95.
[33] Compare here the tables provided by Watson 2010, 262.

If the first of these alternatives were true, then we should also have to explain how the surviving population was able to escape a constitutional crisis after the highly elevated mortality it experienced during the Peloponnesian War; or we would need to explain away the evidence for that mortality (which is something that should be resisted: see below). If the second were the case, and the early classical population was already much larger than it is usually taken to be, then we create another set of problems (although it is worth noting that this is the situation that Moreno seems to endorse in the conclusion to his book).[34]

A relatively minor issue would be that with a citizen population of significantly more than 30,000, it becomes hard to understand why Athens had any difficulty with manning its fleet of 200 triremes in 480. (We are told in Herodotus that they could only fill 180, even with the help of Plataea.)[35] The weak level of military mobilisation that would seem to be implied by a small number of hoplites could be explained away relatively easily by pointing to the greater cost of hoplite panoplies at the beginning of the classical period compared to its end. More seriously, a much larger population in 480 would imply that there had been very significant growth already well back in the sixth century, which sits rather less easily both with Athens' persistent military feebleness and with the archaeological data, which indicate that Athens only came to be 'filled up' towards the end of the century.[36]

The military narrative of the classical period would also be complicated by such a suggestion. That Athens was a military powerhouse in the mid-to-late fifth century is surely unquestionable. While population size is not straightforwardly linked to military power, neither is it irrelevant. Athens' strength in the fifth century was in large part a reflection of her unusually large free population; that she was weaker both before and after this period was also surely due in part to the fact that she did not then have so many men. Athens during the *pentecontaetia* was fighting full-scale wars on many fronts. While those wars were not always successful, the city seems to have had no difficulty in sustaining these losses.

[34] Moreno 2007, 310–16.
[35] Herodotus 8.1.
[36] Foxhall 1997; Morris 2002, 36.

It is also worth explicitly recalling once more that warfare in the classical Greek world was extremely manpower-intensive. This had been true as long as hoplite phalanxes dominated the battle-field. Exactly how long that was in 480 and even what precisely we should understand by a hoplite phalanx remains a matter of some dispute, but influential cases have been made for a close connec-tion between the emergence of hoplite warfare and the peculiar political development of Greek *poleis* in the archaic period.[37]

Much is made by some scholars of the democratic nature of hoplite phalanx warfare, but trireme warfare is surely even more 'democratic', and not only for the usually quoted reason that it gave an important military role to large numbers of even poorer (than hoplites) members of the community.[38] Rihll pointed out that in the Greek world the rulers had no technological advantage over the ruled: there were no water cannons or tear gas. Rihll picks out these mostly non-lethal technologies, but many governments have been prepared to use battlefield technology against their own citizens; we need only think of Northern Ireland or the increasing militarisation of police forces in the United States, let alone any further afield.[39] Charles Napier's (not completely unsympathetic) comment in his diary in 1839 that certain Chartists failed to under-stand the true meaning of 'physical force', given that they did not have any artillery or apparently appreciate its effects, was a usefully blunt one for illustrating the point.[40] Every citizen's house in classical Athens would have contained at least some weapons, and some individuals were clearly able to arm them-selves to the teeth. But still it was possible within a *polis* for organised bodies of well-armed men to terrorise a population and to seize and hold power for a tyrant (or oligarchic junta). Full hoplite panoplies never became universal among the citizens of a *polis*. Naval warfare was quite different. Triremes were com-plex high-technology products. Even if the operation of a single

---

[37] For example, Raaflaub 1999; Hanson 1995; Kagan and Viggiano 2013a; Ober 2015, 136, has a pithy summary. Van Wees 2004 takes a markedly different line; see also Van Wees 2013a and Krentz 2013.

[38] Strauss 1996.

[39] Rihll 1993.

[40] Napier 1857, vol. 2, 69.

ship was within the reach of the wealthiest individuals, useful fleets were made up of dozens or hundreds of such vessels, and these could only be mobilised by the resources of a whole community. Moreover, in themselves they were of no use in suppressing a population. The security they offered looked outwards. Their greatest attraction was the possibility they provided of power projection, and Athens used hers to deprive other Greeks of their autonomy while democracy was preserved at home. From this angle, Athenian democracy was not just compatible with imperialism; it positively invited it.

While Athens' hoplite forces *were* very large in the fifth century, the real source of her power was the trireme fleet, which was still more hungry for men. In spite of the undoubted presence of numerous non-citizens on the rowing benches, still many, if not most, of those men must have been citizens. Patterson pointed out that the 450s represented something of a peak in Athenian imperialism and military activity, and that the scope of its ambition and power projection is consistent with a citizen population that was already very large, and perhaps as large as it was in the 430s.[41] It is quite possible that there was not a period of steady increase from 479 to 431, but instead an explosive growth in the first half of that period to a peak, which then levelled out or even fell back before rallying again. This is, after all, what we might infer if we could be sure that the scale of the operations about which Thucydides tells us was more or less directly related to the size of the citizen population: major operations against the Persians came to an end around 450; peace was made with Sparta in 446.[42] These observations alone do not make the case, but they are suggestive.

All of this does not really prove anything about the historical demography of classical Athens. Nonetheless, the evidence that we have seems, at least superficially, best to be explained by a genuinely explosive expansion in the Athenian citizen population. To some extent, that could (as we shall see) be explained by immigration and the incorporation of immigrants into the citizen body. Still, it is important to decide whether a growth rate of 2–3 per cent per

[41] Patterson 1981, 64.
[42] Watson 2010.

annum in the short term (which here means 30 to 50 years) is really possible by endogenous means.

Here, Scheidel's conclusions turn out to be rather more equivocal. He rightly points out that comparative data from modern developing nations are of no direct relevance to the ancient world, since in the latter there was no possible source of the 'exogenous input of medical knowledge' which could have caused a sudden massive decrease in mortality rates.[43] However, Sallares (like Snodgrass) also drew on data from colonial populations in North America, and here rates of natural increase up to 3 per cent per annum were sometimes sustained for several generations. Given that ancient populations in mainland Greece were not in quite the same economic and social situation as those in colonial North America, there is some scope for questioning the appropriateness of the parallel. On the other hand, Sallares' original point was just that, given sufficient resources, pre-industrial human populations *are* capable of rates of increase well above 0.5 per cent per annum. Scheidel was happier to accept, on the basis of early modern census data from Greece, that 'short-term demographic surges of up to 1 per cent per year may have been feasible in a pre-modern Greek ecosphere'.[44]

What may be more important here is what he goes on to say, when he stresses the degree of regional differences in growth rates (something that Sallares was also keen to emphasise).[45] A little earlier in this piece, Scheidel had already observed that while the available evidence for medieval and early modern Europe suggested maximum rates of (long-term) increase of 0.3–0.5 per cent per year, these were 'almost an entire order of magnitude lower than the rates envisioned by Snodgrass, Sallares, and Tandy [for eighth-century Attica]'. Nonetheless, he was prepared to accept that 'it is possible that smaller geographical units may deviate from these broad averages: after all, Attica covers only a thousand square miles'.[46] This seems to be an important concession in the context of the fifth century. Even Scheidel's robust and sensible

[43] Scheidel 2003, 128.
[44] Scheidel 2003, 129.
[45] Sallares 1991, 107–29.
[46] Scheidel 2003, 128.

scepticism leaves the door ajar for a very rapid population expansion within a small region and over a period of, at most, half a century – and which had no great impact on the overall size of the population when looked at in the long term. This is, again, not the same thing as *proving* that it took place, but it shows that the possibility cannot be excluded. Given the possibility that the population *did* expand very rapidly during the *pentecontaetia*, we still have to explain why this period saw such a sudden explosion.

There are only two ways that a population can increase. The first way is by generating an excess of births over deaths. Ancient historians tend to call this 'natural increase', which is slightly misleading, as it implies both that the alternative was somehow 'unnatural' and that it is inevitable that populations tend to increase over time. Such an excess can, obviously, be the result of increased fertility, lowered mortality, or a combination of the two. The second way is by immigration. One or both of these mechanisms must have been operating in Athens if its population really did grow so quickly.

Jones argued that in fact the population as a whole need not have increased as much as the army figures in Herodotus and Thucydides imply, since they refer only to hoplites. Because Athens was becoming increasingly wealthy as a result of the empire, many poorer citizens would have become wealthy enough to afford a hoplite panoply, thus increasing the total number of hoplites and Athens' military power, without necessarily a commensurate increase in the total number of citizens. It is possible that something like this was going on, and it must be the case that some poor Athenians gained significantly from the empire, and new hoplites were added to Athens' ranks. However, this was not necessarily a period of unalloyed good news for the poorer citizens, as we shall see (Chapter 7). In any case, increasing the number of hoplites cannot be the whole story. Apart from the fact that this argument would seem to be inconsistent with the picture presented by Hansen (which, as we have seen, there are good reasons for accepting), Athens' military adventures during the *pentecontaetia* demanded at least as much naval as land power. The key point of difficulty in accepting Jones' argument is that it reopens the problem of understanding how Athens' losses in the Peloponnesian War could have been sustained without provoking severe difficulties in maintaining the operation of the institutions of democracy, a plausible solution to which has been provided by Hansen.[47] Unless we think that those fleets were overwhelmingly manned by non-Athenians, the number of citizens must have been very large, not just the number of hoplites. Earlier authors such as Gomme and Jones seem to have believed that the growing wealth of imperial Athens would have led almost inevitably to a growth in the population by 'natural' means. As Patterson pointed out, this idea, that wealthier automatically equals bigger, is not one that is given much credence by demographers.[48] Something like this attitude has, however, resurfaced in Ober's *The Rise and Fall of Classical Greece*, where in addition to making the claim that 'Athens was a highly desirable destination for economic migrants', he suggested that 'conditions of improved welfare also promoted increased natural population growth', without much in the way of explanation of how that might have happened (although perhaps he had Bresson's suggestions about lowered mortality in mind).[49] The note he provides here to support his claims about Athenian demography in the fifth century directs the reader to Hansen's work on the fourth century.

A huge increase in Athens' citizen population demands more explanation than this. It is surely likely that the explanation lies in a combination of enhanced fertility and immigration. Assessing the relative importance of the two is difficult, however. Even before the citizenship law of 451/0, it cannot have been altogether straightforward in normal circumstances for an outsider to become an Athenian citizen (albeit not impossible, and circumstances were not always normal). As for 'natural' increases, it is, in spite of Bresson's cautious optimism, hard to see any real improvements in Athenian medicine or sanitation that could have led to a meaningful reduction in mortality. Fertility within a population is subject to change, however, and the circumstances of fifth-century Athens may have allowed for such change.

[47] Hansen 1988.
[48] Patterson 1981, 69–70.
[49] Ober 2015, 205; Bresson 2008, 50–6; 2016, 43–9.

The Persian Wars were vitally important for determining the later course of events in Athens. There are good reasons for using them to locate the start of the classical period, and they firmly established Athens as a major player in the Greek world and beyond. Still, our perception of them has been coloured by hindsight and by centuries of mythologising. For those who lived through the war and the invasion and occupation of Attica, these must have been traumatic and disruptive times, to say the least. Events like this can have marked demographic effects. It is natural to think about elevated mortality, but fertility can be affected too. The consequences for fertility can tend in different directions. High levels of risk and uncertainty tend to depress fertility, as people fear for the future and avoid committing scarce or vulnerable resources to increasing the size of their families. The successful resolution of a crisis or the removal of a terrible threat, however, can also lead to an increase in fertility that may not just reverse a reduction but actually overcorrect. War and crisis, when successfully resolved, can then lead to a 'baby boom'.[50] In the Athens of the early 470s, it is tempting to consider at least the possibility of a significant increase in fertility. Part of this would have resulted from deferred decisions about having children now being made. The Athenians were also now able to take advantage of vastly greater resources. In the immediate aftermath of the war, the spoils of victory would have enriched many individual Athenians.[51] Though the Athenians were not in a 'colonial' situation similar to that of the European settlers of North America, as their *arche* expanded they clearly were able to draw on (or rather forcibly co-opt) the agricultural resources of a much larger area than Attica itself, and this could have allowed for a fertility increase.[52] This was Sallares' explanation in passing for the rapid growth of the Athenian population in the *pentecontaetia*, and it would also help Ober. Moreno has eloquently demonstrated the importance of the agricultural resources of the Aegean islands (and most of all Euboea) to, and the scale on which they were

---

[50] Wrigley 1969, 68–70.
[51] Miller 1997, 29–62.
[52] On the economically exploitative character of the empire right from the start, see Kallet 2013.

exploited by, the Athenians in this period – even if we need not accept all his arguments about the mechanisms of exploitation.[53] We need not, and should not, think of anything on the scale witnessed by the United States at the conclusion to the Second World War, but neither is the parallel wholly inappropriate.[54] Athens did not gain materially as much as the US then, but the influx of wealth was real. The men serving in her army and fleet were not absent for years, but they were gone for more extended periods, and in greater numbers, than seems to have been normal at the time. The existential threat to the community of Athens was very much more immediate and apparent, on the other hand, than it ever was to the continental US; it is not obviously absurd to think that relief at victory and survival may also have been felt as intensely.

The idea of a 'baby boom' itself is, of course, a familiar one in modern western countries. If something similar, if less dramatic, did take place in Athens in the 470s, then it may be even more interesting than simply forming part of the explanation for Athens' power and confidence in the *pentecontaetia*. Such booms tend to have 'echoes' in succeeding generations – for fairly obvious reasons, as the children who are born in large numbers in the initial boom grow up to have children of their own, who in turn grow up to have children ... and so on. This is one illustration of 'Sundt's Law', the observation by the Norwegian sociologist Eilert Sundt that where the age structure of a population is disturbed for some reason (usually a crisis), the irregularity that is produced will recur in future generations (unless it is overwhelmed by another major crisis).[55] Children conceived soon after the shattering victory of Plataea, or after the capture of Sestos (and the cables for Xerxes' bridge across the Hellespont), would have been turning 20 in 458, just in time to provide the pick of Athens' manpower for the attempt to create land empire, for the Egyptian expedition, and for the first Peloponnesian War. This group would also be the group on the threshold of entering the *boule* and perhaps being

---

[53] Moreno 2007, 77–143.
[54] Watson 2010 takes a different view, but seems to me to be too dismissive of the appropriateness of the comparison.
[55] Wrigley 1969, 69; Tandy 1997, 58.

more assertive in the assembly when the citizenship law was passed. If (and it is admittedly a big if, even more so given the generally parlous state of our knowledge about ages of marriage in Athens) they started having children in their twenties, then their children would have been coming of age in the 430s, when after an apparent lull Athens started to expand aggressively again (leading to the outbreak of the Peloponnesian War). The same pattern repeated again would see the next bulge appearing in the 410s. The relevance of this would be in helping to provide a further possible explanation for Thucydides' rather mystifying remark that the Athenians had 'recovered' from the plague by the time of the Sicilian Expedition. In more general terms, it is worth pointing out this echo effect as a further illustration that restricting discussion to 'mean long-term trends' may obscure short-term variations which can have important effects on *l'histoire événementielle*, and which we might still want to care about.

This also reinforces the point that, while the use of model life tables is worthwhile, it is nonetheless limited. A rapidly expanding population is going to be very much younger on average than one that is static or declining, or even just growing more slowly. Hansen's chosen model assumed a 0.5 per cent per annum growth rate, and for ease of comparison this is the growth rate that was employed in the alternative models that were presented in Chapter 2. However, in the years 480–431, the actual 'natural' growth rate *could* have been higher than this, perhaps even as high as 1.5–2.5 per cent. This would have resulted in a very different age structure. This would, it must be stressed again, have very little effect on Hansen's conclusions about the political institutions of the fourth century, but it illustrates the futility of applying such a model to the Athenian citizen population in any actual given year during the classical period. Even as an average figure, the 0.5 per cent per annum growth rate is completely arbitrary, and has no basis in evidence. It was chosen only because it is the lowest rate of positive growth in the Princeton tables (which were not, of course, designed with ancient historians in mind). The actual growth rate of the citizen population between 480 and 320, averaged for the whole period, was probably closer to zero. At no stage, however, need the age structure of the population as a whole have closely resembled any of the stationary models provided by Coale and Demeny (or anyone else) or that could be devised.

Nor would it be surprising that many people moved from elsewhere to Athens during the *pentecontaetia*, too. Athens after the Persian Wars was a place that had almost overnight acquired a new injection of wealth, and it would have been rife with economic opportunities of various sorts: the monumental temples were left in ruins at first, but there would have been all kinds of other reconstruction to be done, and Athens, after all, remained on a full war footing. Furthermore, with the evacuation to Troezen and disruption of normal civic life at all levels, there would surely have been confusion about exactly who was a citizen. There may also have been little desire to exclude men whose legal claims were weak but who had (or could plausibly claim that they had) fought in Athenian ranks or on Athenian ships.[56]

Some increased immigration should probably be inferred earlier in the 480s.[57] When the Athenians decided to build a fleet of the still relatively newfangled and high-technology triremes, they must have brought in the necessary skilled labour to help build them. Even if the ships were bought ready-made, the infrastructure to support them and to train the new crews must have led to some newcomers arriving, some of whom could well have wanted to stay.[58] How many of these men came to Athens is impossible to know, but for the fleet to have been put together so quickly and (given its performance in the Persian War) efficiently, they must have been fairly numerous. Where they came from is another matter. Had these men remained in Athens as metics, then they are the kind whom one could easily imagine becoming citizens after the war. Clearly however, there were others who did not fall into this category. The necessity every so often to purge the citizen lists of those who were not entitled to be enrolled indicates that the citizen/non-citizen boundary was not always as carefully or

---

[56] Watson 2010, 265–6.
[57] Or even in the late sixth century: Van Wees 2013b, 64–8.
[58] Meiggs 1982, 122; Bissa 2009, 117–40, for some discussion on the origins of this expertise. Meiggs may underestimate the difficulty of finding skilled manpower, however. See also Strauss 1996, 317–20.

successfully policed as we sometimes think.[59] The money to pay for the fleet also reflected a substantial level of immigration, of course, but among those who had no chance of becoming citizens: the slaves who mined the silver.

It is clear that if a significant contribution to a high rate of increase in the citizen population were due to an increase in fertility (to the extent that the citizen population doubled), then the age structure of that population in 451 would have been very different from the ones we have been using. To double the number of adults would have required an even larger number of young people. In fact, to achieve this in the space of 30 years would imply a rate of increase of about 3 per cent rather than 0.5 per cent. There are two points to make here about the implications of such a high rate of increase. One is just that rapidly increasing populations have a much lower average age than those that are stationary or decreasing. The other is that such a high rate of increase, even if it is not wholly implausible, really looks astonishing. Whatever we accept as a reasonable natural rate of increase, however, the short-fall must somehow have been made up by non-citizens becoming citizens. In this light, the citizenship law would presumably have helped to mitigate any further tendency to rapid increase, whatever the original impetus for its passage.[60] Slower growth, driven principally by 'natural' increase, could well have continued until the early 420s, before being curtailed and reversed by the massive casualties inflicted by the plague.

Population Contraction during the Peloponnesian War

Probably no one would dispute that there were fewer people in Athens and Attica at the end of the Peloponnesian War than there had been before the war's start. As with population growth, there were two mechanisms responsible, but this time, in addition to migration, the other was *mortality*. Fertility may well have been affected negatively during the war, but here we cannot begin to assess the scale of the effect. However, it seems likely that the

---

[59] Figueira 1991, 142–3, 231–6; Patterson 2005; Watson 2010.
[60] Watson 2010, 273–4.

effects of changing fertility were dwarfed by the effects of elevated mortality. The effects of each would obviously have varied across the different sections of the population. However, every section of the population would have been exposed to some degree of elevated mortality.

Combat and campaign fatalities will have been suffered primarily by (youngish) adult males. Citizens may have been more likely to die in a pitched land battle than slaves or metics, but it is now clear that both these groups actively participated in warfare. It is possible that the casualties suffered in sea battles were usually drawn from different social groups from those who died in land battles.[61]

Increased disease mortality will likewise have affected different age groups depending on the diseases responsible.[62] Migration too will have affected different age groups differently. Few citizens will have left Athens voluntarily, and some will actually have returned from overseas garrisons and settlements.[63] At least some metics will have left Athens. One way or another, large numbers of slaves seem clearly to have been lost to the city, and replacing them would not necessarily have been easy.

Trying to quantify the effects of all this is not easy, but we can make a start. For reasons which will now be familiar, previous studies have concentrated on the citizen population. Most important here are the accounts of Strauss, in his *Athens After the Peloponnesian War*, and of Hansen, in the 1988 article we have already met.[64]

Clearly for the citizen population, or at least that portion of it that fought as hoplites or cavalry, the two factors about which we are best informed are combat casualties and the numbers of men who died as a result of the 'plague' of Athens. Strauss was rather more interested in the former than in the latter, since one of his arguments is that different sections of the citizen population suffered to different extents and at different stages of the war, whereas the plague killed everyone more or less indiscriminately.[65]

[61] Strauss 1986, 1996, 2000 is convinced of this.
[62] Sallares 1991, 221–90, especially 237 and 258, for examples; Lancaster 1990.
[63] Well discussed by Jones 1957, 161–80.
[64] Strauss 1986; Hansen 1988, 14–28.
[65] Strauss 1986, 75, on the importance of the plague.

As a result, Strauss performed the extremely useful service of ploughing through Thucydides and the relevant bits of Xenophon and Diodorus, totalling up all the hoplite figures they mention, reaching a total of 5,470.[66] As Hansen noted, this figure can only be a minimum; it is clear (not least from the evidence of surviving casualty lists inscribed on stone) that these authors are not telling us about *every* fight where Athenian hoplites fell.[67] Strauss, however, felt (perhaps over-optimistically) that this would be more or less compensated for by the fact that his figures for hoplite casualties would have included some metics.

Strauss' figures do contain a lot of guesswork, although exactly how much is only clear in his appendix. It does, however, seem reasonable to believe the precise figures we are given when they appear. The identification and proper treatment and commemoration of the battle dead was clearly taken seriously by the Greeks, as the very existence of casualty lists would imply.[68]

Strauss claimed that 'the greatest agent of increased mortality in wartime is generally death in battle'.[69] This seems, however, to be a rather dubious claim for periods before the advent of the machine-gun and modern artillery, along with armies with properly (or at least somewhat) organised medical and logistical services. It seems likely that thousands more Athenians must have died of disease amid the squalor of armies on campaign. Roth has made the same point, specifically for the Hellenistic period.[70] We may also get a glimpse of the scale of the issue (which was clearly a particular problem in sieges) in the highly elevated plague mortality of Hagnon's troops before Potidaea in Thucydides 2.58, and in the Athenian camp at Syracuse at 7.47. If Strauss' guesswork has yielded a figure that is roughly right for hoplites, then it still might have to be doubled to reflect more accurately war casualties rather than battle casualties.

For sections of the military population other than hoplites, Strauss found himself on even shakier ground, the principal reason

---

[66] Strauss 1986, 71, with the appendix at 179.
[67] Hansen 1988, 15.
[68] See also Vaughn 1991.
[69] Strauss 1986, 71.
[70] Roth 2007, 395–6.

for which was that casualties in naval battles are almost always reported in terms of numbers of ships lost rather than men. Granted, we think we know the size of the crew of a trireme, but as we have seen, the proportion who were *citizens* is much less clear. If we are interested in the population in general rather than just the citizens, this is less of a problem. What is more serious is the simple fact that we do not know how many men survived the sinking of their ships.

Occasionally, we are given *some* idea, but only in exceptional circumstances – most obviously the 25 triremes lost with all hands at Arginusae, or the Athenians executed by Lysander after Aigospotamoi.[71] Generally, Strauss assumes (on what basis is unclear) that 20 per cent of the crew of a sunk ship died. Whether this is an over- or underestimate or about right is impossible to determine. Strauss' figure of 12,600 dead *thetes* may well be of the right order of magnitude, but we have no way of knowing.

Hansen, in fact, argued that Strauss had probably underestimated Athenian casualties, although this was inevitable, since Strauss was aiming to establish minimum figures. Hansen's estimate was that over the whole of the war, including losses due to the plague and emigration (the sending out of an estimated 2,000 colonists), the Athenians lost something in the order of 43,000 citizens.[72] He then went on to observe that these losses were sustained over a period of 28 years, and attempted to create a model for the size of the (adult, male) citizen population throughout the years of the war.

Before we can assess this attempt, we need at least briefly to consider the other major causes of population loss. In terms of increased mortality, the most important single factor was the plague. A great deal of ink has been shed on the identification of this disease. Certainty will probably continue to elude us (although it seems clear that it was not actually plague of any kind) as long as all we have to go on is the literary account provided by Thucydides. For what it is worth, smallpox does seem to be one of the more likely candidates, as suggested by the Littmans in the 1960s, and vigorously, though not uncritically, supported by

---

[71] On Aigospotamoi, Xen. *Hell.* 2.1.28; according to Plutarch (*Lysander* 13.1) there were 3,000, but according to Pausanias (9.32.9), there were 4,000.
[72] Hansen 1988, 19.

Sallares in 1991.[73] Another plausible alternative would be epidemic typhus, however.[74] The suggestion of typhoid fever made in 2006 by Papagrigorakis et al. is not impossible, but it fits less well with the testimony of Thucydides, and the methodology used to identify it is controversial.[75]

There seem to be fewer problems with understanding what Thucydides has to say in his comments on the effects of the plague, especially at 3.87.1–3, where he says that 300 of the *hippeis* died, and 4,400 hoplites *ek ton taxeon*. Notoriously, he is unable (or unwilling?) to give figures for the rest of the population, but we do already have his account of the numbers of cavalry and hoplites (at 2.13). The cavalry are relatively straightforward. Thucydides tells us first that there were 1,200 – including the *hippotoxotai* – and later that 300 of them died. This implies a casualty rate of 25 per cent. If there were only 1,000 citizen cavalry, then the rate would be 30 per cent, but that requires us to make assumptions about both the status and the number of the horse-archers, about whom there is virtually no other information.

The hoplites are slightly more problematic. We are told that 4,400 died. But are these 4,400 from the 13,000 hoplites of the field army (in which case the casualty rate would be about 34 per cent), or of all the citizen hoplites, or even all of the hoplites, including metics (in which case the rate would be much lower)? A lot depends on the translation of *ek ton taxeon*. Jones was inclined to take it as meaning 'from the tribal regiments', implying, for him, *all* citizen hoplites, and total casualties of around 20 per cent.[76] Obviously, the exact casualty rate depends on how many of the 16,000 'garrison' hoplites are taken to be citizens. The apparent discrepancy between hoplite and cavalry was accounted for just by observing that the cavalry were a small sample, and in any case might have suffered disproportionately just because they were kept in an almost permanent state of

---

[73] Littman and Littman 1969. Sallares 1991, 241–90, has a summary of other suggested identifications. Langmuir et al. 1985, and Holladay and Poole 1979 (with Holladay and Poole 1982, 1984) are generally despairing about the chances of identifying the disease.

[74] Littman 2009.

[75] Papagrigorakis et al. 2006a, 2006b; Shapiro, Rambaut, and Gilbert 2006.

[76] Jones 1957, 165.

mobilisation. (Jones was happy to accept that there were 1,000 citizen cavalry.) For Jones, *ek ton taxeon* 'is presumably added either to exclude the ephebes, or more probably *thetes* equipped as hoplites for service in the fleet as marines'.[77]

As Strauss noted, however, Jones' argument, although in itself perfectly reasonable, rests on what would be a rather unusual (in fact unique) use of the word *taxis* by Thucydides.[78] In other contexts, Thucydides always uses it in the sense of a battle line, or fighting troops, and not as the total number of hoplites in the (essentially administrative) 'regiments'. Particularly important here is the passage at 8.69.1, where *taxis* must refer to the men in the field, distinguished from those on garrison duty. Strauss also observed that if Thucydides had meant what Jones thought he meant, he could have used the word *katalogos*, which he uses in this sense at 6.26, 6.31, and 6.43.[79] As Strauss notes, Gomme seems to have been right in his inference that the losses inflicted on the militarily active population of Athens were in the range of one-quarter to one-third, rather than the one-fifth suggested by Jones.[80]

Gomme and Strauss were probably also justified in assuming that similar casualty rates applied across the rest of the population. True, the hoplite figures are elevated by the staggering losses suffered at Potidaea (1,050 in 40 days), but the part of the population for which we have the numbers were reasonably affluent, fit young men – hardly the most vulnerable group of society. There seems little reason to assume that the old and young would have suffered to any lesser extent. However, Sallares' observation about the age-specific mortality of smallpox is an interesting one. In summary, children aged 5–19 are more likely to survive than other age groups. This may make some sense of Thucydides' odd claim that Athens' manpower had recovered by the time of the Sicilian Expedition (6.26.2), as the boys who had been in these age groups at the time of the plague would now be forming the core of Athens' military forces.[81] Poorer citizens and the women of

[77] Jones 1957, 166.
[78] Strauss 1986, 76.
[79] Strauss 1986, 84 note 33.
[80] Gomme 1933, 6–7.
[81] Sallares 1991, 258–9.

citizen households (pregnant women would presumably have been particularly vulnerable), along with metics and slaves, probably also suffered casualties of the same magnitude; clearly, it would have been harder for Thucydides (or anyone else) to arrive at firm figures, even if they had wanted to.

If we accept Thucydides (and we would need a good reason to reject him on this), we seem to have to accept a staggering loss of population over the four-year period of the plague. As Hansen's attempts at a year-by-year analysis indicate, no other single factor contributed as much to the fall in the citizen population – even when very pessimistic assumptions are made about the loss of life incurred in the Sicilian Expedition.[82] Before going any further, it is worth asking if what Thucydides' account implies is really plausible. Could the plague have caused casualties on this scale?

In short, the answer seems to be yes. Virgin-soil epidemics of smallpox and typhus do seem to have been responsible for very high mortality rates, at this kind of scale, in historical times.[83] The most recent standard text on smallpox notes some examples, without any objections to the plausibility of mortality at this kind of level. They note that, in some cases at least, the high mortality apparently caused by the epidemic will have been exacerbated by dislocation in the food production and distribution systems of these societies. This does not seem to have happened to any great extent in Athens, but on the other hand the authors, not having access to Garnsey 1988, may have exaggerated the vulnerability of pre-industrial societies in this regard.[84] Henige has cast doubt on the scale of the casualties caused by disease in the wake of European contact with native American populations.[85] However, the estimates of the 'high counters' he is seeking to attack dwarf anything suggested for Athens, and are based on significantly flimsier evidence than that of Thucydides.

In more recent times, where epidemics of these diseases have caused much lower numbers of deaths and much lower mortality rates, the key difference is that they were afflicting populations in

---

[82] Hansen 1988, 22, 27.
[83] McNeill, 1976, 3–4, 105–6; Sallares 1991, 250–2; Walker and Raoult 2011.
[84] Fenner et al. 1988, 209–44.
[85] Henige 1998.

which smallpox was already endemic (where acquired resistance was much higher) or in which its spread was limited by vaccination programmes (and in fortunate countries, sophisticated public health systems that knew how to respond).[86] There is no particular reason, in short, to doubt that the implications of Thucydides' account were as severe as they appear.

The apparent reticence of our contemporary literary sources other than Thucydides cannot be used as an argument against the reality of the plague or the level of casualties as he describes them. Robin Mitchell-Boyask has argued both that the lack of other direct accounts like Thucydides' is not altogether surprising, and that in fact the impact of the plague can be seen elsewhere in Athenian literature, specifically in the tragedies of the post-plague period.[87] On a smaller scale and simpler level, I have argued that the plague may help to explain an otherwise puzzling feature of the development of Aristophanes' comedy.[88]

The important point about the plague for the current purpose is that it probably affected the whole population. It is also worth bearing in mind that, although the precise effects are incalculable, throughout the war, sections of the population other than the citizens will have suffered elevated mortality for other reasons. In spite of Thucydides' lack of interest, both metics and slaves will have been exposed to many of the same risks of warfare as citizens. The non-combatant population will also have been exposed to increased risk of disease if and when they took refuge inside the Athens–Piraeus fortress. There is no reason to doubt Thucydides' picture of the squalor and misery endured by refugees, or that this would have had consequences for their health. This situation will have been compounded by the occupation of Decelea.

To return briefly to emigration, we have already seen that many slaves ran away. But what about metics? What we think happened to them will depend on what kind of people we think they were, and the range of options that was really available to them. Clearly the label of 'metic' covered a wide range of people, as we saw in

[86] Fenner et al. 1988, 169–208; Walker and Raoult 2011, 329.
[87] Mitchell-Boyask 2008.
[88] Akrigg 2013.

Chapter 4. Some may well have wanted to leave at the outset of the war, although it is hard to believe that all that many would. Athens was quite often at war, after all, and for many metics it is surely likely that the opening of hostilities would have reinforced their reasons for being in Athens in the first place. What Whitehead, in his discussion of this issue, refers to as the 'more general assets of Athens – which, for the majority, meant the economic activities of a large city and major port'[89] will, if anything, have increased. Athens' need for imported food, timber, and skilled manpower, the factors that drove its economic dominance, would only have become more intense.

The coming of the plague and, eventually, Athens' declining fortunes in war, will have changed this picture. At the end of the war, the size of the population will have been reduced, and along with it the scale of demand for basic imports; the wherewithal for more luxurious goods will also generally have been lacking. The once-mighty fleet was reduced to a mere dozen vessels for local defence. The economic opportunities for metics would have been sharply reduced accordingly. That later in the fourth century the number of wealthy metics in Athens was (at least partly) responsive to the level of economic opportunity is suggested by Xenophon in the *Poroi* and Isocrates in *On the Peace*.[90] It is likely that such was the case in the immediate aftermath of the war, too. Whatever we think about the number of such metics, either absolutely or relative to the citizen population, the emigration of at least some of them will have come on top of the effects of the elevated mortality experienced by those who could not or chose not to leave.

The Fourth Century, and Conclusion

While Hansen's essentially static picture of the citizen population in the fourth century may reflect the scattered and partial nature of the evidence that we have (which encourages the creation of composite pictures which smooth out short-term variations), it

[89] Whitehead 1977, 18.
[90] Xen. *Poroi* 3; Isocrates 8.21.

may reflect reality quite well. During the fourth century, Athens experienced neither the exogenous shocks of epidemic disease and total war nor the abundant resources of empire to anything like the degree that it had during the fifth century.

This does not mean that this story is unproblematic, at least when one looks outside the narrow boundaries of Hansen's interests in fourth-century political history. The low point of the size of the citizen population was taken by Hansen, not unreasonably, to be in the immediate aftermath of the Peloponnesian War; after that, the picture is one of steady if unspectacular recovery. Still, late fourth-century Athens was a prosperous and, as far as we can tell, well-populated place. In the Hellenistic period, however, there seem consistently to be far fewer people around. Where did they all go? Recently Oliver, picking up on this problem in his account of early Hellenistic Athens, has pointed out that Athenian citizens at the end of the fourth and beginning of the third centuries can be found all across the newly expanded Greek world, and so the likely explanation is a significant increase in emigration.[91]

From the snapshot-like evidence discussed in Chapter 3, it was clear that the citizen population of Athens in the second decade of the fifth century was probably comparable in size to that of most of the fourth century – roughly 30,000 (implying a total citizen population including women and children of roughly 120,000). However, by the 430s, the citizen population was about twice this size, before being cut down again during the Peloponnesian War. This implies *both* a very rapid increase and a very rapid decrease in quick succession. Such changes should have had quite profound and far-reaching effects. In practice, however, there has been little interest in discussing what the effects might have been. Patterson's is the standard account of fifth-century historical demography, but she is only interested in the immediate context of the Periclean citizenship law. While that does make her interested in the scale of the increase in the citizen population, she needed neither to consider very far what the *sources* of that increase were, nor to take the story any further than 431 and the evidence of Thucydides, which provided

---

[91] Oliver 2007, 87–100.

a terminal fixed point for her discussion. While there has been some interest in the scale of losses suffered during the Peloponnesian War, in the most important and influential accounts, the final few decades of the fifth century are not so much interesting for themselves but become a prologue to the political narratives of the fourth. While there is nothing intrinsically wrong with these approaches, they have left the years of the Peloponnesian War, which should be seen as a watershed in the historical demography of Athens, somewhat in the shadows. In this chapter, I have tried to reassert the scale of the demographic changes of the fifth century and start to draw out why they are of more than pedantic interest. In this light, the Peloponnesian War has emerged as a real watershed in Athenian demography. In the 50 years before its start, the citizen population seems to have doubled; barely 30 years later it was reduced by half again. These were colossal changes, which must have made huge impacts on the economy and society of Athens. What should we make of them?

CHAPTER 6

IMMEDIATE IMPLICATIONS OF POPULATION
CHANGE: WAR AND FOOD

In the preceding chapters, the main focus has been on quantifying the population of classical Athens. In this chapter and in Chapter 7, I turn to the implications of the results of that exercise. In this chapter, I look at the implications of the absolute size of the population. Most of the questions here will be familiar. While this will reduce the need for detailed discussion, one point I want to make is that, as with consideration of population numbers, the answers that have been provided to those questions even in the quite recent past have tended to be directed towards very specific and limited goals.

For ancient observers, the most obvious consequence of a large population, and one that has been mentioned several times already, was that it provided an abundance of military manpower. This is clearly recognised by Thucydides when he is summarising the effects of the plague.[1] Not only does he provide casualty figures from among the hoplites and the cavalry (which may have been because these were the only figures available), but he comments that losing these men was the biggest single blow to her *dunamis* that Athens suffered during the war. As we saw in Chapter 5, this is at least a justifiable claim; it is also not a trivial one.

Scheidel has observed that if military power were straightforwardly linked to population, then we should all be speaking Chinese.[2] This is a fair comment, although presumably the United States, for example, is more concerned by the military potential of China than that of, say, Luxembourg. However, when technologies and the institutions that allow the mobilisation

---

[1] Thuc. 3.87.3
[2] Scheidel 2001b, 67.

of military manpower are comparable – as they were in the Aegean world of the fifth and fourth centuries – then numbers do count.

While we need not go quite so far as Sallares suggested in his biologically determined model of ancient history, military success often does seem to have been dependent on manpower.[3] The conquests of Alexander would have been impossible had it not been for the apparently limitless supplies of high-quality manpower that Macedon could provide in his generation. Likewise, Rome was able to defeat Carthage in the Second Punic War not because of any superiority in technology or leadership but because she was able to absorb the most horrific casualties and still raise more legions. When we turn back to classical Greece, it is worth comparing the positions of Athens and Sparta. One constraint on the latter's foreign policy was always her lack of citizen manpower, and it was the casualties from a single battle that led to her permanent eclipse. Athens, by contrast, seems already in the fifth century to have suffered significant casualties in the Egyptian debacle even before the outbreak of the Peloponnesian War. After open hostilities between the two broke out in 431, Athens was almost immediately hit by the plague, which killed a significant fraction of the population on its own. Combat casualties seem to have run at a pretty high rate throughout the war, but there were presumably upward spikes in casualty numbers at the end of the Sicilian Expedition and the battle of Aigospotamoi. In spite of all of this, however, Athens was still able to re-establish herself, not perhaps to her former glory, but as a major military player again for most of the fourth century. The forces that were mobilised for the Lamian War in the late fourth century were quite impressive by Athens' own previous standards: the problem by then was that they were less so when compared to what Alexander and his successors had available to them. Taken together, this seems a compelling argument in favour of a picture of a fifth-century Athens that was overflowing with people.

For both Plato and Aristotle, however, there were negative consequences to having *too* large a population. In the former's *Laws*, for example, the size of the citizen population is to be

---

[3] Sallares 1991, 47.

maintained at an (notionally) ideal and convenient 5,040. The concern that the citizen population should not be so large that it becomes unstable is tempered by the awareness that if it is too small it will not be able to defend itself or come to the assistance of its neighbours when required.[4]

While it is important to bear all of this in mind, thinking about military power will not take us very far here. This is not because the scale of Athens' military is in any way unimportant, but because it is precisely the scale of her armed forces and military activity that lie behind so much of our picture of the size of its population. Explaining Athens' military history by using its historical demography would clearly then be circular. As often, it is the perceptive Aristotle who points the way to more fruitful lines of enquiry.

In the *Politics*, Aristotle points out in passing that Plato's suggestion of maintaining 5,040 citizens in what amounts to a state of leisure (which would allow them to meet their various commitments to the community) will actually imply an extremely large number of non-citizens, and so in practice such a *polis* would be of an unwieldy size. Aristotle also argues that communities above a certain size can no longer count as a true *polis*.[5] He further explicitly notes that there can be a correlation between a large population and poverty, which in turn leads to political instability. This has been discussed less often, but as we shall see in Chapter 7, it is important for understanding Athens.

In the remainder of this chapter, I shall review the implications of the demographic arguments I have presented in the one area other than politics where population size has always been recognised: the food supply, and the perennial question of how far Athens was dependent (or otherwise) on food (especially cereals) imported from overseas. In fact, even these kinds of questions have often been motivated ultimately by more traditional military-political concerns to do with explaining or understanding Athenian foreign policy, whether in the northern Aegean, the Black Sea, Egypt, or the West, and the development of her naval

---

[4] Plato, *Laws* 737d, 740b1–741a5.
[5] Arist. *Pol.* 1265a1–17, 1276a22–34.

empire. I shall argue here that the domestic consequences of this large market for foodstuffs are at least as important and interesting. I shall also suggest that other forms of consumption, although they are much harder to quantify even than that of cereals, will have been significant too.

In answering these kinds of questions, it is clearly necessary to quantify both the scale of the demand for food and how much of that demand could be met by domestic production. Exact figures will remain elusive; the best that we can do is to establish reasonable parameters for the relevant variables. Both the demand for and the supply of food in Athens are governed primarily by two variables. The components of demand are the overall size of the population (nothing more needs to be said at this stage on this subject), and per capita requirements. The components of supply are usually taken to be the amount of cultivable land available and what the productivity of that land was. However, the latter two are not wholly independent of each other, as both will of course be affected by views of *how* the land was worked.

Two relatively recent accounts have addressed many of these issues: those of Moreno and Bissa.[6] Both accounts have to draw on the same, limited material. Both are also determined to show that (almost) whatever assumptions we start from, Athens' demand for grain throughout the classical period far outstripped its capacity to produce it. Their intention in making this point is at least in part (and wholly reasonably) to emphasise the importance of their respective projects: Bissa's on the scale and scope of governmental intervention in trade in Greece in the archaic and classical periods, and Moreno's on the centrality of the grain trade to Athenian politics. It is therefore not very surprising that they reach generally similar and compatible conclusions. There is also little point in duplicating every aspect of their discussions here. Some comments are, however, in order before we can adopt their conclusions wholesale.

First, when it comes to food, both are primarily concerned with the consumption of grain. (Bissa also pays attention to two other

---

[6] Moreno 2007; Bissa 2009. There is also a brief but clear treatment, focusing on the late classical and early Hellenistic periods, in Oliver 2007, 74–110.

non-food commodities that were important to Athens – silver and timber – and we shall return to one of them in more detail later.) While this is perfectly sensible, since cereals really were an important trade item and one about which we are *relatively* well informed, it is also important to remember that the grain trade was not completely alone in its importance. Even if it is accepted that it was the single most important commodity to classical Athens, the production and consumption of other goods were not necessarily all that *much* less important, especially when taken in aggregate. Limiting the discussion to grain has obvious benefits for clarity, but what both Moreno and Bissa provide are models developed to illustrate their arguments, not necessarily descriptions of what was going on in classical Attica.

Second, both Bissa and Moreno adopt a rhetoric that is appropriate for making their points but also inevitably affects their arguments. Both are concerned to demonstrate the importance and the significance of the grain trade. This means that when it comes to establishing parameters for the relevant variables, they have a natural tendency to make minimising assumptions about the scale of demand, but maximising ones about the limits of production. Effectively, they are both saying 'even if we assume both that the population was quite small, and that the land productivity of Attica was quite high, still the demand for imported food would have been substantial and significant'. This is surely the right conclusion, but as with Hansen's arguments about the size of the citizen population in the fourth century, the route used to arrive at it does not provide us with a complete story.

This becomes clear when we consider their estimates of the total population of Attica. Both, incidentally, accept Hansen's figures, with Bissa going so far as to say that 'Hansen's figures are an estimate but his method is based on well-established figures for political participation and on comprehensive demographic evidence, and as such is more reliable than other estimates based on incomplete figures for military manpower'.[7] Bissa uses a range of four figures, but the range is pitched quite low. Her minimum figure is 150,000, while her maximum is 300,000 – although she

---

[7] Moreno 2007, 29–31; Bissa 2009, 172.

remarks in a footnote that it might have been better to use a maximum of 400,000.[8] Moreno, not unreasonably, thinks that 150,000 is too low a figure for a minimum in the classical period (and the people whom he attacks for having suggested such a figure in the 1980s probably would no longer defend it), but also suggests a 'conservative' total of 337,000 for (an implied peak in) 431.[9] This last figure includes a large number of slaves, as it treats Sargent's maximum estimate as a minimum. The conclusion that I think has to be drawn from the survey in earlier chapters is that a realistic minimum for the classical period has to be 200,000, as Moreno suggests, but also that 400,000 is perfectly plausible, on the evidence we have, for the pre-Peloponnesian War figure (again, recall that Hansen's suggested 60,000 citizens is meant to be another minimum; see 142–143 above). Bissa and Moreno have other fish to fry, but it is worth considering what the implications of a population of this size would have elsewhere in our picture of classical Athens. Strictly for the purposes of making their arguments, there is a real virtue for them in adopting 'conservative' maximum figures; in any other context, however, a conservative figure is just one that is known to be likely to be wrong (as too low) and has no greater intrinsic value than any other estimate. This is not really a problem for Bissa in her account; Moreno, however, has grander ambitions in the direction of characterising the Athenian economy as a whole. His consistent preference for conservatism could then sometimes be problematic if we were to use his conclusions in other contexts.

The most obvious instance of this comes in assessing the production potential of Athens. Both Bissa and Moreno, on comparative grounds, are prepared at least to contemplate a theoretical maximum land productivity figure for barley of 800 kg/ha; this is quite a high figure (as their rhetoric requires), but is comfortably within the bounds of possibility.[10] There is slightly more scope for debate when it comes to the amount of cultivated land in Attica. The area of Attica is more or less known, even though its political

---

[8] Bissa 2009, 172 note 24.

[9] Moreno 2007, 28–31.

[10] Bissa 2009, 175; Moreno 2007, 26–8; on the 'bounds of possibility', it is useful to compare Halstead 2014, 242–3, 250.

boundaries were not fixed. Estimates of the amount of it that was suitable for cereal cultivation, however, vary from a very pessimistic 20 per cent to an optimistic 40 per cent (with 50 per cent, including some very marginal land, as the absolute maximum that anyone has seriously suggested). Moreno is committed to the idea that a biennial fallow regime was universal in classical Attica, and pours scorn on any suggestion that more than 20 per cent of the total land would be cultivated in any one year. He therefore thinks that 17.5 per cent is an altogether more likely typical figure.[11]

Bissa observes that the evidence is not nearly as strong as Moreno maintains (and, contrary to his explicit claim, there is none that is actually fifth-century in date) and is not adequate to deal with Garnsey's point that the temptation for small farmers to break biennial fallow would at times have been extremely strong.[12] Having allowed at least the possibility that more than half of the cultivable land of Attica was under grain in any one year, however, she retains a figure of 20 per cent as a maximum, on the grounds that this is half of 40 per cent. Again, this does not particularly weaken her argument, as there would have been diminishing returns involved in bringing more, increasingly marginal land into cultivation.

The point, however, is that we do not have a set of independent variables here; the entries in Bissa's (undeniably clear and useful) matrices are not all equally plausible.[13] The larger the population, the greater the likelihood of more land being brought into cultivation. In turn, average land productivity would have been lowered if poorer quality land were being used. Furthermore, the productivity even of good land would have declined if abandonment of the 'ideal' fallowing regimes resulted in declining soil fertility (that is, if they were not replaced by effective crop rotation). On the other hand, the abundant labour in a large population could have been employed to maximise land productivity, albeit at the expense of labour productivity in the agricultural sector.[14] A large population

---

[11] Moreno 2007, 12–15.
[12] Bissa 2009, 174; again, compare Halstead 2014, 246.
[13] Bissa 2009, 176.
[14] But not necessarily labour productivity overall. Erdkamp 2016 draws out some of the complexities for the slightly different case of the Roman empire.

would also have generated significant pressure to adapt methods of cultivation on its own. The combined impact on land productivity is hard to assess; the meaningfulness of an average figure is debatable in a dynamic situation.

All these minima are too low, in any case; farmers could never have counted on good years, and must have planted more than the minimum needed to achieve an average crop.[15] Such figures also assume perfect distribution and no wastage. This applies not just to grain, but to all the other commodities we might try to quantify.

Moreno clearly has a preference for the 'traditional' picture of Greek agriculture as represented by Isager and Skydsgaard.[16] However, his own rich and fascinating discussion of the evidence for the deme of Euonymon surely calls the applicability of that picture to classical Athens seriously into question.[17] The terracing that Moreno stresses was surely the product of the classical period, as he argues. Although they are features that are intrinsically hard to date, terrace walling on the scale which emerges so clearly from the aerial photographs must have been the product of a time when labour was abundant and cheap, as Foxhall observes.[18] This in turn obviously complicates what we might think about the value of labour, levels of wages, and average standards of living in Attica. A peculiarity of Moreno's account is that he clearly recognises this, but at the same time still seems to want Isager and Skydsgaard to be right, and Garnsey, Halstead, and Gallant to be wrong.[19] What he presents as emerging from his description of Euonymon is a straight choice between subsistence farming using biennial fallow, on the one hand, and intensive olive (and honey) cultivation, on the other. While he makes an excellent case for the likelihood of the latter, the possibility of any other strategy is simply ignored, regardless of plausibility. A simple, even obvious, example would be intensified wine production.[20] Similarly overlooked is the point made by Foxhall that arboriculture is a very

---

[15] Halstead 2014, 191–251.
[16] Moreno 2007, 14–24.
[17] Moreno 2007, 37–76.
[18] Terraces: Moreno 2007, 46–57; Foxhall 2007, 61–9; see also Price and Nixon 2005; Grove and Rackham 2001, 112–13.
[19] Moreno 2007, 15–28.
[20] Hanson 1992b lays out the advantages well; see also Halstead 2014, 286.

good fit with small-scale animal husbandry – which Moreno has already decided was not a significant feature of Attic agriculture. He also downplays the uses of livestock beyond meat animals and plough oxen.[21] It is also worth pointing out that the debate over the different reconstructions of Greek agriculture has tended to obscure the fact that (as all the protagonists have been aware) one of the advantages of a biennial fallow regime is that the fallow fields can be used for grazing animals (although only very few could be supported without additional sources of food). The difference is often one of emphasis rather than a fundamental disagreement. At this point, however, we should turn to some positive arguments about the scale of consumption in classical Athens.

Quantifying Consumption: Grain

I think that it would be a good idea to start with food; for everyone has to eat.

(XENOPHON, *Memorabilia* 2.1)

Aristippus was not one of Socrates' more brilliant interlocutors, but he had a point here. Athens' food supply was important for many reasons. Food production was central to the continued survival of the *polis*; it was the principal occupation of the majority even of Attica's inhabitants, and was fundamental to the economy even of this exceptionally commercialised city. Unfortunately, when it comes to quantifying the consumption of food, the problems are at least as great as they are in assessing population size.

The staple food in Attica, as elsewhere in Greece, was cereal, whether consumed as bread or in some other form.[22] Immediately when we go beyond this, however, we run into some problems. When we talk about cereals in a Greek context, we are talking about varieties of wheat and barley.[23] Wheat and barley have different nutritional and growing characteristics, and these differences can have a significant effect even on the 'order of magnitude' calculations that we might want to attempt. There are also social factors to

---

[21] Foxhall 1998, 2007, 82–3; Moreno 2007, 18.
[22] Braun 1995; Von Reden 2007, 390; Bresson 2016, 119–22.
[23] Jardé 1925; Amouretti 1979; Sallares 1991, 313–89.

be considered. Wheat was generally considered to be 'better' than barley, both nutritionally and socially, although the Greeks were not (partly out of necessity) nearly as contemptuous of barley as the Romans were.[24] For Hesiod (*Works and Days* 590) and Archilochus (fr. 2), barley cakes or bread form part of idealised meals. These meals take place out of doors; we could compare Telemachus in the *Odyssey*, who takes barley with him on his cruise round Greece, along with the finest wine in the palace (2.349–355), in spite of the fact that wheat is available to him (17.343; 18.120).[25] In the classical period, the references to barley in Aristophanes (for example), while they may not be as 'affectionate' as Braun has them, certainly confirm the impression that it was a major staple. Wherever there was a choice, wheat was consumed by preference (and in fact its relative scarcity at Athens compared to the dependable barley can only have added to its appeal as a marker of status). But our evidence suggests that Attica could not produce as much wheat as it did barley. As Garnsey observed, the thin soils and low rainfall of Attica can be tolerated reasonably easily by barley, to the extent that Theophrastus, somewhat hyperbolically, could claim that 'at Athens the barley produces more meal than anywhere else, since it is an excellent land for that crop'.[26] By contrast, the wheat crop, much more vulnerable to drought, might be expected to have failed as often as one year in four. This often-quoted figure may be somewhat overspecific. It was probably worth routinely trying to grow some wheat in Attica on lower-lying and better irrigated land, and we should expect a variety of practices in cultivating cereals.[27] Still, wheat was certainly more vulnerable to drought than barley.[28] On the other hand, if Athens in the classical period was importing large quantities of grain from overseas, a large proportion of that grain could have been wheat.[29]

[24] Foxhall and Forbes 1982; Braun 1995, 29–34; Garnsey 1999, 119–22; Foxhall 2007, 91; Von Reden 2007, 390–4.

[25] Braun 1995, 30.

[26] Theophrastus, *Historia Plantarum* 8.8.2; Garnsey 1988, 96.

[27] Halstead 2014, 57–61.

[28] Garnsey 1988, 105; Bresson 2016, 64–5, 158.

[29] 'Traditional' views, according to which Athens always depended on such imports, were defended against Garnsey by Whitby 1998 and Keen 1993.

Even granted that cereals of one kind or another formed the staple of the Greek diet, what does that actually mean in terms of consumption levels? How much wheat or barley was consumed by a typical inhabitant of Attica (if there was such a thing)? This is a question that can be approached both in absolute terms and relative to the other parts of the diet. The major role of food in ensuring survival is in providing energy. Both the other two products of the traditional Mediterranean triad – wine and olives – have considerable calorific value (especially olives), and will have contributed to the diets of almost everyone; but we are even less well informed about the consumption of these.[30] We are further in the dark about the consumption of legumes, which certainly had the potential for making significant contributions to calorific intake.

Obviously, the rate of cereal consumption will not have been uniform, either across the population or across time. The range of possibilities in ancient diets is illustrated at one extreme by the young man whom Xenophon's Socrates chides for eating his *opson* without *sitos*, and at the other, by Cato's chain-gang slaves, who seem to have eaten very little apart from bread (though because of the arduous nature of their work they were given plenty of it).[31] This contrast of extremes is not meant entirely seriously, although it is conceivable that some of the mining slaves at Laurion would have had a similarly cereal-heavy diet to Cato's slaves. But, clearly, there will have been differences across society. As one moved up the social scale, more wheat would have been consumed, and non-staple foods would have formed a larger part of the diet. Of course, once the Peloponnesian War was underway, the range of foodstuffs available to the Athenians would have become increasingly restricted. This is reflected even in Aristophanes' *Acharnians*, produced at a fairly early stage in the war. When Decelea was occupied and the Athenians at least partially lost control over their countryside, and when Euboea was lost and their naval superiority came to be challenged, diets would have changed a great deal even before the close siege that ended the war.

---

[30] Sarpaki 1992.
[31] Xen. *Mem.* 3.14; Cato *De agricultura* 56.

There are no actual figures for how much cereal was consumed by anyone in ancient Greece. There are a number of scattered figures for amounts supplied or distributed, but these are not quite the same thing.[32] Moreover, all of these figures apply to organised distributions to particular groups – usually soldiers on campaign, or prisoners – who probably should not be taken as representative of any wider population. The references do seem to indicate the widespread existence of a rule of thumb that one man should receive one *choinix* of wheat, or its equivalent in barley meal, per day. As Foxhall and Forbes pointed out, however, rations on such a scale seem to be quite generous, providing the bulk of the calories required even for men engaged in the most strenuous activities. It is unlikely that every inhabitant of Attica was consuming grain at this rate.[33]

The problem is that even if all we did was simply to multiply the size of the population by one to give a number of *choinikes* consumed every day, it would not give us even a useful maximum figure. A lot of the interest in thinking about grain consumption rates lies in the implications for production and distribution. A maximum is hard to obtain, because some people will have had access to far more food than they needed. Distribution will not have been wholly efficient, and it would have been necessary to supply more than was actually consumed, but how much more is impossible to recover. We are also completely in the dark as to how far animals other than humans would have been fed on cereals, and there are further difficulties in establishing how much livestock there actually was in Attica. The amount of grain that was fed to animals was surely highly variable but must always have been more than zero. Cavalry horses would have needed their diets supplemented with grain; oxen, too, would have worked best if their diets were supplemented, and presumably sometimes were fed grain.[34]

A minimum figure may be more interesting and useful, because it can give us some idea of how much grain was definitely *needed*,

[32] Collected in Foxhall and Forbes 1982, 86–9, table 3.
[33] Foxhall and Forbes 1982, 56. See now O'Connor 2013, who takes a critical attitude to Foxhall and Forbes, but still concludes that a *choinix* of wheat would be a largely sufficient ration for active men of military age (349).
[34] Engels 1978, 126.

whether it was produced locally or imported. Knowing how much grain was needed will have implications for how much was likely to have been produced locally, as it will have been one of several competing pressures on the land of Attica. It is easier to establish, because we have reasonably good information about how much food is required to sustain human life at different ages and at different levels of activity in the modern world.[35] We should be wary of adopting too optimistic a position about the nutritional status of any past population, but with the exception of the close siege at the end of the Peloponnesian War, actual starvation does not seem to have been prevalent in classical Attica.[36] Geoffrey Kron takes a generally very optimistic view of the nutritional status of Greek and Roman populations on the basis of anthropometry; little of his material is from Attica, but there is no reason to think that Athens was particularly badly off.[37] Ian Morris was once more cautious, and emphasised that the picture is generally quite unclear.[38] Anna Lagia provides some isotopic data, including from a classical cemetery at Laurion, that suggest a generally good diet in Athens in the classical period.[39] So if we could work out the calorific value of the available food, we could arrive at some kind of estimate of how much would have been needed.

First, we have to address the question of what proportion of the Athenian diet cereals actually constituted. At the risk of labouring the point, this is something that cannot be known for sure. However, it is unlikely that we can improve significantly here on the conjectures of Foxhall and Forbes that grain contributed about 70–75 per cent of the calories in the 'average classical diet'.

There are essentially two reasons for their adoption of this figure. The first is that the 'standard' allowances of one *choinix* per day per man would provide about this percentage range of the calorific requirement of adult males at the very highest levels of activity ('extremely active' in the World Health Organization/Food and

---

[35] For obvious reasons, this has been the focus of considerable attention from the FAO and WHO since 1949; see FAO 2004 for a summary of the current position and of the complexity involved in dealing with this kind of question in detail.

[36] Garnsey 1988, 17–39; Von Reden 2007, 388–90.

[37] Kron 2005.

[38] Morris 2007, 220–6.

[39] Lagia 2015.

Agriculture Organization scale they were using).[40] The significance of this is that these standard allowances were intended to be enough for anyone in any circumstances; for most people most of the time, they would be more than sufficient, although some allowances may have been made for losses and wastage. The second is that such a range would also be very close to modern maxima for grain consumption, even in developing countries where grain is the staple and consumed in very large quantities. It seems unlikely, therefore, that a higher rate of grain consumption prevailed in classical Attica. On the other hand, the central and highly visible importance of grain in our sources makes it hard to argue for a much lower figure, and certainly not less than 60 per cent.[41]

It is also worth noting in passing at this point that it is in this kind of calculation that our choice of age distribution model might make some difference, if we could be sure about it. Energy requirements vary according not only to levels of activity but also to age and sex (to mention only the most important factors that can vary between individuals). Men have higher requirements than women, and adults than children. If we are working with a pattern of age distribution that reflects lower childhood and higher adult mortality than has usually been assumed in the past, then the total energy requirement of the population might have been lower, even if the overall size of that population was the same.

Another problem with this kind of calculation has to do with the processing of cereal grains, which cannot be eaten in the form in which they are harvested. Usually, this means removing the hulls and grinding the grains into flour or meal. Braun notes that the processing of barley in Greece seems to have involved roasting the grains before grinding them into meal; barley seems not usually to have been ground into fine flour like wheat.[42] Exactly how this was done in classical Athens is something else about which we are disconcertingly ill informed. However, given what information we

---

[40] Foxhall and Forbes 1982, 48 note 24; FAO 1973, 25. O'Connor 2013 revisits aspects of this issue, and uses more recent data (348 note 112), but is really only interested in militarily active men. On the contribution of cereals to the energy content of the diet, he retains the range of 60–75 per cent (342).

[41] Foxhall and Forbes 1982, 56–71.

[42] Braun 1995, 27–8, on barley processing; 30–1, on wheat.

have (including a very little experimental and comparative evidence), a flour extraction rate of around 60–70 per cent seems to be likely, although higher rates cannot be excluded.[43] This is relevant, because the extraction rate has consequences for the nutritional value that is contained within a given quantity of flour or meal, or that can be provided by a given quantity of flour or meal. The flour extraction rate is the percentage of the original weight of grain that is left after grinding and winnowing/sifting. At higher extraction rates, the indigestible portion will be larger. The hope expressed by Foxhall that more thorough experimental research would be carried out has resoundingly been ignored by historians of ancient Greece, who just continued to cite this article.[44] There is a related problem here in using such literary evidence as we have. Ancient measures for cereals are units of volume, rather than the weight units that we tend to use today. The potential for variation is obvious. They also varied between cities, although this is a relatively minor problem, since we are focusing on Athens, about whose dry measures we are reasonably well informed for the classical period.

A variety of methods could be used to reach figures for consumption of calories. Foxhall and Forbes' 'hypothetical household' yielded a mean total calorific requirement of 2,583 kcal per person per day.[45] Foxhall and Forbes make no particular claims to the accuracy of this model, and in fact they note that this estimate of requirements is probably very overgenerous. The most detailed information on a relatively modern, but still usefully comparable, Greek diet was provided by Allbaugh's study of the area around Khania in Crete.[46] The situation he encountered in the immediately post-war years can hardly be considered typical, but the comparison is interesting: he found an average per capita intake of 2,554 kcal per person per day (with an actual variation from a low of 829 in the bottom 10 per cent to a high of 5,707 for the top 10 per cent).[47]

---

[43] Foxhall and Forbes 1982, 75–81. O'Connor 2013, 341–2, again in the context of armies on campaign, suggests rates of 70–90 per cent.

[44] Summarised by O'Connor 2013, 328–31; see 351 note 121 for the potential for further experimental work.

[45] Foxhall and Forbes 1982, 49 note 26, using 1973 FAO figures.

[46] Allbaugh 1953.

[47] Compare the recommendations in FAO 2004.

The problem with using figures like those developed by the FAO is that they require you to have an idea not only of ages and sexes, but also of size (weight) and metabolic rate. Archaeological (skeletal) evidence can help to a certain extent with stature (Foxhall and Forbes drew on Angel's analysis of skeletons from Attica).[48] However, there are always problems both with ascertaining how much skeletal material can tell us about soft tissue and in establishing how representative excavated samples of material are of any living population. Trying to improve on the figures calculated by Foxhall and Forbes in detail would at best add a spurious air of precision to the whole exercise. At worst, it would be completely misleading. However, since Foxhall and Forbes think that their household figure is excessively generous, especially to the children, and because the number of children in the population may have been understated in the past, it might be preferable to use a lower figure for average per capita calorie intake. For the moment we could keep both the relatively generous 2,500-odd kcal figure and use 2,000 kcal as a (purely arbitrary) alternative minimum and see where they take us.

According to the FAO tables used by Foxhall and Forbes, 1 kg of 60–70 per cent extraction barley meal (made from hulled barley) will provide 3,320 kcal.[49] If an individual is getting 70 per cent of their calories from cereals, this will be 1,750 kcal (if they are getting 2,500 total per day) or 1,400 kcal (at 2,000 total per day), which would have been provided by 527 g, or 422 g of such meal. Over the course of a year, therefore, an average person will consume just over 192 kg or 154 kg of the meal. In turn, assuming an average 65 per cent extraction rate, each person will have consumed c. 296 kg or c. 237 kg of unprocessed barley over the year.[50]

We could compare this to the estimates put forward by Garnsey, who suggested that the yearly minimum requirement of cereals was about 150 kg, with a total minimum requirement in food of around 200 kg 'wheat equivalent'.[51] Whitby, however, observed

---

[48] Angel 1945, 1975.
[49] Foxhall and Forbes 1982, 46.
[50] Compare Von Reden 2007, 390, 403–5. Bresson 2016, 120.
[51] Garnsey 1988, 91. Note also that Jardé suggested c. 230 kg of wheat per year. Foxhall and Forbes 1982, 46 note 15, observe that the nutritional value of processed wheat and barley is not greatly different.

that Garnsey does not appear to have differentiated between processed and unprocessed barley. If Garnsey means processed barley meal, then in the end everyone seems to be making roughly similar kinds of estimates.[52] The general range seems to be between 150 kg and 200 kg of processed barley meal, or 200 kg to 300 kg of unprocessed barley. To give an indication of order of magnitude, if we assume a per capita requirement of 250 kg, then a population of 250,000 will have needed over 60,000 tonnes of barley a year, and a population of 350,000 nearer 90,000 tonnes. To these figures might be compared the suggestions made by Garnsey for production of wheat and barley in Attica in a 'standard year' of 5,250 and 25,872 tonnes, respectively.[53]

Assuming area yields of 800 kg/ha, enough barley for a population of 250,000 would require nearly 80,000 ha, or about one-third of the total land area of Attica, to be cultivated. In practice, of course, such good returns could never have been counted on, even if they were achieved fairly regularly (and even if they could have been counted on, the distribution of grain would never have been 100 per cent efficient). The structural need for Athens to import grain from elsewhere is clear, but so too is the colossal pressure *not* to farm according to Hesiod's recommendations.

It is worth bearing in mind, too, that it is likely that the FAO's figure for the calorific value of 60–70 per cent extraction barley meal is actually too high. Their samples were probably quite efficiently milled; ancient processing would probably have led to a greater inclusion of inedible hull and greater loss of edible grain in the end product. This *may* indicate that we should be looking at the higher end of these ranges rather than the lower. It is also the case that about 200 kg of naked wheat, were it available, would produce about the same calorific value as the 296 kg of unprocessed barley that was suggested as a figure for a year's consumption for one person. While the nutritional content of the *edible* portion of wheat and barley is very similar, wheat is a lot easier to process. It is also rather denser, and so a given volume of whole wheat will certainly provide a lot more useful food than the same volume of barley.

---

[52] Whitby 1998, 118 note 29.
[53] Garnsey 1992, 148.

Olives

It is not at all clear that the Greeks fully appreciated the olive as a valuable source of nutrition.[54] Galen (in the second century AD, and so a late source for us, but one who held classical authorities in high regard) explicitly states that he believes olives to be of little value as food.[55] Closer in time to our period, Diocles of Carystus (an approximate contemporary of Aristotle) wrote that fruits from fruit trees were of little value, presumably including the olive.[56] In fact, the olive is an exceptionally useful foodstuff, high in calories, essential fats, vitamins, and minerals.

We have no figures for the consumption of olives or olive oil in antiquity. Curiously, the most complete literary pictures of an ancient Greek diet that we have do not refer to the consumption of olives at all, although that might explain Gallant's suspicions about vegetables. These are the accounts we have from Plutarch and Athenaeus of the monthly contributions made to the Spartan *syssitia* by their members.[57] Again, these are both late sources, although Athenaeus claims to be quoting the fourth-century writer Dicaearchus, an approximate contemporary of Theophrastus. Plutarch gives figures for the amount of barley meal (*alphita*), wine, cheese, and figs that a Spartiate had to provide. Athenaeus also gives figures for *alphita* and wine (larger than Plutarch's) but not for cheese or figs. He goes on, however, to talk about the voluntary contributions that were made for the second course or *epaiklon*. He mentions that most members would have shown off their hunting prowess by providing meat and game, but also adds that the wealthier members also sometimes provided wheat bread (*artos*) and seasonal produce from the fields – presumably fresh fruit and vegetables. Neither source explicitly mentions olives or olive oil in either course.

In his work on Greek households, Gallant minimised the role of olives in the diet. While he accepted Foxhall and Forbes' arguments about and suggested figures for grain consumption, he

---

[54] Sallares 1991, 285; Foxhall 2007, 91.
[55] Galen *Peri trophon dunameon* 2.27.
[56] Diocles of Carystus fr. 141.
[57] Plutarch *Life of Lycurgus* 12.2; Athenaeus 4.141c.

differed from them by observing that their suggestion that olives would have provided a lot of the remaining calories is not the only one possible.[58] Instead he suggested that these calories would have been derived from vegetables, fresh fruit, and legumes, on the basis both of comparative studies and of the prominence of these foodstuffs in the literary sources: '[their explanation] is of course quite possible, but other explanations come to mind as well. Quantitative analysis of data from around the Mediterranean seems to suggest greater consumption of vegetables.'[59] On the basis of data from Clawson, Landsberg, and Alexander (1971), he suggested that oil consumption is fairly consistent but cereal and vegetable consumption are correlated negatively. Vegetables seem to have been consumed at all levels of society in Greece: 'thus, while we cannot put a precise figure to it, it seems clear that vegetables and fruits made up an important part of the ancient diet ... we can postulate a dietary regime for the ancient peasant consisting of approximately 65–70 percent cereal products, 20–25 percent fruits, pulses and vegetables, 5–15 percent oils, meat and wine'.[60] A couple of pages later, this is resolved into 65 percent (of calories) in cereals, 25 percent in vegetables and pulses, and only 10 percent in olive oil and wine.[61]

It cannot be inferred that the classical Athenians never consumed any olive oil in their diets – there are enough references in Attic authors to make this impossible.[62] There is a nice illustration in Plato's *Republic*, where oil turns up as one of the 'luxuries' that Socrates is prepared to allow the inhabitants of his utopia, along with salt, cheese, and vegetables. Grain and wine are among the key necessities, on a level with shelter and clothing. For actual levels of consumption, we could try looking at later periods. Cato gave his farm labourers a single *sextarius* of oil a month.[63] In modern terms, this is a shade over 0.5 L, and it implies a weekly consumption rate of c. 135 cm^3; it was to be supplemented by doles of windfall olives

---

[58] Gallant 1991, 67–8, with 198 note 9.
[59] Gallant 1991, 198 note 9.
[60] Gallant 1991, 68.
[61] Gallant 1991, 72.
[62] Plato *Republic* 372c.
[63] *De agricultura* 58.

for as long as they were available. Much later, Forbes' study of Methana in 1972–4 found that Methanites worked on a rule of thumb of a consumption rate of about 1 L a week (or 50 L per year) per person, together with quantities of pickled olives.[64] Allbaugh's study on Crete found that while the Cretans 'counted on' similar quantities to the Methanites, they actually consumed only about 0.6 L per week, though they were reputed to be among the keenest consumers of olive oil in Greece.[65] This figure still represents more than four times what Cato's slaves received.

But Cato's figure presumably only includes oil for consumption as food. The figures from both Methana and Crete included oil for non-food uses, including soap-making (irrelevant for the ancient world), lubricant, and for the Cretans at least, lighting.[66] In the ancient world, oil was also used as a base for perfumes and cosmetics. The demand for oil for other purposes may well have contributed to a relative reluctance to use it (or even 'waste' it, if the perception was widely held that it had little nutritional value) as food. On the other hand, this would not depress *overall* demand and consumption. Demand for oil and for table olives – which seem to have been relatively widely consumed as a foodstuff – may also have gone up in the winter months, when other supplements to the cereal-based diet would have been in relatively short supply.[67]

If we are interested in a *minimum* figure, however, we would probably not want to assume that Athenians were consuming less than Cato's slaves, which would have meant about 6 L a year. The calorific value of this would have been about 48,000 kcal, or c. 130 kcal per day – or about 5 per cent of a daily intake of 2,500 kcal, or 6.5 per cent of 2,000 kcal.

---

[64] Forbes 1982.

[65] Allbaugh 1953.

[66] On the manifold uses of the olive and its products, see Amouretti 1986. In a Roman context, Mattingly 1996, 222–6, considers this issue. In particular, at 224, on lighting, he notes 'the principal form of domestic illumination in the Roman world was the oil-lamp ... my own experiments suggest that 1 L of oil might provide c. 134 hours [!] of light for a single-nozzle lamp'. He suggests (as a rough order-of-magnitude guide) that a population of 10,000 might consume nearly 30,000 L of oil in a year just for lighting. Compare Foxhall 2007, 92–3.

[67] Foxhall 2007, 90–1, on table olives, especially black ones, as a staple for the poor at Athens.

Foxhall has suggested that a 'wealthy' household might consume as much as 200–300 kg of olive oil in a year.[68] She observes that such a quantity could be provided by 185 to 306 trees, assuming a low average productivity of 2.16 kg of oil per tree per harvest, and with harvests coming every other year. On what appears to be a normal spacing, of about 80 to 100 trees per ha, this number of trees would need 1.9–3.8 ha, if they were evenly spread (which of course they were not).[69] How many such wealthy households there were is of course unknowable, but there must have been hundreds, even if 'wealthy' is restricted to the 'liturgical' class. If we assume for the sake of argument a round thousand such families, then Foxhall's figures would imply an aggregate demand for oil of around 200,000–300,000 kg per year, and (roughly) 200,000 to 300,000 trees, requiring somewhere between 2,000 and 4,000 ha of land.

Foxhall's focus is mainly on the production and consumption of elite households. If we also reckon with an additional 200,000 people consuming a minimal 6 L per head per annum (like Cato's slaves), they would imply a demand for more than an additional 1,000,000 kg – around 4 times as much as the elite households alone, and requiring something in the order of an additional 10,000 ha. Clearly, a population of 400,000, such as we might envisage in the 430s, could easily have generated a demand for the produce of well over 20,000 ha. That in turn could represent as much as a quarter, and at least a fifth, of the cultivable area of Attica. It is worth noting, as Foxhall points out, that it is extremely difficult to arrive at meaningful average yield figures for olives, so this is all highly speculative.[70] Foxhall's yield figures tend to be minimising. This is appropriate for her argument, but yet again this should make us cautious about extrapolating from her conclusions to support arguments in other contexts. Very little weight should be placed on the illustrative figures provided in Table 6.1.

---

[68] Note that Foxhall talks in weight terms, where volume measures are used by most other scholars. The density of olive oil varies according to a number of factors but is generally about 0.9 g/ml; so 6 L will weigh about 5.5 kg, 200 kg will have a volume of roughly 220 L, and 300 kg about 330 L. Foxhall, 118 note 9, suggests that 1 L = 0.96 kg.

[69] Foxhall 2007, 216.

[70] Foxhall 2007, 212–13.

6.1 Estimates for consumption of staples at different population size levels

Population	Barley		Olive oil		Wine	
	Consumption (tonnes)	Land needed (ha)[*]	Consumption (L)	Land needed (ha)[**]	Consumption (L)	Land needed (ha)[***]
200,000	50,000	62,500	1,150,000	10,222	18,000,000	9,000
250,000	62,500	78,125	1,450,000	12,889	22,500,000	11,250
300,000	75,000	93,750	1,750,000	15,556	27,000,000	13,500
350,000	87,500	109,375	2,050,000	18,222	31,500,000	15,750
400,000	100,000	125,000	2,350,000	20,889	36,000,000	18,000

[*] Assuming area yield of 800 kg/ha.

[**] Assuming area yield of 2.16 kg per tree per harvest and 100 trees per ha.

[***] Assuming area yield of 2,000 L/ha.

Having discussed elite consumption, Foxhall suggests that

levels of production of olive oil may have been relatively low compared to the high levels which have been generally assumed in assessments of Attic farming. Indeed, most of the olives grown may well have been made into table olives, which probably were an important staple.[71]

This may well be true, although the key word is perhaps 'relatively'; even at very low levels of per capita consumption, the population of classical Attica was large enough to create a voracious demand for olive oil, and surely some of that demand was met by local agriculture. What is clear is that classical Attica was very unlikely to be generating any genuine surplus of oil; while oil clearly was exported, this picture reinforces the suggestion that it was effectively an expensive luxury, not a bulk commodity.[72] Attica may in fact have been a net importer of oil.

Wine

The importance of wine in classical Athens is impossible to dispute. Again, however, actual consumption rates are rather more elusive. One place to start is the same comparative sources we used for olive oil. Plutarch claims that the Spartiates contributed 8 *choes* to the *syssitia* each per month; Athenaeus gives the figure as 11 or 12. The range is from about 24 to 36 L per month. This compares to 1 L a day among Forbes' Methanites, although among them women drank considerably less than men.[73]

Our sources for Athens do not give us definitive figures for wine consumption. Nonetheless, its frequent appearances in our sources enable us to say something about what was expected or considered normal, even though there is a limit to how much confidence can be placed on this kind of argument. However, complete abstinence was clearly regarded as somewhat eccentric. At the other extreme, drinking a whole *chous* at a sitting seems to have been regarded

[71] Foxhall 2007, 95.
[72] Foxhall 2007, 17–18, on the Solonian legislation allowing the export of olive oil. The relative scarcity of Attic oil would only have elevated its value as a prize for Panathenaic victors.
[73] Forbes 1982.

(not surprisingly) as a sign of being utterly dissolute.[74] It may well have been the case that, as in 1970s Methana, women drank considerably less than men. If there was a difference, it is unlikely that we should be able to quantify it. Our evidence for women drinking is problematic (most of it coming from comedy), but nothing, I think, suggests that women generally did not drink at all. For the population as a whole, average per capita consumption in the order of a *kotyle* (c. 250 mL or about half a pint) a day does not seem wholly unreasonable. It would certainly have taken a substantial number of pretty heavy drinkers to get the average above two *kotylai*. The wine would usually have been drunk diluted, and the wines of classical Greece, left undiluted, would probably have had a high ethanol content: 15–16 per cent compared to the 12 per cent typical today (or in 1970s Methana). One *kotyle* per day would work out at an annual per capita consumption of 30 *choes*, or about 90 L. For a population of 200,000, this would imply a total of about 18 million L or 20 million kg; for a population of 400,000, the total would be 36 million L or about 40 million kg.

The scale of wine production in Athens has received virtually no attention, though some very rough estimates are possible. It is slightly surprising that both Bissa and Moreno almost completely neglected wine, even though it seems highly relevant to the concerns of both: the wine trade of Thasos was clearly subject to some kind of public intervention, and vines would have provided an obvious and surely attractive option for the small farmers of Euonymon, alongside or instead of olive production. In a Roman context, Sallares notes that Columella discusses grape productivity in terms both of yield per vine and yield per unit area.[75] Sallares uses this observation to stress that while it was possible to think in terms of area yields, it is significant that Columella has not abandoned the yield per vine, because in the modern world we are much less likely to think in terms of yield per plant than yield per area. In fact, it may be even more remarkable that Columella is prepared to think in terms of area yield for vines at all, since

[74] Davidson 1997, 36–69.
[75] Sallares 1991, 375.

modern grape yields are in fact often considered in terms of yield per vine as well as per area. This is in contrast to cereal crops, of course, where area yields are much more normal.[76] In any case, purely for the sake of argument we could consider his figures, which imply a range of, very roughly, 20,000–4000 L/ha. For the sake of comparison, a modern rule of thumb is 5,000 L/ha – which happens, for what it is worth, to be very close to the average figure for Greece in 2008 according to FAO figures. In order to meet Attica's demand for wine when the population was 200,000, it would have taken about between 5,000 and 10,000 ha of vines to be cultivated. For a population of 400,000, between 10,000 and 20,000 ha of vineyards would have been necessary. Again, clearly much of Attica's wine was imported, but there would also have been a ready cash market for cheap local wine. Even at relatively low levels of productivity, it does not seem out of the realms of possibility that a significant portion of this demand could have been met by domestic production.[77]

Meat

It is a truism that meat did not usually form a significant part in the diet of the ancient Greeks. This, as Garnsey notes, is in the first instance, a straightforward consequence of climate and geography.[78] The short spring growing season means that grass and fodder crops for animals were in short supply; so too was arable land, and only the wealthiest could even contemplate turning such land over to pasture. Mass production of meat was simply not feasible, especially since in terms of the production of food (measured by calorific content), meat production is an extremely wasteful use of land. The technology for both the transport and the preservation of meat was primitive, and so there was less scope for bringing meat into the Greek world from elsewhere than there was for bread wheat, even if the demand had been there.[79] Animals

[76] Although see Halstead 2014, 244, on area yields.
[77] Bresson 2016, 124–5. Morley 1996, 55–82, brings out some of the complexities that might have been involved in practice in the case of Rome.
[78] Garnsey 1999, 6–7, 122–3.
[79] Primitive, but not completely absent: see Frost 2001.

were raised, but not necessarily principally for meat production: oxen as draught animals, and sheep and goats for textile production and cheese. Pigs provided the only real exception to this rule.

Where meat clearly did enter the diet was as the result of religious sacrifice. For Athens, the Old Oligarch notoriously makes the claim that 'as for sacrifices and victims and festivals and sanctuaries, the people, who realise that it is not possible for each of them individually to sacrifice and to hold a feast and to make offerings and to make a city that is beautiful and great to live in, have discovered how to make these things happen. The city then sacrifices many victims at public expense, but it is the people who hold the feast and apportion the victims.'[80] It is in this aspect of meat consumption that some attempts can be made at quantification. Even if the role of meat in the diet was small, there may be some implications for the amount of livestock available to the Athenians.

There exists some epigraphic evidence that allows us to get some idea of the frequency with which the Athenians sacrificed, whether as a *polis*, as in the Old Oligarch, or as a deme, or as another corporate group that was obliging enough to leave some record on stone.[81] Unfortunately, much of the relevant evidence comes from the fourth century, but it can give an indication of a likely order of magnitude for meat consumption in Attica.

The principal evidence is provided by the (partially surviving) ritual calendars from three demes – Marathon, Thorikos, and Erkhia – and is discussed by Jameson and, in a little more detail, Rosivach.[82] Rosivach arrives at slightly lower figures for the numbers of animals consumed in deme sacrifices, partly because he is explicitly trying to establish minimum figures. For this reason, I follow him here.

Rosivach's arguments lead to the conclusion that the demes annually sacrificed something in the region of 214 oxen and 2,531 sheep and goats, along with an indeterminate number of

---

[80] [Xen.] *Ath. Pol.* 2.9.

[81] For example, *IG* ii² 1496, which records the sums received from the sale of the hides of the victims sacrificed at certain festivals, and the deme calendars of Erkhia (*SEG* 21.541), Thorikos (*SEG* 33.147), and Marathon (*IG* ii² 1358).

[82] Jameson 1988; Rosivach 1994.

pigs.[83] Rosivach also observes that all three demes are fairly large, and there were many more smaller demes, and smaller demes probably sacrificed more of the smaller victims; as a result, he thought it likely that the figure for oxen is too high and that for sheep and goats possibly too low, if anything. It is worth noting, with Jameson, that the situation at Erkhia, where no oxen were slaughtered, was more likely to be 'typical' than Marathon, which appeared to be quite extravagant with oxen: 'local conditions are relevant. There was good pasturage for cattle on the plain (Pausanias 1.32.7), and it was the Marathonian bull that Theseus captured and brought to the Acropolis to sacrifice, a story commemorated by the deme of Marathon with a dedication (Pausanias 1.27.10).'[84]

In addition to these, there were the victims sacrificed at higher levels than the deme: the *polis* itself, but also the tribes and presumably the trittyes (although there is little evidence concerning the latter); likewise the *gene* (for example, the Salaminioi), and the Marathonian tetrapolis.[85] Quantification for these other groups is harder, with the partial exception of the *polis* as a whole. Rosivach argues for

more than 873 oxen annually at its *epithetoi heortai*, and an additional, undeterminable number at is major penteteric festivals and *ad hoc* celebrations.[86]

Rosivach's estimates for the number of cattle sacrificed come principally from the accounts for the sale of hides; on the same basis, Jameson reckoned a figure of between 1,400 and 1,700, and a *total* annual minimum of 2,000. This requires making some arguably rather tenuous assumptions to get to a total figure, rather than accepting a minimum figure known to be too low (like Rosivach's 'more than' 873). For the smaller animals, at least the 500 goats sacrificed by the *polis* to Artemis Agrotera have to be added to the notional deme sacrifices calculated by Rosivach,

[83] Rosivach 1994, 76. On his own figures, the total should be 2,534 (but the discrepancy is minor).
[84] Jameson 1988, 95.
[85] There is a dubious but possible sacred calendar for a trittys at *IG* i[3] 255.9. For tribal sacrifices, there is *IG* ii[2] 1165.5 (Erechtheis). It is possible that tribal sacrifices were limited to those for the eponymous hero. Parker 1996, 103–4; also 1994, 343 note 19.
[86] Rosivach 1994, 72.

even before such groups as the Salaminioi[87] (6 swine, 4 sheep, plus another every other year, in addition to 'whatever the *polis* provides'; which we only find out about because the Salaminioi still have to pay for the firewood), and the tetrapolis are considered. A minimum annual sacrifice of nearer 4,000 would seem more likely than the 3,000 that Rosivach is prepared to commit himself to. Around 60 *gene* are known to exist; if they were all sacrificing at the same rate as the Salaminioi, then that is another 600-odd animals a year at least. Rosivach excludes holocaust sacrifices from his calculations, because they provided no meat, but it is worth remembering that the victims still had to come from somewhere. It is also worth pointing out Jameson's argument (1988, 60) that the story about only 500 goats being sacrificed to Artemis instead of the 6,400 technically due (one for every Persian killed at Marathon) does not testify to any particular shortcomings in the goat supply in the early fifth century.[88]

All this activity is not sufficient to establish meat as a significant part even of an Athenian citizen diet in the fifth century. Jameson and Rosivach use 'roughly comparable' figures for the meat provided by sacrificial animals.[89] Two thousand cattle would have provided about 200,000 kg of meat; sheep and goats might each have provided something of the order of 20 kg each; 4,000 of them would therefore produce around another 80,000 kg. This takes no account of pigs, but at a population of about 250,000, we are still only looking at less than 2 kg per person per year. Citizens would, of course, have gotten most of this meat, but even assuming that there really were only about 30,000 of them in 431 (which is a much lower figure than seems plausible), and they ate all of the meat from these sacrifices, that is still only about 1 kg each per month. If they ate it once or twice a week, that would mean citizens were familiar with the taste of meat, but it would hardly be a major part of their diet. Fred Naiden has observed that, if anything, Jameson and Rosivach may have been too optimistic in their estimates of how many people could have been fed by public sacrifices in Attica. Naiden also points out that not all meat was consumed in ritual

---

[87] Xen. *Anabasis* 3.2.12; Rosivach 1994, 57–8, for Artemis Agrotera.
[88] Jameson 1988, 60.
[89] Jameson 1988, 95; Rosivach 1994, 157–8.

contexts, but sacrifices were still probably the largest ultimate source of meat.[90]

There would have been other consequences of this level of meat consumption, however. Not the least of these is that quite large total numbers of animals must have been involved in providing even small quantities of meat per capita, which would have posed challenges of transport and processing.[91] Meat, like cereals, had to be cooked before it could be eaten. The mention of firewood by the Salaminioi raises the question of one more resource whose consumption was of enormous importance to Athens.

Wood: Timber and Fuel

Assessing the demand for and consumption of wood in Athens is much more difficult even than for foodstuffs, but a number of points can be made. In themselves, they may appear trivial or obvious, but the cumulative effect does have some interest. Demand for wood in Athens, and perhaps especially in the years leading up to the Peloponnesian War, must have been prodigious. That there seem not to have been any serious difficulties or problems in supplying that demand has important implications in itself.

Perhaps most obvious were the demands of the 'wooden walls' of the fleet – allegedly with 300 triremes fit for service, according to Thucydides. The reconstructed trireme *Olympias* weighs about 25 tonnes unladen.[92] The whole fleet would therefore represent about 7,500 tonnes of timber. But assuming that a trireme's life was about 20 years, and a steady replacement rate, the fleet would only have *needed* about 400 tonnes of timber a year. Pretty much all of this would have had to be imported, although the difficulties were probably more to do with securing supplies of sufficient

---

[90] Naiden 2013, 258–74, on the optimism of Jameson and Rosivach; 241–50, on contexts for consumption.

[91] MacKinnon 2014, 226–40, on the implications of the animal remains from the Agora in the classical period.

[92] Morrison, Coates, and Rankov 2000, 210: 'The weight of [the] basic shell was only about 15 tonnes. The addition of outriggers, seats etc. for oarsmen, decks, stanchions and braces to complete the hull added another 10 tonnes or so to make a weight of 25 tonnes, a little more than half the weight of the fully manned and equipped trieres.'

quality rather than sheer quantity. The same may not have been true of the timber for oars, flax for sails, and pitch for water-proofing the hulls – all of which, again, would have had to have been imported.[93] Major structural timbers for other building projects (temples, mainly) would again have posed problems of quality rather than quantity, however.[94]

Bissa discusses the Athenians' need for imported timber. However, her discussion is framed almost entirely around the Athenian fleet. As we saw above in the discussion of labour demands (191), she brings out well the colossal logistical demands of shipping large quantities of timber around the Aegean, and makes a good case for the Athenians' building (or having built for them) most of their ships not in the Piraeus but in the areas where the timber grew, it being much more convenient to move a trireme than its constituent timber. (Here the fact that triremes need not always have been fully crewed was a good thing for the Athenians, as full crews would not have been needed for 'ferry' duties.)[95] But the scale of demand for new ships is surely under-stated in her account. Triremes do seem to have lasted on average about 20 years, but a fleet of 300 would have needed more than 15 replacements every year. The twenty-year lifespan of Athenian triremes is generally accepted, but in comparative perspective is quite long: as noted above (see 130 above), the lifespan of the galleys built by the Venetian Arsenale seems only to have been about 10 years.[96] Gabrielsen has observed that the Athenian fleet would have been supplemented periodically by the capture of enemy vessels. This is true, although captured ships might well have required additional maintenance before they could be accepted into service.[97] Losses to storm and accident, let alone in battle, must also have inflated such an average figure. In practice, the Athenians would have experienced peaks in demand as large batches of ships wore out together (what is now

---

[93] Sallares 1991, 340, for the inability of Attica to produce much in the way of flax. Pausanias (5.5.2, 6.26.6) seems to claim that the only part of Greece which produced flax was Elis (which experiences significantly more precipitation than Attica).

[94] Salmon 2001, 203–4.

[95] Bissa 2009, 117–40.

[96] Lane 1934, 263.

[97] Gabrielsen 1994, 131–6.

called 'block obsolescence'). By the late 460s, if not before, any ships that had survived from the original Themistoclean construction programme would have had to be replaced, for example.

Timber would also have been required in large quantities outside of the fleet. A great, though essentially unknowable, quantity of timber would have been required for the roofs and many fittings of humbler dwellings.[98] The construction of public buildings would have required timber for ladders and scaffolding.[99] The uses of small pieces of timber in agricultural production are legion – most impressive quantitatively perhaps are the 10,000 vine props mentioned in the Attic Stelai.[100] The mines of Laurion seem to have used substantial quantities of pit-props.[101]

All of this, however, seems to pale into insignificance compared to the demand for fuel, most of which would have been provided by wood.[102] Estimating domestic fuel consumption is an exercise fraught with difficulty and uncertainty, but Forbes suggested a rough figure of 6 tonnes per household per year for 'a single traditional Methana family's needs' – of which he thought that about a tonne would be generated as byproducts of agriculture – for both cooking and heating. This figure may be too high for classical Athens (where the absence of bread ovens would have made a difference), but if we take a total of three or four tonnes as being in the right order of magnitude for household needs, and with tens of thousands of such households, we could be looking at a figure of well over 100,000 tonnes of firewood needed every year.

The other big fuel requirement would have been industrial. Again, the industry about which we are best informed is the

[98] Forbes 1996, 79–80.
[99] Thompson 1980.
[100] Uses of timber: Forbes 1996, 80–1; Hesiod *Works and Days* 420–36. Vine props in the Attic Stelai: Pritchett 1956, 305–6.
[101] Shepherd 1993, 24–6, is cautious about how many would actually have been needed, but perceptions of need were probably different at the bottom of the shafts.
[102] Although a certain amount could, of course, be derived from other sources – for example, the press-cake that is left at the end of olive-pressing. Some fuel will also have been produced as a byproduct of other agricultural activities, including the prunings from olive and other fruit-trees and vines, apparently a preferred fuel for pottery kilns (Matson 1972, 213, 219). Olive stones have remained a source of charcoal, especially for firing kilns, to the present day (*AR* 1994–5, 5). All of these sources, however, are relatively trivial in scale.

Laurion mines. The production of silver required colossal quantities of wood, processed into charcoal. Rihll has estimated that every drachma produced required about 18 kg of wood.[103] Conophagos estimated that in the 'golden age' of the *pentecontaetia*, when silver production was at its peak, as much as 20 tonnes were being produced every year.[104] This is about 750 talents, and would have required over 80,000 tonnes of wood every year. Over 200 tonnes would have been required every day. This would have been *in addition to* the 4 tonnes of food that Rihll observes would have been needed every day to feed the workforce, and the logistical strain of supplying which she stresses. Two hundred tonnes is about 4,000 donkey loads, if the fuel was being carried on donkeys, as it was on Phaenippus' estate. Mules or pack horses can carry about twice as much as donkeys (in the region of 100 kg), but that is still around 2,000 loads. The 4 tonnes of food to which Rihll refers would be about 80 donkey loads or 40 mule loads.

Rihll refers her readers to Rackham (1996, 29–30) 'for sane comments on the environmental implications'.[105] This is what Rackham has to say, and it is worth quoting in full:

Theodor Wertime ['The furnace versus the goat', *JFA* 10, (1983) 445–52] claims that fuel-using industries were the prime factor in the deforestation of Mediterranean lands during antiquity. He works out that all the silver produced by the Laureion mines would have called for one million tons of charcoal, implying that this is an unreasonably large amount and proves deforestation. But the figure is of no value without knowing how long it took the wood to grow; it does not, in itself, prove deforestation. Wertime does not ask whether 'industrial' Attica was more deforested than non-industrial Boiotia.[106] In reality, a million tons of charcoal over 500 years implies about 14,000 tons of wood a year. Even if one hectare of maquis produced only a ton of wood a year, Laureion could have kept going for ever on 14,000 hectares of land. Maybe we should double this area, to allow for most of the smelting being done over a shorter period (c. 480–300 BC). Even so, was it really unreasonable for the Athenians to use one-seventh of their land area as a fuel supply for what was by far their biggest industry and the sole means of keeping Attica solvent?

---

[103] Rihll 2001, 133.
[104] Conophagos 1980, 101, 349.
[105] Rihll 2001, 140 note 66.
[106] Meiggs 1982, 206, for the observation that Boeotia was believed to be a poor place to live during the winter because there was a great shortage of wood, according to Dicaearchus (1.21).

For the most part, this is undeniably true; Rackham may well have been right (like Meiggs before him) to cast doubt on the scholarly fiction that Greece in the classical period was disastrously deforested.[107] But it is at least possible that even his doubling figure would not have provided sufficient wood for silver production during the very high peaks of production that are generally assumed to have taken place in the fifth century. Even if Conophagos' estimate is too high by a factor of two, more like 40,000 ha, or a full sixth of the 2,400 km^2 of Attica in the fifth century, would have been required: and of course, if this were the case, the mines would also be precisely half as important as Conophagos argues, and they would only have been producing 10 tonnes of silver a year. If Conophagos is right, however, then we are looking at a full third of Attica's land area being used to generate fuel for Laurion. And this is in addition to domestic fuel consumption. Even if every household needed barely a tonne of wood every year, this domestic demand (which would have persisted throughout the classical period) would have been equivalent in scale to the demand generated by the mines when the latter were at peak production. Then there all the other industrial purposes, including ceramic production and, probably rather more significant, other metal processing, including the production of agricultural tools and armaments.

It is also worth pointing out that Laurion did not in fact keep going for ever. After the Peloponnesian War, production ceased. Even when it got going again, it was probably not until the 370s and then at a low rate. If silver mining was 'by far' Athens' biggest industry and her sole means of balancing the books, this seems rather surprising. One obvious explanation would be a shortage of labour. But Rackham's point suggests a couple of alternative lines of explanation, neither of which is actually mutually exclusive with the labour shortage hypothesis. One is that, actually, silver production in the fifth century was not always as crucial as has been made out. Another is that there was real difficulty getting the necessary fuel after the war, and that whatever expedients were

---

[107] Grove and Rackham 2001, especially 8–22 and 361–5. The opposite view has been stalwartly maintained by Hughes 2014, 68–87. Harris 2013 provides a summary and presents something of a compromise. Specifically on charcoal, see Veal 2013.

being employed to meet demand in the fifth century were no longer being employed, perhaps because they could not be. Rackham considered the evidence for management of wood supplies in ancient Greece, and reasonably argued that it did take place to a generally underappreciated extent. If anywhere would have provided the incentive to put into widespread practice the knowledge and skill that clearly existed, it would have been fifth-century Attica; even so, the pressure on the available land would still have been enormous.[108]

In any case, the overall conclusion has to be that Olson's comment that 'classical Athens was a fuel-hungry society' is a drastic understatement.[109] The implications of this voracious hunger may well have rivalled the food supply in their importance. It is deeply unlikely that many of the inhabitants of Attica would have been able to get as much fuel as they would have liked. Winter in many households must have brought persistent discomfort that is scarcely imaginable to most of us today. All of Athens' industries, including and perhaps especially those needed to sustain her armed forces, may have been as vulnerable to shortages in fuel as the population was to shortages in food.

[108] Rackham 1982, 1983.
[109] Olson 1991, 419.

CHAPTER 7

BEYOND FOOD AND FUEL

In Chapter 6, we saw how the population of Attica generated intense demands for the most basic essential commodities. Those demands were often in conflict, as the same agricultural land could be used to produced food, drink, or fuel. The scale of demand for agricultural products is the obvious source of connection between population and economy in classical Athens, and so it has attracted a great deal of attention. More, and more complex, connections appear as soon as we start to ask how those demands were actually met. These questions take us immediately beyond the purely economic realm, precisely because these demands could not be met from the land of Attica alone. One way or another, the Athenians had to secure imports from overseas, which complicated their policies and their relationships – peaceful and otherwise – with other peoples and communities.

As Moreno's work has very eloquently demonstrated, the need to deal with outsiders, sometimes over very long distances, had implications for how Athens' political institutions worked. This brings us back to the political life of Athens, but there were also economic consequences for Attica, where, after all, most Athenian citizens still lived. An obvious place to start is with how the land was owned. Land continued to be the most visible and prestigious form of wealth, and agriculture remained a dominant sector in the economy, even as the non-agrarian sector grew. How land-ownership was distributed had important consequences not just for the social and economic structure of the population, but for how the land was worked.

There is a connection here, too, to the issues of economic growth, and economic performance more generally, which have been prominent in ancient economic history since the turn of the millennium. In a very basic way, population size is itself an indicator of economic performance and of aggregate growth. If the population of Athens in 430 was much larger than it had been 50 years previously, then the total size of the economy would have been greater too. At some level, the simple possibility of sustaining such an increase in the population must be counted as an economic success for fifth-century Athens. Harder questions to get to grips with are whether the economy grew in per capita terms, and how wealth was distributed within the population. However, the ownership of land is once again the clearest starting point.

Unfortunately, we are largely in the dark about the distribution of land in classical Attica. Neither archaeological nor historical evidence seem able to provide much direct illumination. Archaeological field survey could tell us a fair amount about the occupation of and activity on the land, but projects of this kind are lacking for most of Attica, and in any case would tell us little directly about ownership, quite apart from any other problems of interpretation. Literary historical sources, as usual, tend to focus on the exceptional and reflect the preoccupations of the relatively wealthy (in practice, this turns out to be almost as true of epigraphic sources as it is of oratory, history, or moralising philosophy). There are few explicit considerations of the actual sizes, or even values, of individual landholdings. The clearest exception is the account of the estate of Phaenippus in [Demosthenes] 42.5–7, which has naturally attracted a great deal of attention.[1] The 'Attic Stelai' provide values of estates held by Athenians, but what is perhaps most notable about these is how much property is held *outside* Attica.

The fact that geographical and climatic forces coincided with a dominant system of partible inheritance to produce small plots of land rather than consolidated estates clearly would not have prevented a single man or household owning several such plots across Attica. And this is in fact the picture implied in the fictionalised portrait of a wealthy man's estate in Xenophon's *Oikonomikos*; even for the estate of Phaenippus, there is no reason to assume that the land under discussion represented the whole of his property.[2]

---

[1] De Ste Croix 1966 remains key; see now also Bresson 2016, 146–8.
[2] Davies 1981, 52–4; Osborne 1985; Pomeroy 1994, 41–67.

Attempts to draw a likely picture of the distribution of land in Attica therefore have to rely on inferences from other features of Athenian economy and society and on (more or less) plausible *a priori* assumptions. Inevitably, when such attempts have been made, they have concentrated on the fourth century, about which we are much better informed in many key respects.

Two important efforts to do exactly this, which both appeared in the early 1990s, reached similar conclusions and drew similar inferences, even though they started from different premises. Robin Osborne estimated that about 7.5 per cent of the population owned about 30 per cent of the land.[3] Lin Foxhall reckoned that about 9 per cent of the population owned about 35 per cent and were likely to have controlled about another 10 per cent via leases.[4]

It is worth briefly looking at the arguments used to reach these figures, since they have been and continue to be widely cited and used.[5] This is partly to illustrate the assumptions that underlie them and partly to show how approximate they are. This is not necessarily to contest their plausibility; in fact, as with Hansen's demographic arguments, it may help to defend them against some objections.

Osborne started from the demands imposed by the *polis* on the wealthy in the form of liturgies, trierarchies, and capital levies.[6] These demands can be roughly quantified; Osborne suggested that the *average* demand each year from the richest Athenians was in the order of 50–100 talents:[7]

Demands of this order of magnitude for cash could not be met out of savings or met for long by selling off ancestral land. That the city could regularly demand such sums shows that at least as great a surplus was being created by the

---

[3] Osborne 1991, 1992.

[4] Foxhall 1992, arguing that 'public' land was mainly cultivated, in practice, by the wealthy, drawing on Osborne 1988. Foxhall observes that there is almost no evidence for private tenancy in classical Athens; see also Foxhall 2007, 72–5.

[5] Most recently in Scheidel 2017, 196–7. See also Taylor 2017, 86–90.

[6] One of the reasons for restricting this kind of calculation to the fourth century is our almost complete lack of any direct evidence for how the Athenian fleet – which imposed some of the heaviest financial burdens – was actually funded in the fifth century. See Gabrielsen 1994.

[7] Osborne 1991, 129–31. On the scale of the expenses in classical Athens, see Pritchard 2015. Pritchard is not, however, all that concerned about where the money was coming from.

economic activities of the rich. Some rich men certainly made their money out of activities other than agriculture – from the mines and from bottomry loans – but a large proportion of the Athenian rich must have had to generate an agricultural surplus with an annual market value of approaching 100 talents simply in order to meet their civic obligations ... we should reckon private expenditure as being at least as great ... Then we should probably assess the *normal* demand for cash by the rich at 200 talents.[8]

Osborne further reckoned that raising this sum would have required the sale of roughly one-third of the barley crop of Attica, or its equivalent. This could be taken as the minimum extent to which wealthy fourth-century Athenians engaged with the market in agricultural products.

Osborne went on to speculate about the total landholdings of the rich, starting from the assessment for the *eisphora* in 378/7. Here, the total capital value of the property assessed was 5,750 talents, and probably represented the property owned by about 1,200 men with estates worth a talent or more.[9] Unfortunately, we do not know how much land area such a value represents, so Osborne had to 'work indirectly', as he put it. Taking rents as 8 per cent of capital value, 5,750 talents of property would have been rentable for 460 talents. This sum could be raised by the sale of 552,000 *medimnoi* of barley at 5 drachmas a *medimnos*. Assuming a barley yield of 12 L/ha, this would be the product of just over 24,000 ha.[10] This was taken by Osborne to be a highish barley price and assumes that the land only had to cover its rent.[11] Thus, for Osborne this was likely to be an underestimate of the amount of land represented in the capital assessment – although land was probably not in fact the only capital item included: 24,000 ha is (obviously) about 10 per cent of the total land area of Attica, and, according to Osborne's estimates, about a quarter to a third of the cultivated area.[12]

[8] Osborne 1992, 23.
[9] Harding 1985, 54–6 (39), gathers the references.
[10] The same figure adopted by Garnsey 1992, 148; see 186–187 above.
[11] A highish price for barley: see now Rathbone and Von Reden 2015, especially 194, table 8.3.
[12] Osborne 1992, 24; see 115 above. Osborne notes that this is consistent with a plausible picture for the sum of *individual* capital holdings. A minimum liturgic capital seems to have been around four talents, but some men must have exceeded this by far; assuming

On this basis the richest 2,000 Athenian citizens will have owned between one-quarter and one-third of the cultivable land in Attica [. . .] Of the other 25,000 or so Athenian citizens in the fourth century [. . .] we may accept, for want of a better figure, Lysias' guess that 5,000 owned no land, and we can reckon on some 8,000–10,000 being hoplites. If we give 10,000 hoplites 4 ha of land each they will account for 40,000 ha. If the remaining citizens, 10,000 in number, are allowed 1.5 ha each they will account for 15,000 ha. Adding together the holdings of the rich, the hoplites and the poor we get a figure of 79,000 ha or practically one-third of the total area of Attica. This is a plausible enough figure and it leaves us with the rich occupying just over 30 per cent of the cultivable land of Attica. That 7.5 per cent of the population owned 30 per cent of the cultivated land of Attica suggests that we cannot automatically assume that material remains recovered from the countryside are indicative of peasant free landowning agriculture.[13]

Foxhall's approach was different. She started from the land area of Attica, which she took to be about 2,000 km^2. She thought that at least half of that would have been 'usable' or worth owning for broadly agrarian purposes.[14] She then (cautiously) adopted 5.5 ha as the size of 'the subsistence holding' of the average Attic peasant. Taking 22,000 as a reasonable figure for a number of citizen households, she too reckoned that 5,000 owned no land at all, and that a further 5,000 owned less than the 'subsistence holding'. At the other end of the scale, she inferred from Plato and Aristotle that 'in ordinary, non-utopian Greek *poleis*, the largest landholdings differed from the smallest by considerably more than a factor of 4 or 5'.[15] Taking Phaenippus' estate to be around 45 ha (500 *plethra*; note that this is a minimising assumption), she inferred that the largest holdings of land by Athenian households may have been well above the 45 ha mark; how many is impossible to tell. However, she estimated that about 1,000 of her 22,000 households had holdings of 10–20 ha and another 1,000 had holdings of 20–50 ha. Foxhall here was working essentially from Davies' count of 800 men in the liturgical class known over 250 years, and assuming that a lot of families left insufficient

a mean average (median and mode would have been lower) of eight talents, and about 500 such properties at one time, the liturgical class will have owned about 4,000 talents of property, more than two-thirds of that assessed for the *eisphora*. Another 1,000 individuals could have had an average capital of 1.7 talents to give a total capital for those liable to the *eisphora* of 5,700 talents.

[13] Osborne 1992, 24.
[14] Foxhall 1992, 156.
[15] Plato, *Laws* 744b–e; Arist. *Pol.* 1266b (2.4.2); Foxhall 1992, 156.

marks on the record to allow estimates of their wealth, this left about 10,000 citizen households owning 5.5–10 ha each.[16]

What is notable about these two accounts, beyond the similarity of the results, is the rhetoric of the two pieces. Both Osborne and Foxhall have set themselves up to argue *against* a pattern of more egalitarian landholding. Foxhall was more explicit about this, as it was her main aim; Osborne was frying slightly different fish, but the general point holds for him too. As a result they both, at various stages, made claims that their results were *minimising* the extent to which the distribution of land was polarised, in order to make their claims more compelling and plausible to an assumed sceptical audience that believed in a democracy of more or less equal peasant-citizens.[17] This is important, because one line of response to both sets of figures is that, in a broader comparative context of other societies in other times and places, the picture painted by Osborne and Foxhall is not one of a particularly polarised distribution of wealth, but rather the reverse. Ian Morris made this point most explicitly:

Osborne and Foxhall have tried to estimate the distribution of land in fourth-century Athens on the basis of the income that the wealthiest 2,000 families would need to meet their obligations. Their reconstructions depend on taking at face value upper-class claims to be simple farmers who generate their wealth in the time-honoured way from the land, entirely within the visible economy. But as Cohen has shown so well, this is unjustified.[18] Osborne and Foxhall both conclude that 7.5–9 percent of the citizens held 30–35 percent of the land. This would be an extremely egalitarian distribution; and if elite involvement in the invisible economy was as high as Cohen suggests, the rich might need even less land, and middling and poor citizens could own a still large proportion of Attica.[19]

And:

Both Osborne ... and Foxhall ... seem to think that their calculations point toward significant elite economic domination, but they do not see their results in comparative terms.[20]

---

[16] Her results are displayed in chart form at Foxhall 1992, 158.
[17] Foxhall 2002, 209, provides examples of how such a view has in fact been espoused as an orthodoxy 'by scholars working from a surprisingly broad range of political and ideological perspectives'.
[18] Cohen 1992. See also Davies 1981, 38–72, for a survey of alternative sources for the income of the wealthy.
[19] Morris 1994a, 362.
[20] Morris 1994a, 362 note 53.

This latter comment is only partly fair. More than one comparative perspective can be adopted. It is not obvious that the comparisons that Morris suggested are the best or even good ones. In this piece, he compared the Gini coefficients derived from Osborne and Foxhall with those presented for the Roman empire by Duncan-Jones, along with thirteenth-century AD Orvieto to demonstrate that 'broader comparison'.[21] He did not explain why he chose these examples. It seems to be just implicit that Rome must, again, be usefully comparable to Greece, and that a single (apparently arbitrarily selected) medieval city-state is usefully comparable to the classical *polis* of Athens. In fact, as Foxhall quite rightly pointed out in a later article, it is hardly surprising that, measured like this, the distribution of wealth in the Roman empire appears more polarised:

The Roman elite could and did acquire land and other property throughout Italy and across the empire. Archaic-classical Greek city-states were effectively closed systems: the privilege of land-ownership was generally limited to citizens, and usually political barriers were erected to stop economic (or any other kind of) integration with other, similar polities. Certainly the richest were richer in Rome than in Athens or Corinth, though whether the poorest were any poorer in Athens than in Rome is probably an unanswerable question, though I personally doubt that there was much difference.[22]

Both Osborne and Foxhall were effectively arguing against a model where the Gini coefficient was even closer to zero, and so they made conservative assumptions about the relevant variables to make their case. In Osborne's case, these were the price of barley and the amount of income a farm would need to generate; in Foxhall's case, they were about the sizes of landholdings at all levels of citizen society but especially among the richest. That fourth-century Athens looks, by their accounts, to be a place where wealth was distributed in a comparatively egalitarian fashion is largely a reflection of the rhetorical strategies they have adopted, which in turn is the result of adopting a different comparative perspective from Morris.

---

[21] Duncan-Jones 1990, 129–42; Waley 1968, 28.
[22] Foxhall 2002, 215. Taylor 2017, 94–5, demonstrates vividly just how much less egalitarian the Roman empire of the second century AD was than the citizen population of late fourth century.

It is worth considering how 'extremely' egalitarian the Foxhall–Osborne model really is in yet another comparative perspective. Morris generates a Gini coefficient of 0.382–0.386. This would make Athens (superficially – in fact the following figures are for income distribution rather than wealth distribution, which is always more polarised) more egalitarian than the United States in 2004 (0.408), but slightly less so than the United Kingdom (0.360), and a good deal less so than other European countries such as Germany (0.283) and Denmark (0.247), or than Japan (0.249).[23] Whether the UK, for example, would count as a country with an 'extremely' egalitarian wealth distribution is moot.[24] It is also worth commenting that, useful as it can be, the Gini coefficient is something of a blunt instrument in this kind of case. Different countries or societies with the same coefficient can have very different patterns of wealth distribution. An extreme case would be where half the households in one economy held no property and all the rest shared wealth equally, giving a coefficient of 0.5; the same coefficient would be given by an economy where all the households were equal, except for one that held half the available property.[25] The importance of this should be clear for a situation where one of the key issues is the existence or viability of a 'hoplite class' of independent farmers.

It is also worth recalling that just because elite involvement in the 'invisible' economy was at a high level and that they might not have needed as much land as Osborne suggested, that does not mean that they did not actually own it, value it, and try to get more. There is still a great deal of evidence that suggests that land was ideologically crucial to the Athenian elite, and that it was the most secure form of property investment.[26] Almost any comparative perspective would show that Athens was not so unlike any other pre-industrial society in this respect. Just because we know about the property of Demosthenes' father in some detail should not lead us to infer that it was typical of that of elite citizens. The fact that it requires such detailed description might encourage us to infer the

[23] UN 2004, 50–3.
[24] Kron 2011, 134.
[25] See now Scheidel 2017, 11–13, and Taylor 2017, 86–90.
[26] Foxhall 2007, 55–83; Bresson 2016, 142–9.

reverse; although perhaps the diversity of elite practice is the most significant point.[27]

A key aim of Osborne's argument was to highlight one of the difficulties of interpreting material remains in the Attic country-side, rather than the distribution of wealth within Attica as such. However, he was also pointing out what looks like a structural requirement for widespread involvement in market transactions in classical Athens. Far from making any mistaken assumptions about the nature of the Athenian elite, Osborne was pointing up the pressure towards the development of a monetised market economy, even without appealing to the operation of the invisible economy (which by its nature is rather hard to get a grip on). There also had to be two sides to the transactions suggested by Osborne; if wealthy Athenians were selling (for cash) large quantities of agricultural produce, someone had to be buying that produce.

Another account of the distribution of wealth in Attica deserves some comment: that provided by Davies, in his fundamental account of Athenian property holding, *Wealth and the Power of Wealth in Classical Athens*.[28] Davies argued that

the liturgical system of public financing was so stable and integral a part of the Athenian democratic constitution that it is reasonable to infer that the dispropor-tionate burdens which it imposed on the narrow liturgical class corresponded to an equally disproportionate distribution of property. Albeit with a very large margin of error, it is possible to construct a property distribution graph for the fourth-century Athenian citizen population which shows this inference to be well-founded.[29]

He added:

I doubt if the general pattern was very different in the fifth century. It is true that the citizen body was larger, being certainly not less than 30,000 for much of the century, but the distension thereby involved in the graph is probably cancelled out by the existence of a somewhat larger and richer liturgical class. A major difference to the distribution pattern between the 5th and 4th centuries can be taken as unlikely.[30]

[27] Acton 2014 has some valuable discussion of this estate.
[28] Davies 1981.
[29] Davies 1981, 34; the graph in question is presented between 36 and 37.
[30] Davies 1981, 37.

Davies' conclusions are plausible, but they are not as secure as he implied. Writing at a time before Hansen's key contributions on the size of the population, he somewhat understated both the extent of the demographic changes between the fifth and the fourth centuries, as should already be clear, but also, crucially, the extent of the demographic pressures experienced during the fifth century.[31] This should make us hesitate before we retroject his (or for that matter anyone else's) model for the fourth century back into the fifth without modification.[32]

In general terms, of course, Davies is very likely to be right: the shape of the curve on his graph of wealth distribution probably would not have been that different, especially because it is a fairly loose approximation to reality in any case. But the experience of individual Athenians on the ground might well have been noticeably different, and the consequences of that elsewhere in the economy and society could well have been significant.

Davies' account has largely been endorsed by Geoffrey Kron, who has placed it in the kind of broader historical context that Morris recommended.[33] Kron's main refinement to Davies' picture is to accept Hansen's conclusions about the size of the citizen population in the fourth century as superior to those of Ruschenbusch. Kron's first resort for a comparative model is fifteenth-century AD Florence, and specifically the data provided by the famous *Catasto* of 1427. A major function of this comparison is to demonstrate that both the absolute level of wealth and the pattern of its distribution that Davies and Kron suggest for Athens are, in fact, plausible. There is a parallel here with Hopkins' use of model life tables.

As it turns out, in this case the comparative test shows that the reconstruction of Athenian wealth distribution proposed by Davies is plausible. The average net wealth of the citizens per capita seems very similar (although, as Kron acknowledges, there are a number of methodological complications here), and, more significantly, the wealth distribution curve of the two cities is also quite close, with Florence appearing to be 'more inegalitarian, but

---

[31] Davies 1981, 27–8, for 'the standard fifth-century figure of 30,000 for the male citizen population of Athens' and 'the figure of 21,000 attested for Athens in 316'.

[32] This is compatible with the conclusion of Taylor 2017, 96–111.

[33] Kron 2011. Kron dismisses Foxhall and Osborne as 'almost entirely conjectural'.

not radically different'.[34] Kron concludes that 'the Florentine results tend to show that the Athenian wealth distribution curve is credible for a pre-industrial city-state'.[35]

Kron also puts Athens into a wider set of comparisons, including various industrialised countries (which provide suitably detailed information about their wealth distribution) from a number of points in the twentieth century, pointing out that Athens seems not obviously less egalitarian than the post-war democracies. An important part of this article is to correct 'the common assumption that Athenian political democracy coexisted with a basically aristocratic and inegalitarian social structure'.[36] As a genuine contrast, he suggests that 'the curve for England prior to World War I shows the sort of profound inequality which marked truly aristocratic societies'. One might counter, in a similar way to Foxhall replying to Morris, that the profound inequality which prevailed in Edwardian England was only possible in a country that was at the centre of a world empire and which had experienced an industrial revolution, but the point stands.[37] All societies are unequal to some degree. The interesting questions usually concern the direction in which inequality is moving.

The choice of quattrocento Florence as a comparison for Athens is appealing for a variety of reasons, including their roughly similar size, although Kron does not go into this in detail. Still, the most compelling reason for looking at Florence has to be precisely the unusual richness and detail of the information provided by the *Catasto*. It is worth noting that the comparison Kron makes is explicitly between late fourth-century Athens and fifteenth-century Florence. Both cities had major demographic upheavals in their relatively recent pasts. The Black Death had ravaged Florence along with the rest of the Mediterranean and Europe 80 years before

[34] Kron 2011, 134.
[35] Kron 2011, 135.
[36] Kron 2011, 134.
[37] Note also Kron's observation that the gradual but not insignificant political democratisation of England in the late nineteenth and early twentieth centuries does not seem to have had much of a retarding effect on economic inequality. This is compatible with Scheidel's argument (2017, 345–66), but note that Kron still thinks that it would be natural for the wealth distribution of aristocratic Florence to be less equal than that of democratic Athens.

the *Catasto*; Athens in the second half of the fourth century had its own plague and the end of the Peloponnesian War a similar distance in the past. The Black Death does not play a particularly prominent part in the accounts of Florence's economy on which Kron relies, especially Richard Goldthwaite's *The Economy of Renaissance Florence*.[38] Nonetheless, it is clear that the possibility for social mobility that existed in the 1400s in Florence, and the shape of the wealth distribution curve that can be reconstructed from the *Catasto*, were substantially the result of demographic shock. If we had a snapshot equivalent to the *Catasto* from before 1348, it would probably look very different.

We can accept Kron's argument that Athens in the late fourth century was not particularly unequal in its distribution of wealth. That does not, however, mean that we can infer the same about Athens in the middle of the fifth century, or indeed about 'classical' Athens in general. It also does not explain why Athens had the economic structure that it did. This is a question that is too complex to address fully here, but the demographic background is an important factor to take into consideration.

Changes in the distribution of wealth are the focus of an important recent and very wide-ranging study by Walter Scheidel. In his *The Great Leveller: Violence and the History of Inequality from the Stone Age to the Twenty-First Century*, Scheidel argues that economic inequality has tended to increase over the course of human civilisation. The only factors that he identifies as having reduced inequality, even temporarily, are what he calls the 'four horsemen': mass-mobilisation warfare, transformative revolution, state failure, and lethal pandemics.[39]

Scheidel's picture is a distinctly bleak one. His horsemen all represent 'violent ruptures', and the book ends with this observation:

[38] Goldthwaite 2009. Goldthwaite is mainly concerned to note how very temporary the interruption to business activity was in 1348, and to explore the new opportunities for entrepreneurship it provided (548–9). He also notes, interestingly in the context of a comparison with Athens, that the fluidity of wealth ownership was partly 'a function of partible inheritance practised by men who continued to have many male children without much thought about laying the foundation for an enduring dynastic patrimony' (550).

[39] Scheidel 2017, 6.

All of us who prize greater economic equality would do well to remember that with the rarest of exceptions, it was only ever brought forth in sorrow. Be careful what you wish for.[40]

Again, this is not the place to evaluate the full scope of Scheidel's claims in detail, but it is worth noting that classical Greece provides one small chink of light through the mostly unremitting gloom:

The ancient Greek city-state culture, represented by Athens and Sparta, arguably provides us with [the] earliest examples of how intense popular military mobilization and egalitarian institutions helped constrain material inequality, albeit with mixed success.[41]

Scheidel's account of Athens accepts Foxhall's and Osborne's versions of Athenian wealth distribution as starting points.[42] Once again, it is the structure of (mainly late) fourth-century Athens that is his main focus and the basis for comparison with other times and places. Scheidel is not interested in the differences between the fifth and the fourth century (unavoidably in a book of such chronological scope), and sometimes this leads to a lack of clarity about exactly what he is claiming. In the picture he presents here, the relatively egalitarian structure of classical Athens was due principally to the mass military mobilisation required by hoplite and trireme warfare, reinforced by the system of liturgies, which

were bound to reduce – or in extreme cases, perhaps even prevent – wealth accumulation in the Athenian elite. This matters because in this period Athens experienced rapid economic growth, especially in the non-agrarian sector. Liturgies thus served as a brake on inequality in an environment that was otherwise conducive to increasing disparities [. . .] For what it is worth, the notion that fiscal interventions checked inequality is consistent with what we can say about the distribution of wealth in classical Athens at the time.[43]

Exactly how rapid Athens' economic growth was in the fourth century (which must be the period Scheidel is talking about,

[40] Scheidel 2017, 444.
[41] Scheidel 2017, 7.
[42] Scheidel 2017: on Athens generally, 192–9; on Foxhall and Osborne, 196–7. Other models of wealth distribution, including Kron's and Ober's (Ober 2015) are noted by Scheidel here, but none 'rises above controlled conjecture' (197).
[43] Scheidel 2017, 196.

since the wealthy were significantly shielded from the demands of liturgies both directly by imperial revenues and indirectly by the greater opportunities for enrichment in the fifth century), and the reasons for that growth, are not obvious. The evidence for economic growth that relates specifically to Athens in the 300s is fairly tenuous, to say the least. Nothing Scheidel says here is unreasonable. However, it elides the point that it is also consistent with a rather different picture for the mid-fifth century, when the liturgy system would have been a much less effective brake, and there is no reason to think that Athens' economic growth was any slower, and the population was growing much more rapidly. There is, on Scheidel's own terms, every reason to think that Periclean Athens was seeing increasing disparities. If fourth-century Athens was relatively egalitarian, the explanation has to include reference to the demographic upheaval caused by war and plague at the end of the fifth. That makes Kron's choice of Florence as a comparison look more apt, but it also makes the glimmer of light in Scheidel's seem more like a retinal after-image of Polanyi's hopeful vision of a civilised Athenian alternative. The apparent egalitarianism of fourth-century Athens may have more to do with the other horsemen than with the institutions of the *polis*, and supports Scheidel's overall thesis better than it provides a counterexample.

Davies was not quite explicit about how he thinks his graph might have been (expected to be) 'distended' by the presence of a larger population. But what he says about the 'existence of a somewhat larger and richer liturgical class' implies that he thought, quite reasonably, that the bulk of that extra population would have been able to own very little wealth.[44] Now, it is almost certainly true that the richest men in Athens in the fifth century were richer than their counterparts for most of (if not all) the fourth century. It is also quite likely that there were more men who would have qualified for membership of the 'liturgical class'. But to go from there to saying that the overall pattern of wealth distribution

---

[44] Strictly speaking, even on Davies' own terms, the graph *should* have been distended, as he is assuming a population in the fifth century that is about 50 per cent bigger than that in the fourth century, whereas his assumption about the size of the liturgical class is that it was only 33 per cent bigger (400 as against 300) (33).

in Athens was therefore essentially the same, in spite of the difference in population size, seems a little more dubious.

There are two reasons for thinking this. The first has nothing to do with the size of the population but more to do with the source of much of this extra wealth. Athens in the fifth century was rich largely because it was an imperial power. Again, it is certainly true that the ordinary inhabitants of Attica benefitted materially from the empire, whether directly or indirectly. It was imperial revenues that made possible (one way or another) the fleet and the 'Periclean' building programmes, which must have provided a certain amount of gainful non-agricultural employment. The people best placed to take advantage of the opportunities presented by the building programme would presumably have been those who lived close to Athens and who had draught animals that could be rented out. It was also these revenues, surely, which made possible in the first instance the introduction of pay for jurors. The fleet also had the benefit of ensuring that food supplies could be secured from overseas with less risk of interdiction from enemies or pirates.

However, it is also surely the case that the wealthy were in a position to do far better out of the empire – as is revealed, for example by the Attic Stelai and the colossal holding of Oionias, and that of Adeimantos on Thasos. We should probably include Thucydides' family. There is also the Brea decree (*ML* 49, *OR* 142). Foxhall notes that, while it makes provision for the appointment of *geonomoi*, it says nothing about how the land is to be distributed.[45] The restriction of participation in the colony to the *thetes* and the *zeugitai* comes only in the amendment of Phantocles. All kinds of possibilities are open for how this amendment changed the substance of Democleides' original proposal, but it is conceivable that Foxhall is right to suggest that 'this could be an attempt to block the efforts of wealthier men to dominate in terms of both landholding and political power'. Jones had argued that the intention of the colony (or at least one intention) was to increase the size of the 'hoplite class' by increasing the property of a number of the *thetes*, and this is the explanation that is accepted by Davies and

[45] Foxhall 2002, 214.

Jameson.[46] Jones actually thought that this was the original intention of the colony, and that the original decree probably restricted
membership to the *thetes* only. Meiggs and Lewis, however, thought
it 'most likely' that originally membership was unrestricted, but that
if it had been restricted it was more likely to have been to *zeugitai*
only, given the reference to *stratiotai* in line 27. If Jones is right,
then Phantocles' amendment may have been an attempt to restrict
the extent to which the poorest Athenians would benefit. On the
other hand, it might reflect a situation where some of the *zeugitai*
were not at all well off either, and there was a concern not to exclude
them unfairly. Jones (prompted by De Ste Croix) also observed that
presumably few of the wealthiest Athenians would have wanted to
give up their Athenian citizenship to go off to live in the 'wilds' of
Thrace.[47] This is not implausible, but perhaps it does not say much
for the condition of the poor in Attica. Alternatively, if we abandoned the idea that the plots were all equal, there may have been
some appeal to being a big fish in a little pond. The connections of
the Athenian aristocracy with some of their Thracian counterparts
may also have meant that the 'wilds' were not always so unappeal-
ing. Whichever way it is played, it is hard, I think, to take the Brea
decree as unambiguous evidence for the Athenian poor benefitting
hugely from the empire. That in turn is not necessarily to say that
this inscription shows the rich benefitting disproportionately in this
case, of course.

The second point is linked directly to demographic observations,
and to what is perhaps one of the most important issues that arise
from them. The usable agricultural land of Attica was finite, even if
we have to assume that more was being used than has sometimes
been assumed in the past. The scope for capital investment in Greek
agriculture was not zero but was quite restricted. That would suggest that as one of the other factors of production (land and labour)
became more abundant, and so relatively less valuable, the other
would have become scarcer and relatively more valuable.

A situation where labour is abundant and cheap (because of
a large population) and land is scarce and expensive tends to be

---

[46] Jones 1957, 168–9; Davies 1981, 56; Jameson 1994, 59 note 21.
[47] Jones 1957, 168.

bad news for those people who rely on wages for some or all of their income. For those who can subsist entirely off the produce of their own landholding, the situation is more favourable. But given the interannual variability of agricultural production in Attica, a holding that was large enough to ensure this kind of security over the longer term (more than a decade, say) would have to have been quite substantial. Foxhall's 60 *plethra* or 5.5 ha may have been at the bottom of this range rather than the top – which is not to say that there were not many people eking out a more precarious living on plots only half that size or less.[48] Whatever size we go for, however, there clearly cannot have been enough land for all the citizens to have so much, even at fairly low estimates of population and assuming an entirely equal distribution of the usable land. So, if we assume that the area of Attica was 240,000 ha, and that 40 per cent of that was cultivable, there would only have been 4 ha each for 24,000 households. Even in a situation where initially land had been equally distributed (which was never the case), some households will, inevitably, just have died out; others, whether as a result of the vagaries of fortune or because (like Hesiod's Perses) they were lazy or incompetent, will have failed economically, while other households will have been able to take advantage and increase their own share.

The denser the population on a given area of land, the higher the stakes will have been for the failures, and the greater the chances of their falling into dependence on their more fortunate neighbours. The less land there is to go around, and the smaller the shares, the greater the chance of failure in the first place. The less the value of one's labour to those with larger holdings, the harder it will be to survive or to adapt to a failure of one's own crops. In the worst case, when one loses one's land completely, the less the value of one's principal remaining asset.

All other things, such as the availability of land, being equal, a bigger population will result in a more polarised distribution of

---

[48] Jameson 1994 for some indications that on the ground many landholdings were well above this minimum threshold. See also Van Wees 2006, 383. Elsewhere in this article, Van Wees suggests some different minimum figures in the context of trying to understand the 'Solonian' property classes.

wealth, as the rich will become richer at the expense of the poor. If the population of Athens in the fifth century was much greater than it was in the fourth, then there is every reason to believe that the difference in wealth distribution would have had more signifi- cance than forcing Davies to lengthen the axes on his graph.

Of course, all other things were not equal. The poorer inhabi- tants of Attica would have been shielded from the worst conse- quences of this grim economic logic. In the first place, the institutions of the democracy, and the strong local association embodied in the deme, would have acted to some extent to prevent the poorer citizens falling into total dependence on their richer neighbours. Classical Attica may provide a partial exception in this regard to the distinctly gloomy picture painted by Gallant of the prospects for Greek peasant farmers.[49] In the second place, there was of course the empire, which provided some cash hand- outs, but probably more importantly, generated a significant demand for non-agricultural labour and other opportunities for subsistence. On the other hand, the fact that the wealthy were probably getting even more benefit out of the empire meant that it would not have retarded the polarisation of wealth distribution *per se*. It just helped save some of the worst off from falling into utter destitution.

This is another issue that needs to be returned to, but the democ- racy of the fourth century was remarkable for its resilience and stability, especially by Greek standards and given the legacy of the oligarchic revolutions. A contributory factor here may have been that economic inequalities were not so extreme as to make nonsense of a political ideology of equality. But this does not entitle us to infer that the fifth-century democracy also saw such a balance, or that that stability was inevitable, or due to the inherent niceness/civilization/ clarity of vision of the Athenians.[50] Had the Peloponnesian War not happened, or taken a different course, or had the plague not struck

[49] Gallant 1991; see also Ober 2008.
[50] Strauss 1986, 1–6, rightly stresses the need to *explain* the relative success of the post-403 amnesty. Pointing out that it was adhered to for reasons of *Realpolitik* (Carawan 2001, 2005) rather than any genuine reconciliation is not an explanation, as it essentially involves an appeal to the superior rationality of the Athenians compared to the likes of the Corcyrans. Xenophon's comments at *Hell.* 2.4.43 are not wholly without irony, but irony cannot explain them away completely either.

Athens, then the democracy would have come under increasing strain and might not have lasted so long.

Existing accounts of change in the classical period in Athens tend to emphasise the development of economic institutions. Edward Cohen's book *Athenian Economy and Society* (which Morris was reviewing in 1994) typifies some aspects of this approach. The book opens with a strong claim:

> The fourth century at Athens witnessed two startling, and perhaps interrelated innovations: the transition to an economy governed (in Aristotle's words) by 'monetary acquisition' rather than by traditional social motivations, and the development of the world's first private businesses ('banks', *trapezai*), which accepted from various sources funds ('deposits') for which they had an absolute obligation of repayment while being free to profit from, or even lose, these monies in their own loan and investment activities.[51]

Not everything here is substantiated in the text that follows. Cohen talks about the nature of the fourth-century economy and Athenian *trapezai*, but he never justifies the first part of his statement, that all this happened in the fourth century. In fact, it seems likely that it could, even should, already have taken place long before 400 BC.

The Athenian elite, after all, would presumably have been under just as much pressure to raise cash in the fifth century as in the fourth, and so the structural necessity for involvement in market exchange outlined by Osborne would have been just as important. What changed here between the fifth and fourth centuries was not that the Athenian elite had to find more cash for the *polis* in absolute terms. Rather, the loss of the empire and (for a time at least) the cessation of silver production at Laurion meant that the resources they had available to meet those demands were considerably reduced. The banks that Cohen entirely reasonably, and surely correctly, argues were crucial to the grain trade in the fourth century would presumably have been even more important in the more densely populated and richer fifth, even if the grain was coming from different suppliers.[52] The probable demographic reality of the fifth century provides further compelling reasons

---

[51] Cohen 1992, 3.
[52] Cohen 1992, 111–83.

for thinking that this 'transition' to a more commercialised economy should have happened then.[53]

First, it is relevant that a densely settled population in itself is conducive to the emergence of market exchange systems, as has been observed in discussions of economic change in other times and places.[54] Put very crudely, the more people there are living nearby you, the easier it is to find someone to exchange with, and the less far your goods have to be transported.

More importantly perhaps, such a large and dense population would also have meant that a commercialised economy was positively necessary. The more people there were, the less land there was for each person. Even if my suggestion about the implications for the distribution of the land is wrong (for example, if the rich were contenting themselves with building up estates only outside Attica), this would have meant that a lot of people had plots that were barely able to provide subsistence in an 'average' year, and must in practice frequently have failed to do so. These people would have needed some alternative survival strategies. For them, the possibility of engaging in some forms of market activity would have been crucial, even if it was something as simple as hiring out their own labour. It might be relevant to point out that there is at least one apparently clear example of a labour market operating by the late fifth century – that for skilled trireme crewmen, which is taken for granted in Thucydides and Xenophon.[55] Even when their situation was not critical, producing crops for sale may have been a better strategy than trying to maintain an autarkic existence.

---

[53] Quite apart from the existence of several indications that concern about 'monetary acquisition' of the type expressed by Aristotle can be found (for example, throughout Aristophanes' *Acharnians*). Schaps 2004, especially 93–123 and 150–74, illustrates this point very clearly. Note also that while Schaps is (obviously) mainly interested in pursuing (and emphasising) the significance of the invention of coinage, he makes an interesting remark early on: 'there is no doubt that economic transactions tended, as Greek society developed from the archaic age to the classical and the Hellenistic, to be more a matter of immediate mutual economic benefit and less a form of discharging social obligations. The invention of coinage certainly facilitated this change, which may, however, have been propelled more by simple population growth than by any technological or cultural development.'(33)

[54] Persson 1988 for medieval Europe provides a clear example; see also Persson 2010, 21–39, and Erdkamp 2016, who makes important points about the mobilisation of labour.

[55] Thuc. 8.29, 8.45; Xen. *Hell.* 1.5.4.

The tendency in the fifth century would have been to accelerate the adoption of such strategies. As the urban centre of Athens and the Piraeus became larger, there would have been a ready market there for food and fuel products, quite apart from anything else. We do not have to take Thucydides entirely literally when he claims that all the Athenians lived in the countryside before the war (2.16). Even if we did, there must have been a lot of metics in the centre, not least, as we have seen, because of the demands of the fleet and its facilities (Pseudo-Xenophon *Athenaion Politeia* 1.12). Clearly here I have a good deal of sympathy with the conclusion reached by Moreno, and would be less reluctant to make generalisations from his account of Euonymon to other regions of Attica, where the challenges faced would have been similar in kind if not always in detail. Euonymon's relative fertility and proximity to the *astu* itself must have had an effect on its agricultural economy, but it is worth recalling that Athens and its agora were not the only urban centre and market in Attica. A major centre like Athens could have a variety of effects – but effects nonetheless – on different areas in its hinterland, according to both distance and terrain. Morley's *Metropolis and Hinterland*, though mainly concerned with Rome, contains useful insights for other smaller centres too.[56]

There is an important issue of cause and effect here: how far was the increasing size of the population responsible for an increasingly commercialised economy, and how far was it enabled by it? This, however, is a problem that is not easy to resolve for any period of history, especially if more general technological development is considered.

Up to this point, I have not said anything that is explicitly in conflict with what Morris has to say about the development of Greek economies between the sixth and the fourth centuries. He sees a shift in the nature of settlement patterns and in agricultural exploitation towards greater intensification, and genuine, significant economic growth, starting from the beginning of this period.[57] We might ask how far it is possible to generalise across

---

[56] Morley 1996, 55–82. See also Jones 2014, 440–515, and Erdkamp 2016 on the importance of stable markets and the reduced volatility of prices.

[57] Morris 1994a.

the Greek world – what appear to be similar observed phenomena in field surveys need not all have the same explanation in different places. But a sharper difference in our positions emerges, I think, when Morris suggests that 'we might . . . link the new agricultural history and the history of representations in an economic explanation for democracy'.[58]

Morris rapidly concedes that cause and effect might have operated differently, but it is possibly revealing that his first instinct was to assert that the emergence of democracy was dependent on an increasingly market-driven economy. Morris seems, like Cohen, to have an absolute faith in the idea that Athens, and Greece generally, becoming more commercialised was straightforwardly a Good Thing, something to be celebrated and connected directly to other aspects of Greek society that we find admirable, such as democracy.[59]

Morris notes that

a general rise in prosperity around 500 might or might not have changed the distribution of wealth between rich and poor, but in absolute terms the spectre of economic failure and hunger would no longer have hovered so closely over so many of the poorer citizens. In the new situation patronage may have lost much of its power.[60]

This is a possible reconstruction, but not necessarily what happened. Whatever the initial spur, intensification of agricultural production would rapidly have become necessary just to ensure survival for many of those poorer citizens; it is hard to see how this represented the increased altitude of any spectres over them. Overall economic growth would not necessarily have benefitted the poor at all, if the avenues for the generation and exploitation of that wealth were dominated by the elite. If there was any change in the distribution of wealth, it is unlikely to have been to the benefit of the poor.[61] True, the institutions of democracy and the empire might have prevented many peasant farmers from falling into complete dependence on their wealthier neighbours, but it is

[58] Morris 1994a, 365.
[59] Ogilvie 2007. Did Athens just happen to have the right answers?
[60] Morris 1994a, 365.
[61] Scheidel 2017, 25–112, on the general tendency of growth of this kind to be attended by increased inequality.

worth recalling Kron's comments about nineteenth-century Britain here. It is not immediately obvious how an Athenian farmer with a plot too small to maintain subsistence and forced to depend on market transactions was personally better off than his ancestor with (possibly) a bigger plot, without appealing to political explanation, even if overall labour productivity was improved. It is also important to remember that any gains the Athenians made from the empire were at the expense of their allies. I do not think we have to share in the optimism of Cohen and Morris, at least as far as the fifth century is concerned.[62]

It is likely that intensification of farming would have been adopted at all levels of Athenian agriculture in the fifth century, although not always for the same reasons. For poorer Athenians, more intensive strategies may have been adopted out of sheer necessity. The small plots of land that were available could only have been made to support a household if they were worked as intensively as possible. On the estates of the wealthy, the pressures were slightly different.

If the ownership of land was becoming more polarised, then one might have expected the larger estates to be less intensively worked, since extra labour would have had to have been brought in from outside, and paid for somehow. Even if the elite acquired the land of their less successful neighbours, they could not also automatically claim their labour. But Athens did have a substantial urban centre that would have provided a ready market for agricultural produce.[63] In particular it would have provided a market for wine.[64] Added to this, labour is of course going to have been

[62] Again, this interpretation is compatible, I think, with the picture of Athenian agriculture painted by Moreno 2007, although Moreno rapidly moves on to discuss the more glamorous political and diplomatic machinations of the Athenian elite.
[63] Not to mention the mines, which in this context acted as quasi-urban in that the people employed there could not produce their own food.
[64] See 193–195 above. This is where Sallares' arguments against widespread viticulture (the attractions of which are advocated by Hanson 1992b) seem to fall down (Sallares 1991, 303): 'it seems reasonable to suggest that in the pre-modern period the proportion of farm land in Attica devoted to viticulture was never more than a small fraction of what it is today, in the absence of urban demand on the modern scale. This suggestion is strengthened if it is recalled that Athenian wine, which was ignored by Athenaios in his catalogue of fine wines, was apparently not a connoisseur's delight and is not known ever to have been exported in antiquity. Its probable resemblance to retsina accounts for

relatively cheap, whether in the form of hired hands or slaves (or both). The elite experienced a constant demand for cash expenditure, whether public or private, which had to be met, at least partly, from the agricultural produce of small and scattered plots of land. Intensification and cash-cropping for market sale would have made perfect sense for them.

The question of settlement patterns arises here, although Morris' reference to 'definitional squabbles' is perhaps apt. An intensified regime of production across the board would tend to produce a picture of dispersed farmsteads rather than nucleated settlements. That such a picture is hard straightforwardly to map onto Attica has long been pointed out by Osborne. However, the sole intensive survey of a part of Attica proper found just such a dispersed pattern for Atene.[65]

It is hard, however, to justify the extrapolation of the Atene model across Attica. There are several reasons for this. Some of them have to do with the interpretation of survey results, as Osborne has pointed out.[66] Survey evidence of activity in remote rural areas does not necessarily indicate permanent residence rather than the existence of storage or processing facilities. It is also worth considering how spread out a nucleated settlement can be before it stops being nucleated and becomes dispersed, or even whether there is a linear progression from one to the other.[67] In this context, it is worth noting that with an average population density of over 100 per km², no one is going to be as remote as all that from his neighbours. And as Osborne has also pointed out, economic pressures are not the only ones operating – there are considerable civic, social, and political advantages to living in a nucleated centre.

this.' Urban demand may not have run at modern levels, but it would still have been high enough to repay local wine production. All Sallares' observations establish is that Athenian wine might not have been of the highest quality (but plenty of cheap and presumably nasty wine was drunk in Athens in the form of the *trikotylos*). If there was a large demand at home, it is unsurprising that it was not exported. This does not mean that it was not being produced in large quantities. As Hanson (1992b) notes, viticulture is also a good candidate for an intensification strategy, because it responds well to extra labour inputs throughout the year, even if it is not a short-term strategy. Halstead 2014, 286–7, 314–15; Bresson 2016, 170–4.

[65] Lohmann, 1993; with Osborne 1997.
[66] Osborne 1992. See now also Moreno 2007, 72–4.
[67] Forsdyke 2006.

Such a centre does not appear to have existed at all in Atene, of course. But there are some good reasons for thinking that Atene was not in any way typical. Not the least of these is its location in southern Attica. This is relevant for two reasons. One is that this area has only scattered pockets of (relatively) high-quality land to be exploited, so a more scattered settlement pattern is more geographically determined than in other areas of Attica. The other is its proximity to the mines. The demand for food these generated and the likely desire to minimise transport costs would have created even greater than usual pressure towards intensification of production to wring as much as possible out of the land, which may have overcome the pressures to nucleated settlement.[68]

In any case, one of the striking things about the landscape of classical Attica is the variety of settlement forms it seems to have contained. This is, if nothing else, an important reminder that different pressures might work in different directions or have different consequences in different contexts. It is also worth recalling that we can very rarely recover the motivations of people in the past, who lacked our advantage of hindsight; but also that economically rational behaviour is not the only kind of rationality.

It should by now be clear, I hope, why the absolute size of the total population is interesting. If this can be accepted, then the significance of that population experiencing dramatic change, such as that brought about by the catastrophic losses of the Peloponnesian War, can also be agreed and its consequences taken into account.

We have already seen that, for Thucydides, the crucial point about the manpower losses that were due to the plague was that the deaths (and presumably also the disabling) of much of Athens' manpower was a critical blow to her *dunamis*. It is also clear, however, that Athens' ability to wage war was not fatally compromised by this blow, not least because the Athenians were able to score a strategic victory in the Archidamian War and later contemplate the Sicilian Expedition. That is not, of course, to

[68] Rihll 2001. It may also be relevant that Atene seems to have been a late starter as a deme, even possibly a later addition to the Cleisthenic system, in which case, with a weaker sense of local identity, the tendency to maintain an active civic centre may have been weaker than elsewhere, too.

say that Athens' military power was quite unaffected by the demographic losses suffered during the war. The *polis* that could send 16,000 hoplites out of Attica at once in 430 had to face the wars of the fourth century apparently with only half as many. Athens' military difficulties in the fourth century were not purely the result of the cash flow problems associated with the loss of the empire. In fact, it can be argued that the demographic shocks of the later fifth century can be seen as contributing in subtler ways to Athens' strategic options and posture in the fourth century. For example, Ober famously argued that the fourth century saw the land defence of Attica attaining a much higher priority than previously.[69] This he explains as the result of the increased importance of domestic agriculture to the Athenians, as well as the changing nature of warfare.[70] Taylor suggests that the change is also reflective of a shift in the balance of political power, which saw the inhabitants of rural demes playing an increasingly important role in the democracy.[71] But this shift in itself has to be explained by the alterations in the economic situation which were precisely the result of these demographic shocks. The power of traditional elites was weakened, if not broken, by two related demographic factors: at the level of individual households, the threat of extinction was increased; at the level of the city as a whole their economic position was weakened relative to that of their poorer compatriots, and they had lost more along with the empire.[72]

Most of the modern scholarship we have looked at has either focussed on the fourth century or has elided the differences between the 400s and the 300s. The only modern attempt really to engage with the issue of change between the fifth and fourth centuries remains Barry Strauss', in *Athens After the Peloponnesian War*.[73] Strauss was right here to argue that the post-war political history of Athens can only properly be understood within its social and economic context. He was right too to conclude that 'the demographic

---

[69] Ober 1985.
[70] Ober 1985, 208.
[71] Taylor 2005, 171–2.
[72] Taylor 2017, 107–10.
[73] Strauss 1986.

costs of the Peloponnesian War were staggering'.[74] He also makes a number of acute observations about the general post-war economic climate. However, I think that his central argument about the impact of Athens' demographic losses is not convincing.

In summary, what Strauss wants his demographic argument to do is help explain why the amnesty declared after the restoration of democracy actually worked reasonably well and why there was no prolonged and violent counterrevolution of the sort that might have been expected in the light of what happened in other Greek cities like Corcyra. He does this by saying that the poorer Athenian citizens (whom he is happy to label *thetes*) suffered disproportionately heavy casualties compared to their richer countrymen ('hoplites'), and especially towards the end of the war. If they had not died in such great numbers, they would have been more politically assertive in the immediate post-war period and would have exacted a more violent revenge on the supporters of oligarchy. As it was, they were weak, demoralised, and leaderless: 'by 405, a good part of the political class was at the bottom of the Aegean. It is small wonder then that *hoi polloi* were no more assertive after the restoration of democracy in 403'.[75]

The *thetes* in this account are supposed to have been those Athenians who were too poor to afford hoplite equipment, and are assumed to have fulfilled their military obligations primarily by serving in the fleet. This in itself requires some contestable assumptions,[76] but the real trouble is that we do not actually know how many citizens like this there were before the war, we do not know how many there were after the war, and we do not know how many of them died during the war, or when. We can estimate within broad limits, as I have argued above, but Strauss' argument demands a level of precision about all these things that we cannot hope to attain. And even if we could, crucially, we still would not actually know what the political views of these men really were.

That is not however to say that Strauss was necessarily wrong in looking to demographic change for an explanation of the (relative) absence of political tensions in post-war Athens. Strauss concluded

---

[74] Strauss 1986, 81.
[75] Strauss 1986, 42–86, quotation at 80–1.
[76] Gabrielsen 2002.

that the 'staggering' losses sustained by Athens were 'except for the small grace that there were now fewer mouths to feed, immensely deleterious to Athens', although he went on to note that 'the new demography was, however, not without value to those members of the Athenian upper classes who feared a more radical democracy'.[77] In making these comments, Strauss is in part right, I think, but in part he is also perhaps being too pessimistic. To explain this, we need to turn to the wider economic consequences of Athens' experiences and ultimate defeat in the war.

Strauss paid these issues some attention, especially with reference to the last phase of the conflict, the 'Iono-Decelean' War.[78] His account needs to be summarised briefly here, as it attained something of the status of orthodoxy. Much of it remains uncontroversial, I think, but we might wish to revisit some of the conclusions.

Looking at agriculture, Strauss notes:

> even in Attica ... agriculture was of prime importance ... This is not to say that all landowners depended exclusively on agriculture for their livelihood. Many wealthy landowners had diversified their investments ... Before the collapse of the Athenian empire, a poor landowner ... could easily enough supplement his income by serving as a juror, by rowing in the fleet or by working either in the shipyards of Piraeus or on a state building project, but except for the courts (and after 403 the assembly) these opportunities were gone. Nor were there likely to be many opportunities in private industry. Hence, contrary to what some have argued, there is not likely to have been a move to the city in 403. If anything, the country seemed a safer bet, because even the landless could serve as a tenant farmer or as a seasonal labourer. With the loss of imperial revenues, Athenians depended more on agriculture than in several generations.[79]

Strauss seems to be talking a great deal of sense here, and some of what I want to say would actually reinforce this picture. But he goes on: 'the state of Athenian agriculture, then, personally interested a majority of citizens, and in 403 that state was unquestionably bad'. Rightly, and drawing on Hanson's arguments that the extent of permanent damage should not be exaggerated, he continues: 'one should not speak of an irreversible catastrophe'. But

[77] Strauss 1986, 81.
[78] Strauss 1986, 42–63.
[79] Strauss 1986, 43–4.

then he concludes: 'there was, however, a serious depression, if not a universal one, in the post-war/Corinthian War period'.[80]

Two points need to be made here. First, Strauss gives only a vague indication of how long this 'depression' lasted, and no explanation of how or why it ended (presumably he thinks it did) nor why it should have been prolonged at least until 395 and perhaps longer. Second, it is not clear what he actually means by 'depression'. In its normal sense, a 'depression' would imply a severe reduction in agricultural activity, or perhaps a reduction in production, or profitability.[81] But Strauss' own observation about the importance of and the population's general involvement in agriculture after the war would surely have made this unlikely. What, presumably, he means is that some (many?) farmers would have suffered (sometimes serious) losses of capital during the war, but that is not quite the same thing. The logic of his argument is that agriculture should have seen a great deal more activity, and absorbed much of what investment capital was available, as Athenians struggled to recoup the losses inflicted by the war and to exploit the one major area of economic activity and source of profit (or subsistence) that was still available to them.

Strauss is absolutely right that many Athenians would have experienced hardship:

Many an Athenian farmer found it necessary to buy seed, lost draught animals, plundered farming equipment and household tools and furniture, not to mention slaves ... If he had sheep or cattle, he would have to replace them, and perhaps poultry, pigs and goats as well. A small number of olive trees and vines would have sustained partial damage, in some cases enough to interrupt production for seven or more years.[82]

And he continues:

An uneven pattern of suffering resulted. A small farmer near Decelea who had lost his household goods, animals and a slave or two might have been ruined. His counterpart on the Athenian plain, however ... might have suffered little.

---

[80] Strauss 1986, 44–5.

[81] So, for example: 'A prolonged period characterized by high unemployment, low output and investment, depressed business confidence, falling prices, and widespread business failures' (Samuelson and Nordhaus 2009, 761). Stripped of the anachronisms, such a definition might be applied to the Athenian economy as a whole (compared to its pre-war state), but is harder to apply to the Athenian agricultural sector.

[82] Strauss 1986, 45.

However, generally Strauss seems unwilling to go beyond the scale of Athens' aggregate losses to consider the effects on individuals. His one example is that of Ischomachus, whose estate is supposed to have dropped in value from 70 talents to 20 by the end of his life.[83] Even if we were sure about these figures, Ischomachus was hardly typical. Still, the *way* in which it is not typical does point the way to a different interpretation.

It seems clear that at the outset of the war, and at least up to the Peace of Nicias, many of the wealthiest households in Athens held a great deal of property outside Attica, whether this was agricultural land, or mines in the Thraceward region, or something else. Almost all of this property will have been lost after the end of the war. Strauss may also, I think, be a little complacent when he suggests that 'a wealthy farmer who had diversified his investments in urban real estate or nautical loans might have suffered little'. Athens' ultimate defeat had been caused by a stranglehold put on her maritime trade by the Peloponnesian fleet. Many cargoes must have been lost, to the acute detriment of those who financed them. The profitability of maritime loans was, after all, related to their risk. As Athens' need and ability to pay for imports was reduced, new opportunities in this area would not have been abundant, or at least not as abundant as they had been.

Something of the scale of traffic through the Piraeus is revealed by the scale of the contracts for the *pentekoste* over which Andokides and Agyrrhius had their squabble (Andokides 1. 133–4). It is claimed that in the years 402–399, this tax could be farmed for 36 talents (although Agyrrhius and his associates paid only 30; Andokides accuses them of profiting excessively at the expense of the *polis*, but it is also possible, likely even, that the volume of trade in the years immediately after the war started low and gradually increased). If Andokides is truthful in his claim that only a very small profit was made over the 36 talents, then presumably the total value of the goods being taxed as they passed in or out of the Piraeus was not much more than 1,800 talents. This would represent only about one-tenth of the value of the goods moving

---

[83] Lysias 19.46; whether Ischomachus' property actually ever amounted to the 70 talents alleged here is moot.

around the fifth-century empire that the Athenians seem to have reckoned with when they tried to replace the tribute with the *eikoste*.[84] However, 1,800 talents is still a fairly sizeable sum: in total, the value of over 2,000,000 *medimnoi* of barley at 5 drachmas per *medimnos* (the 'highish' price used by Osborne), although the tax was on both imports and exports.[85] On the other hand, it may not necessarily all reflect activity by or for the benefit of Athenians. Part of the attraction of the Piraeus had presumably been its relatively central position and the quality of its facilities, so it may have continued as an entrepôt, at least for commodities other than grain.

Likewise, the value of urban property is unlikely to have remained unchanged. No longer would the citizens of the allied cities by obliged to visit Athens and need to be accommodated. Some at least of the metics who had dwelt in Athens–Piraeus to support the fleet will presumably have left. And as Strauss himself observes, if anything, the poorer citizens who might have rented housing would have been moving out of the city rather than into it. True, there would have been some returning émigrés, but it seems unlikely that they outnumbered or even matched the people leaving the city. Also, their ability to pay rents would not, one suspects, have been all that great.

On the brighter side, however, it is worth recalling that the damage to agricultural holdings in Attica may not have been as severe as Strauss implies. Not all Athenian farmers would have been caught unawares by Peloponnesian League raiders, and some will have been able to save at least the essential tools for cultivation: hoes, mattocks, ploughshares, sickles, spades, and shovels. The loss of bulkier and more expensive items will have been felt keenly but would have affected wealthier farmers more than the poorer. Relatively few farms in Attica would have been big enough to justify plough cultivation. These wealthier farmers would also have lost the expensive draught animals to pull those ploughs, and were more likely to have owned slaves who could have deserted.

The very poorest citizen farmers, whose main asset in any case had always been their own time and labour, may have lost least,

---

[84] Thuc. 7.28.4, with Osborne 2000, 75.
[85] See 208 above.

and not just because they had least to lose in the first place. After all, the great loss of life that the plague and the war brought meant that the material resources of Attica itself would have been divided between fewer people than before the war. This may or may not in itself have produced a redistribution of land among the citizens, but two points are important to keep in mind here.

One is that the elevated rates of mortality during the war must have caused more families than usual to die out completely, or to be left without male heirs.[86] The property of such households could only go to other citizens. The other is that the war clearly did cause considerable disruption and dislocation in the short term in the Attica countryside. In spite of the efforts of the Athenian cavalry, some areas, such as the immediate environs of Decelea, will have remained inaccessible to their owners. Even elsewhere, in wartime conditions it is easy to imagine that, with normal patterns of residence disrupted, with higher-than-usual mortality, and with many demesmen scattered abroad on active duty, keeping track of the ownership of and entitlement to land became very much more difficult.

It is not, I would suggest, coincidence that it was now that the citizenship law was reenacted, or that corporate bodies like the Demotionidai were demonstrating worries about who could rightfully claim to be a citizen.[87] Citizenship, even at Athens, was fundamentally connected with the right to own land. Many of the other benefits of Athenian citizenship – which may have inspired the original passage of Pericles' law – would have vanished along with the empire. Political participation was still important, of course, but the introduction of pay for attendance at the assembly was due, according to the Aristotelian *Athenaion Politeia*, to difficulty in getting people to attend.[88] There was of

---

[86] There are shadowy reflections of this in the stories of Socrates and Euripides marrying twice, and that of Aristarchus in Xen. *Mem.* 2.7, whose household was only one casualty away from such a fate. This *may* also provide *some* of the explanation for the shift in political power that seems to occur in Athens over this period, although other mechanisms clearly were at work. See Taylor 2005, and 33–37 above.

[87] *RO* 5.

[88] [Arist.] *Ath. Pol.* 41.3. That the rate increased throughout the fourth century might indicate that the problem did not go away. Of course, if there really was a tendency for Athenian citizens to move (back) into the countryside, then distance from the urban centre may have made attendance at the assembly less attractive too. If agricultural work was considered more rewarding, or more important, than political participation at the

course jury pay, but this was surely not such a benefit that it inspired this legislative activity. Military service, in an Athens with a greatly reduced fleet and which was at least temporarily a loyal ally of Sparta, will not have been terribly attractive either. Indeed, if the response to Thibron's request for troops in 400 is anything to go by, it was quite the reverse.[89]

But even if many Athenian citizens did not benefit materially and directly from the war in terms of increasing their landholdings, there is a further factor to consider. The economic (and hence social and political) climate of pre-war Athens was conditioned, I have suggested, at least partly by the relative abundance of labour and scarcity of land, and by the latter being much more valuable than the former. This situation will not wholly have changed after the war. By most contemporary standards, Athens and Attica were still heavily populated. But the change may have been significant for some people. Strauss noted that agriculture was now more important to Athens as a whole than it had been for generations. The only way to compensate for the loss of capital items such as tools and animals was to use what was available (land and labour) as intensively as possible. Labour would have become relatively scarce and more valuable. For those whose own land was still too little to support their own households, and for whom the sale of their labour was a vital part of their economic survival strategies, this should have helped at least a little.

Those with larger estates who still needed extra-household labour, at least for some of the year, will have been harder pressed to obtain it. These are also the people who are most likely to have lost slaves, cattle, and overseas possessions. The most severe blow to Athenian agriculture, possibly including the loss of slaves, as Thucydides himself suggests, may well have been the loss of Euboea and all the animals that had been sent there for security.[90] If almost all Athenian households had some livestock

---

centre, then this only goes to reinforce the picture I am trying to draw, and weakens further the case for agricultural depression.

[89] Xen. *Hell.* 3.1.4. Athenian troops were involved in the war between Sparta and Elis (Xen. *Hell.* 3.2.25).

[90] Thuc. 8.95–6; compare 2.14. Moreno 2007, 81–126, establishes the importance of Euboea well, although his reconstructions of Athenian strategy and taxation are not always convincing.

and most of it was on Euboea (though one might question whether it was worth shipping over the handfuls of small animals, especially pigs and sheep, that probably typified the holdings on most farms), then it would have been difficult to replace immediately. If the effects were felt across Athenian society, then again it is possible that the losses suffered by richer Athenians may have been the most important. To the poor householder, the attraction of a few animals was that they were a flexible part of a varied survival strategy. Their loss would have been a blow, but one which could have come in any case through disease and could usually be survived so long as other elements of that strategy did not fail at the same time. For the wealthier farmer (on whom the financial demands made by the *polis* were far heavier and liable to increase as the war went on), the loss of a substantial capital investment, while it would not compromise his day-to-day survival, might be a severe blow to his finances. Also, the loss of draught animals for ploughing on larger estates would have had to be compensated for with human labour, precisely at the time when slaves were being lost and hired labour would have been scarcer and more expensive or lower yields would have to have been accepted. The poor man would only have been slightly more wretched, and at least his main asset was more valuable, but the rich man would have been a lot less rich. In between the two extremes, the situation would have been a lot more complicated. Many men would have lost heavily who could ill afford to do so, but also some of the aspirant would have lost status symbols rather than being threatened with starvation. The general tendency would still have been to flatten out inequalities of wealth distribution to some extent.

Direct confirmatory evidence of the increased value of labour is hard to come by, unless we accept that the relatively egalitarian nature of fourth-century Athens can be taken as such. This picture is also consistent with Loomis' study of wage levels in classical Athens, *Wages, Welfare Costs and Inflation in Classical Athens*, although Loomis himself seems reluctant to consider the relationship between wages and the labour supply.[91] Assuming that he is right in his identification of wage movements in Athens, then he

---

[91] Loomis 1998.

might well also be right to explain a rise in wages between 450 and 432 in terms of increased revenues from the empire.[92] Elsewhere, his monetarist approach is less helpful. For example, I find it difficult to accept that the abolition of pay for public office during the period of the oligarchic regime of the Four Hundred in 411, which is a substantial part of his argument that we should see major cuts in wages between 412 and 403, should be seen solely as a reflection of Athens no longer having the cash to support wages as a result of the Sicilian disaster and the Spartan occupation of Decelea. Yet this is what Loomis suggests, with no hint that the political ideology of the oligarchs might possibly have had something to do with it.[93]

More seriously, his explanation of an increase in wages between 403 and 330 as 'very slight and gradual inflation during a long period of sustained prosperity and growth in the silver supply'[94] is not really an explanation at all. The idea that wage movements might have something to do with the demand for and supply of labour, as well as the money supply and 'the expansion of commercial and banking activity', is not obviously absurd, and the available labour force in the fourth century was after all rather smaller than it had been in the fifth.[95] Further, the pressures to make even more intensive use of the available arable land might have increased the demand for labour.

Consideration of wages is most directly relevant to free workers, of course. But it is also worth pointing out that the condition of slaves will have altered too, and possibly for the better (though whether any of those involved would have seen it that way is unlikely). After all, in crude economic terms, the value of slaves to their masters will have increased. This in itself will subtly have changed the power relations between master and slave. But the fact

---

[92] Loomis 1998, 243: 'The increasing amount and circulation of this money, in the context of a (presumably) less rapidly increasing labor supply, would have been the cause of the wage increases in this period (i.e., the later fifth century).' It is tempting to ask why commercial activity, which Loomis cites as a factor in the gradual increase in wages he traces through the fourth century, was not a factor worth considering – unless, of course, as Cohen seems to, he thinks that commercial activity was a novelty in fourth-century Athens.

[93] Loomis 1998, 244–5. See also Cohen 2008, focusing entirely on the fourth century.

[94] Loomis 1998, 257.

[95] Loomis 1998, 247.

that Athens was experiencing military pressure, and ultimately defeat, externally, and political upheaval internally, will also have made it more difficult for masters to control and keep hold of their slaves.[96] In fact, any one of these factors on its own would have created problems, as they did in other slave-owning societies in history. This pressure is exemplified both by the desertions during the Decelean War and by the enfranchisement of the Arginusae slaves.

The slaves who were lost in these and other ways could not easily be replaced in the straitened circumstances of the post-war period. There would have been consequences for those slaves who remained and who would be bought as the fourth century progressed. The change in relations between master and slave was, if not permanent, not just ephemeral either. I have argued that it is not coincidence that it is precisely during this period that the confident, cocky slave who becomes a stock character in later comedy starts to appear in the dramas of Aristophanes (such as Xanthias in the *Frogs*).[97]

Furthermore, one of the most valuable contributions of Cohen's account of fourth-century Athenian society is the evidence he presents for slaves (and women) gaining increased responsibility and prestige in Athens. One difficulty he faces is that his implication is that all this happened because of the role in a new market economy. This is problematic, first because the 'marketisation' of the economy seems to happen in the fifth century without having this effect, and second because the numbers involved in banking and the continued marginal nature (in social terms) of their activities makes it hard to see how they could have such a widespread effect. If we just abandon Cohen's premises, but retain his observations and place them in a context that is both wider and deeper in terms of what was happening in Athenian society and the underlying causes, we can provide a more satisfying explanation.

Fifth-century Athens is likely to have witnessed increasingly sharp divisions in the distribution of wealth, and perhaps a concomitant decline in average standards of living. It is possible

[96] Patterson 1982, 285–96.
[97] Akrigg 2013.

that early fourth-century Athens, if it did not see a reversal of this trend, at least saw it retarded, as the rich became poorer and some of the poorest became perhaps a little better off. It is here that we might locate a demographic explanation, or at least a partial one, for the surprising stability of the fourth-century democracy, as economic inequality no longer clashed quite so blatantly with the public ideology of political equality between citizens, and social tensions were, if not eased, at least not exacerbated. The 'new demography' may have been of rather more indirect benefit to the conservatives among the Athenian elite than Strauss implies.

Strauss' conclusion was quite different. He reasonably pointed out that

> many of the rich were still rich, or at least still members of the propertied class [but] as one moves down the social ladder, one finds Athenians who lost far less than 50 talents but could hardly afford to lose 50 drachmas.

He went on:

> What did those who had been impoverished by the Decelean War or the defeat of 405 think of the rich who were still rich? The likely answer is that they resented them ... True, Athenian hoplites and *thetes* are well known for exhibiting tolerance toward the property of the upper classes. In spite of post-war economic pressure, there is no evidence of a fundamental change in that attitude. What there is, however, is a series of straws in the wind that add up to a significant increase of tension between have and have-not.[98]

Most of the 'straws' that follow are insubstantial indeed. His evidence from the orators consists mainly of stock complaints about the wealthy that cannot be taken as evidence of any increase in social tension. As Strauss himself notes, Andocides 1.88 on the cancellation of debts could just have been scaremongering, and again, this is a conventional theme. If we had more fifth-century oratory, these items would probably look even less unusual or significant.[99]

The attacks on the 3,000 are as likely to have been politically motivated as the product of economic inequality. Resentment of these particular wealthy men was understandable resentment of oligarchs, which is not necessarily the same thing as evidence

[98] Strauss 1986, 56.
[99] Sommerstein 1984, especially 332–3.

of increasing tension between haves and have-nots *qua* haves and have-nots. His last item (5) – 'on the other end of the scale, consider the resentment of the propertied classes against the *eisphorai* of the Corinthian War (Lysias 28.3–4) and the lack of enthusiasm of some for the reinstituted trierarchy (Aristophanes *Ecclesiazusae* 197–8)'[100] – again seems to reflect an utterly unsurprising reluctance on the part of wealthy Athenians to take up the financial burden left by the loss of the empire when their own resources were depleted, rather than any increased resentment of their poorer compatriots as such.[101]

There is one important item in his list. In Aristophanes' late plays *Ecclesiazusae* and *Wealth* (especially the latter), there is undoubtedly a concern about the unjust way that wealth is distributed. If we are to take this at face value, then even if my suggestions were right, the perceptions of the Athenians (or at least Aristophanes) were very different. At the least, this would vitiate the idea that the stability of the democracy could have been due to a change in economic circumstances.

First of all, however, the usual caveats about the use of comedy as evidence for anything must be issued. We might want to wonder how representative Aristophanes was of the wider citizen population, and so on. More positively, it is certainly important to remember that overall there was a lot less wealth in Attica. As Strauss is quite rightly at pains to point out, the wealthy had lost a lot in absolute terms, but many of them were still rich, especially compared to other Athenians. But I would maintain that it is likely that the very poorest citizens did not get that much poorer, if at all, if only because they could not. Those who experienced the greatest economic pain could well have been experienced by 'middling' Athenians, not the most destitute. In *Wealth*, Chremylus, like so many Aristophanic 'Everymen', does not appear to be all that poor: he still has at least one slave (Karion), and more are implied. Perhaps this is mere dramatic convention, but it is at least possible that while some of the audience identified with him closely, others found him a still

[100] Strauss 1986, 57.
[101] Christ 2006.

recognisable type (the denizen of 'Middle Attica', perhaps?) but one whose concerns seemed a little ridiculous compared to their own situations.

In discussing these items, Strauss was probably yielding too much to the adherents of the 'crisis of the *polis*' school to whose position he was generally opposed.[102] The most important single problem for proponents of this view is that it has become increasingly clear that there is no particular reason to see a crisis in fourth-century Athens at all.[103] Granted, Athens (and the other Greek *poleis*) failed to withstand the new threat from Macedon, but that is not the same thing. The pattern of warring city-states that 'failed' to unite in the face of Philip can also be seen as 'a more effective (and safer) means of maintaining a balance of power than the massive, opposing power blocks of the later fifth century' that produced the Peloponnesian War as well as the Parthenon.[104] It may be going too far to say that fourth-century Athens was more democratic than it had been in the fifth; but the arguments that it was significantly less democratic (before 322) prove difficult to sustain, too.[105]

But the arguments presented here go further: they turn the 'crisis' picture (especially as it is presented in Mossé 1962) almost entirely on its head. It was the fifth century that was heading for a crisis as a result of increasing economic disparity between citizens. Instead of assuming that the fifth century was a 'golden age', if we start asking questions about demography, the upheavals of the Peloponnesian War (terrible as they undoubtedly were to experience) can be seen as purgative, instead of disrupting the political and social equilibrium.

---

[102] Strauss 1986, 4–5.
[103] Davies 1995. Mossé 1972 and 1973 reflect something of a retreat from her earlier position.
[104] Millett 1993, 183.
[105] Millett 2000b.

CHAPTER 8

CONCLUSION

I hope by now to have made both some specific points about classical Athens, and a wider one about the writing and practice of ancient economic history. The specific points start with the fact that we have enough evidence to say quite a lot about the size of the population of Athens and Attica in the fifth century as well as in the fourth. This includes the non-citizen population as well as the citizens. Previous attempts to look at the numbers of slaves and metics have made less progress than they might have, partly because they treated different sections of the population as though their sizes were independent of each other. It is this, as much as the paucity of the evidence, that has led to such wildly divergent estimates for non-citizen groups. Even though the detail of my approach has differed in most ways, Gomme's choice of a starting point, the ambition of his account, and the breadth of the questions that he raised have largely been vindicated against the criticisms that were levelled against him.

Furthermore, when the available evidence is given its due consideration, it seems hard to resist the conclusion that the size of the population of Attic at its pre-Peloponnesian war peak was at least at the higher end of recent estimates, if it did not exceed them. Moreover, this population was the product of a short but explosively fast period of expansion. Although this has sometimes been noted in passing, there has been a distinct reluctance to face up to what it meant. The reasons for this reluctance have ranged from the focus of political historians on the better documented institutions of the fourth century, to the distance of fifth-century Athens from the mainstream of classical Greece.[1] What I have attempted

---

[1] Hansen 1988, 27–8; Sallares 1991, 95.

to show is that in fact these consequences are of the utmost importance for our understanding of the fifth-century Athenian economy. Because the fourth century was the product of what had happened in the fifth, and because we cannot separate the social from the economic or the political from the social, this observation turns out to be essential to our proper understanding of the shape and development of Athenian history throughout the classical period.

I have also argued that we can attempt to quantify the scale of the demographic losses suffered by Athens during the years of the Peloponnesian War. That these were genuinely very heavy has also been noted in the past, but again without much explicit consideration of the consequences. The path that Strauss took in his account makes that account almost a rule-proving exception, as his arguments could only have been advanced in an environment where little serious thought seemed to have been given to the problem. But if we can agree that the size of the population at the beginning of the war was important, then we should also agree that a major change in that population would have had important consequences. Exactly what those consequences were is harder to establish definitively, and could well be disputed; but their existence cannot be dismissed out of hand.

What also seems clear is that, by most pre-industrial standards, Attica was still, even after the shocks of the later fifth century, densely populated. There is no reason to infer that agricultural production was any less intensive in the fourth century; if anything, the tendency may have been the reverse. Instead, the picture that seems to emerge is one where the huge population of the fifth century could only have been sustained because of Athens' access to the resources of the empire. Cause and effect are not easy to disentangle here, however. The population only grew in the first place because of the opportunities afforded by the empire; on the other hand, the ability of Athens to emerge as militarily prominent and to acquire that empire after the Persian invasions was due in part to its already relatively large population.

However, the empire also brought with it some problems for the Athenians, quite apart from its effects on the allies. A densely packed population, especially in a pre-industrial environment, would have experienced strong pressures towards increasing concentration of wealth, especially land, and decreasing average standards of living. To an extent, the empire, coupled with the institutions and ideology of democracy, shielded the Athenians from the worst consequences of this. Not only was the Athenian fleet able to secure imports but, crucially, ordinary Athenians were provided with the means to acquire the cash needed to pay for those imports. This ensured a ready market and provided a powerful incentive for those with food to sell to bring it to Athens. The development of a large urban market, centred on Athens and Piraeus, would also have helped to stabilise prices. The rich were also shielded from the worst of the financial burdens that they would otherwise have had to shoulder, and which they had to bear in the fourth century. But more than this, given access to the resources of the allied cities as well as their own, some Athenians were able to amass colossal fortunes by the standards of the time. This would have exacerbated the degree and visibility of inequality and threatened a rift between the political ideology of equality between citizens and the social and economic reality. Had the Peloponnesian War not intervened, the empire might have caused severe internal problems – just as happened, *mutatis mutandis*, with Sparta in the fourth century.

As it was, Athens lost the empire. The rich, especially, suffered the loss of the economic shielding it had provided. The principle of payment for participation in the democracy, which was principally of benefit to the poorer citizens, and might never have been introduced in the first place had it not been for the empire, was not only retained but strengthened with the introduction of assembly pay. The rich not only lost their property overseas but now were also obliged to take up the financial slack left by the loss of tribute payments. More generally, and potentially more seriously, had it not been for the losses of population inflicted by the war and the plague, the Athenians as a whole would have had difficulty feeding themselves in the post-war years. This rather cold comfort has been noted before, too.[2] But crucially, the combined effect of the loss of the empire and the losses of population must have been

[2] Strauss 1986, 81.

to lessen the inequality of wealth and to reduce the tendency to crisis in the fourth century. This must be at least part, and an important part at that, of the background to both the political stability and to the relatively equal distribution of wealth in fourth-century Athens which has been emphasised so much in recent scholarship.

The wider point is implicit in most of the foregoing. Historical demography, even, or perhaps even especially, at the crude level at which we are obliged to pursue it, is crucial to economic history, especially in pre-industrial contexts, just because levels of consumption and production (and, to an extent, exchange) are closely related to the numbers of people present in a given area. Most basically, for questions of scale in ancient economies, it is important because average consumption will rarely have been much above subsistence levels; production levels, too, are largely tied to the available labour and how it may best be deployed. At the least, historical demography provides the essential background for all other study of ancient economies.

Clearly, by putting demography at the forefront, I suggested an approach to the economic history of Athens that is substantially different from those adopted in the past. While I would not claim that this is the only valid avenue of approach, demography is too important to ignore, and a good deal more likely to be productive and interesting than most of the alternatives. And this is particularly true at the level of this study: a single *polis* over a specific period, of about a century and a half, for which we have some detailed information.

BIBLIOGRAPHY

Acton, P. (2014). *Poiesis: Manufacturing in Classical Athens*. Oxford: Oxford University Press.

Akrigg, B. (2013). 'Aristophanes, slaves and history', in Tordoff, R. and Akrigg, B. (eds) *Slaves and Slavery in Ancient Greek Comic Drama*. Cambridge: Cambridge University Press.

(2015). 'Metics in Athens', in Taylor, C. and Vlassopoulos, K. (eds), 155–73.

Alcock, S. E. (1993). *Graecia Capta: The Landscapes of Roman Greece*. Cambridge: Cambridge University Press.

Alcock, S. E. and Cherry, J. F. (eds) (2004). *Side-by-Side Survey: Comparative Regional Studies in the Mediterranean World*. Oxford: Oxbow Books.

Alertz, U. (1995). 'The naval architecture and oar systems of medieval and later galleys', in Gardiner, R. and Morrison, J. (eds), *The Age of The Galley: Mediterranean Oared Vessels since Pre-Classical Times (Conway's History of the Ship series)*, London: Conway Maritime Press, 142–62.

Allbaugh, L. G. (1953). *Crete: A Case Study of an Underdeveloped Area*. Princeton, NJ: Princeton University Press.

Amouretti, M. C. (1979). 'Les céréales dans l'antiquité: espèces, mouture et conservation, liaison et interférences dans la Grèce classique', in Gast, M., and Sigaut, F. (eds), *Les techniques de conservation des graines à long terme*, Paris: Éditions CNRS, 57–69.

(1986). *Le pain et l'huile dans la Grèce antique: de l'araire au moulin*. Paris: Les Belles Lettres.

Angel, J. L. (1945). 'Skeletal material from Attica', *Hesperia* 14, 279–363.

(1975). 'Palaeoecology, palaeodemography and health', in Polgar, S. (ed.) *Population, Ecology and Social Evolution*, The Hague: Mouton, 167–90.

Appadurai, A. (ed.) (1986). *The Social Life of Things: Commodities in Cultural Perspective*. Cambridge: Cambridge University Press.

Aston, T. and Philpin, C. (eds) (1985). *The Brenner Debate: Agrarian Class Structure and Economic Development in Pre-Industrial Europe*. Cambridge: Cambridge University Press.

Austin, M. M. and Vidal-Naquet, P. (1977). *Economic and Social History of Ancient Greece: An Introduction*. London: Batsford.

Badian, E. (1982). 'Marx in the Agora', review of De Ste Croix, G. E. M., *The Class Struggle in the Ancient Greek World: From the Archaic Age to the Arab Conquests*, New York Review of Books 29(19).

Bagnall, R. (2002). 'The effects of plague: model and evidence', *JRA* 15, 114–20.

248

Bibliography

Bagnall, R. and Frier, B. (1994). *The Demography of Roman Egypt*. Cambridge: Cambridge University Press.

Beloch, J. (1886). *Die Bevölkerung der griechisch-römischen Welt*. Leipzig: Duncker & Humblot.

Bintliff, J. and Sbonias, K. (eds) (1999). *The Archaeology of Mediterranean Landscapes* I: *Reconstructing Past Population Trends in Mediterranean Europe (*3000 BC–AD 1800*)*. Oxford: Oxbow Books.

Bissa, E. (2009). *Governmental Intervention in Foreign Trade in Archaic and Classical Greece. (Mnemos. Suppl.* 312*)*. Leiden: Brill.

Blok, J. and Lardinois, A. (eds) (2006). *Solon of Athens: New Historical and Philological Approaches*. Leiden: Brill.

Boserup, E. (1965). *The Conditions of Agricultural Growth: The Economics of Agrarian Change Under Population Pressure*. London: Allen & Unwin.

Bosworth, A. B. (2002). *The Legacy of Alexander: Politics, Warfare and Propaganda under the Successors*. Oxford: Oxford University Press.

Bowman, A. and Wilson, A. (2009) *Quantifying the Roman Economy: Methods and Problems*. Oxford: Oxford University Press.

Braun, T. F. R. G. (1995). 'Emmer cakes and barley bread', in Dobson, M., Harvey, D., and Wilkins, J. (eds), *Food in Antiquity*, Exeter: University of Exeter Press, 25–37.

Brenner, R. (1976). 'Agrarian class structure and economic development in pre-industrial Europe', *Past and Present* 70, 30–75.

Bresson, A. (2008). *L'Économie de la Grèce des Cités:* I. *Les Structures et la Production*. Paris: Armand Colin.

(2016). *The Making of the Ancient Greek Economy: Institutions, Markets and Growth in the City-States*. Princeton, NJ: Princeton University Press.

Britnell, R. (1996). *The Commercialisation of English Society,* 1000–1500. Manchester: Manchester University Press.

Brunt, P. A. (1971). *Italian Manpower,* 225 BC–AD14. Oxford: Oxford University Press.

Bruun, C. (2003). 'The Antonine plague in Rome and Ostia', *JRA* 16, 426–34.

Burn, A. R. (1953). '*Hic breve vivitur*: a study of the expectation of life in the Roman empire', *Past and Present* 4, 1–31.

Carawan, E. (2001). 'What the laws have prejudged: *paragraphe* and early issue-theory', in Wooten, C. W. (ed.), *The Orator in Action and Theory in Greece and Rome: Essays in Honor of George Kennedy*, Leiden: Brill, 17–51.

(2005). 'Andocides' defence and MacDowell's solution', in Cairns, D. L. and Knox, R. A. (eds) *Law, Rhetoric, and Comedy in Classical Athens: Essays in Honour of Douglas M. MacDowell*, Swansea: Classical Press of Wales, 103–12.

Cartledge, P. (1983). '"Trade and politics" revisited: archaic Greece', in Garnsey, P., Hopkins, M. K., and Whittaker, C. R. (eds), *Trade in the Ancient Economy*, London: Chatto & Windus, 1–15.

(1985). 'Rebels and *sambos* in classical Greece: a comparative view', in Cartledge, P. and Harvey, F. (eds), 16–46.

Bibliography

(1998). 'The economy (economies) of ancient Greece', *Dialogos* 5, 4–24.

Cartledge, P. and Harvey, F. (eds) (1985). *Crux: Essays Presented to G. E. M. De Ste Croix on His 75th Birthday.* Exeter: Imprint Academic.

Cartledge, P., Cohen, E., and Foxhall, L. (eds) (2002). *Money, Labour and Land: Approaches to the Economies of Ancient Greece.* London: Routledge.

Cawkwell, G. (1984). 'Athenian naval power in the fourth century', *CQ* 34(2), 334–45.

Christ, M. (2001). 'Conscription of hoplites in classical Athens', *CQ* 51(2), 398–422.

(2006). *The Bad Citizen in Classical Athens* Cambridge: Cambridge University Press.

Clawson, M., Landsberg, H. H., and Alexander, L. T. (1971). *The Agricultural Potential of the Middle East.* New York, NY: American Elsevier.

Clerc, M. (1893). *Les Métèques athéniens: etude sur la condition légale, la situation morale et le rôle social et économique des étrangers domiciliés á Athènes.* Paris: Thorin & Fils.

Coale, A. J. and Demeny, P. (1966). *Regional Model Life Tables and Stable Populations.* Princeton, NJ: Princeton University Press.

(1983). *Regional Model Life Tables and Stable Populations* (2nd edn, with Barbara Vaughn). New York, NY: Academic Press.

Cohen, E. (1992). *Athenian Economy and Society: A Banking Perspective.* Princeton, NJ: Princeton University Press.

(2000). *The Athenian Nation.* Princeton, NJ: Princeton University Press.

(2008). 'Elasticity of the money supply at Athens', in Harris, E. (ed.), *The Monetary Systems of the Greeks and Romans*, Oxford: Oxford University Press, 66–83.

Conophagos, C. E. (1980). *Le Laurium antique et la technique grecque de la production de l'argent.* Athens: Ekdotike Hellados.

Dal Lago, E. and Katsari, C. (2008). *Slave Systems Ancient and Modern.* Cambridge: Cambridge University Press.

Davidson, J. (1997). *Courtesans and Fishcakes: The Consuming Passions of Classical Athens.* London: Harper Collins.

Davies, J. K. (1971). *Athenian Propertied Families, 600–300 BC.* Oxford: Oxford University Press.

(1981). *Wealth and the Power of Wealth in Classical Athens.* New York, NY: Arno Press.

(1995). 'The fourth-century crisis: what crisis?' in Eder, W. (ed.), *Die athenische Demokratie im 4. Jahrhundert v. Chr*, Stuttgart: Franz Steiner, 29–39.

De Ligt, L. and Northwood, S. J. (eds) (2008). *People, Land and Politics: Demographic Developments and the Transformation of Roman Italy, 300 BC–AD 14 (Mnemos. Suppl. 303).* Leiden: Brill.

Develin, R. (1990). 'Numeral corruption in Greek historical texts', *Phoenix* 44 (1), 31–45.

Dow, S. (1961), 'Thucydides and the number of Acharnian *hoplitai*', *TAPhA* 91, 66–80.

Bibliography

Duncan-Jones, R. (1980). 'Metic numbers in Periclean Athens', *Chiron* 10, 101–9.

(1990). *Structure and Scale in the Roman Economy.* Cambridge: Cambridge University Press.

(1996). 'The impact of the Antonine plague', *JRA* 9, 108–36.

Edwards, M. L. (1996). 'The cultural context of deformity in the ancient Greek world', *Ancient History Bulletin* 10, 79–92.

Engels, D. W. (1978). *Alexander the Great and the Logistics of the Macedonian Army.* Berkeley, CA: University of California Press.

Erdkamp, P. (2016). 'Economic growth in the Roman Mediterranean world: an early good-bye to Malthus?' *Explorations in Economic History* 60, 1–20.

FAO (1973). *Energy and Protein Requirements: Report of a Joint FAO/WHO Ad Hoc Expert Committee.* Rome: Food and Agriculture Organization of the United Nations.

(2004). *Human Energy Requirements: Report of a Joint FAO/WHO/UNU Expert Consultation, Rome 17–24 October 2001.* Rome: Food and Agriculture Organization of the United Nations.

Fawcett, P. (2016). '"When I squeeze you with eisphorai": taxes and tax policy in classical Athens', *Hesperia* 85(1), 153–99.

Fenner, F. et al. (1988). *Smallpox and Its Eradication.* Geneva: World Health Organization.

Figueira, T. (1991). *Athens and Aigina in the Age of Imperial Colonization.* Baltimore, MD: Johns Hopkins University Press.

Finley, M. I. (1952). *Studies in Land and Credit in Ancient Athens, 500–200 BC: The Horos-Inscriptions.* New Brunswick, NJ: Rutgers University Press.

(1953). 'Land, debt and the man of property in classical Athens', *Political Science Quarterly* 68, 249–68.

(1954). *The World of Odysseus.* London: Chatto & Windus.

(1965). 'Technical innovation and economic progress in the ancient world', *Economic History Review* 18, 29–45.

(1972). 'Anthropology and the Classics'. Jane Harrison Memorial Lecture, delivered at Newnham College, Cambridge, 13 May 1972, in Finley, M. I. (ed.) 1975, 102–19.

(1973). *The Ancient Economy.* Berkeley, CA: University of California Press.

(1979). *The Bücher–Meyer Controversy.* New York, NY: Arno Press.

(1981). *Economy and Society in Ancient Greece.* London: Chatto & Windus.

Finley, M. I. (ed.) (1975). *The Use and Abuse of History.* London: Chatto & Windus.

Firth, R. (ed.) (1967). *Themes in Economic Anthropology.* London: Tavistock Publications.

Fisher, N. R. E. (1993). *Slavery in Classical Greece.* London: Bristol Classical Press.

(2001). *Slavery in Classical Greece (2nd edn).* London: Bristol Classical Press.

Forbes, H. A. (1982). *Strategies and Soils: Technology, Production and Environment in Methana.* Unpublished PhD thesis, University of Pennsylvania.

Bibliography

(1996). 'The uses of the uncultivated landscape in modern Greece: a pointer to the value of the wilderness in antiquity?', in Salmon, J. and Shipley, G. (eds), 68–97.

Forsdyke, S. (2006). 'Land, labor and economy in Solonian Athens: breaking the impasse between archaeology and history', in Blok, J. and Lardinois, A. (eds), 334–50.

Foxhall, L. (1992). 'The control of the Attic landscape', in Wells, B. (ed.), 155–9.

(1997). 'A view from the top: evaluating the Solonian property classes', in Mitchell, L. and Rhodes, P. J. (eds), *The Development of the Polis in Archaic Greece*, Routledge: London, 113–36.

(1998). 'Snapping up the unconsidered trifles: the use of agricultural residues in ancient Greek and Roman farming', *Environmental Archaeology* 1, 35–40.

(2002). 'Access to resources in classical Greece: the egalitarianism of the polis in practice', in Cartledge, P., Cohen, E. E., and Foxhall, L. (eds), 209–20.

(2007). *Olive Cultivation in Ancient Greece: Seeking the Ancient Economy*. Oxford: Oxford University Press.

Foxhall, L. and Forbes, H. A. (1982). '*Sitometreia*: the role of grain as a staple food in classical antiquity', *Chiron* 12, 41–89.

Frank, T. (1924). 'Roman census statistics from 225 to 28 BC', *Classical Philology* 19, 329–41.

French, A. (1993). 'A note on the size of the Athenian armed forces in 431 BC', *AHB* 7, 43–8.

Frost, F. (2001). 'Sausage and meat preservation in antiquity', *GRBS* 40(3), 241–52.

Gabrielsen, V. (1994). *Financing the Athenian Fleet: Public Taxation and Social Relations*. Baltimore, MD: Johns Hopkins University Press.

(2002). 'Socio-economic classes and ancient Greek warfare', in Ascani, K., Gabrielsen, V., Kvist, K., and Rasmussen, A. H. (eds) *Ancient History Matters: Studies Presented to Jens Erik Skydsgaard on his Seventieth Birthday*, L'Erma di Bretschneider: Rome, 203–20.

Gallant, T. (1991). *Risk and Survival in Ancient Greece: Reconstructing the Rural Domestic Economy*. Cambridge: Cambridge University Press.

(2001). *Modern Greece*. London: Edward Arnold.

(2015). *Edinburgh History of the Greeks, 1768–1913: The Long Nineteenth Century*. Edinburgh: Edinburgh University Press.

Garlan, Y. (1988). *Slavery in Ancient Greece*. Ithaca, NY: Cornell University Press.

Garland, R. (2001). *The Piraeus: From the Fifth to the First Century BC (2nd edn)*. London: Bristol Classical Press.

Garnsey, P. (1988). *Famine and Food Supply in the Graeco-Roman World: Responses to Risk and Crisis*. Cambridge: Cambridge University Press.

(1992). 'Yield of the land', in Wells, B. (ed.), 147–53.

(1999). *Food and Society in Classical Antiquity*. Cambridge: Cambridge University Press.

Golden, M. (1981). 'Demography and the exposure of girls at Athens', *Phoenix* 35(4), 316–31.

Bibliography

(1992). 'The uses of cross-cultural comparison in ancient social history', *EMC* 11, 309–31.

(2000). 'A decade of demography. Recent trends in the study of Greek and Roman populations', in Flensted-Jensen, P., Nielsen, T., and Rubinstein, L. (eds) *Polis and Politics; Studies in Ancient Greek History. Presented to Mogens Herman Hansen on his Sixtieth Birthday,* August 20, 2000. Copenhagen: Museum Tusculanum Press.

Goldthwaite, R. A. (2009). *The Economy of Renaissance Florence.* Baltimore, MD: Johns Hopkins University Press.

Gomme, A. W. (1927). 'The Athenian hoplite force in 431', *CQ* 21, 142–51.

(1933). *The Population of Athens in the Fifth and Fourth Centuries* BC. Oxford: Oxford University Press.

(1956). *A Historical Commentary on Thucydides: Volume* II: *The Ten Years' War: Books* II–III. Oxford: Oxford University Press.

(1959). 'The population of Athens again', *JHS* 79, 61–8.

Graham, A. J. (1983). *Colony and Mother City in Ancient Greece.* Manchester: Manchester University Press.

(1992). 'Thucydides 7.12.2 and the crews of Athenian triremes', *TAPhA* 122, 257–70.

(1998). 'Thucydides 7.12.2 and the crews of Athenian triremes: an addendum', *TAPhA* 128, 89–114.

Greenberg, J. (2003). 'Plagued by doubt: reconsidering the impact of a mortality crisis in the 2nd c. AD', *JRA* 16, 409–25.

Grmek, M. (1988). *Diseases in the Ancient Greek World.* Baltimore, MD: Johns Hopkins University Press.

Grove, A. T. and Rackham, O. (2001). *The Nature of Mediterranean Europe: An Ecological History.* New Haven, CT: Yale University Press.

Halstead, P. (1987). 'Traditional and ancient rural economy in Mediterranean Europe: plus ça change?', *JHS* 107, 77–87.

(2014). *Two Oxen Ahead: Pre-Mechanized Farming in the Mediterranean.* Chichester: Wiley Blackwell.

Halstead, P. and Jones, G. (1989). 'Agrarian ecology in the Greek islands: time stress, scale and risk', *JHS* 109, 41–55.

Hammond, N. G. L. (1982). 'The narrative of Herodotus VII and the Decree of Themistocles at Troezen', *JHS* 102, 75–93.

Hannestad, N. (1988). 'The Athenian potter and the home market', in Christiansen, J. and Melander, T. (eds), *Proceedings of the Third Symposium on Ancient Greek and Related Pottery, Copenhagen, August* 31–*September* 4, 1987. Copenhagen: NY Carlsberg Glypotek.

Hansen, M. H. (1981). 'The number of Athenian hoplites in 431 BC', *Symb. Osl.* 56: 19–32.

(1982). 'Demographic reflections on the number of Athenian citizens 451–309 BC', *AJAH* 7, 172–89.

Bibliography

(1985). *Demography and Democracy: The Number of Athenian Citizens in the Fourth Century* BC. Herning: Systime.

(1988). *Three Studies in Athenian Demography. Hitorisk-filosofiske Medelelser* 56. Copenhagen: Royal Danish Academy of Sciences and Letters.

(1991). *The Athenian Democracy in the Age of Demosthenes: Structure, Principles, and Ideology.* Oxford: Blackwell.

(2006a). *Studies in the Population of Aigina, Athens and Eretria. Hitorisk-filosofiske Medelelser* 94. Copenhagen: Det Kongelige Danske Videnskabernes Selskab.

(2006b). *The Shotgun Method: The Demography of the Ancient Greek City-State Culture.* Columbia, MO: University of Missouri Press.

Hanson, V. D. (1992a). 'Thucydides and the desertion of Attic slaves during the Decelean War', *Cl. Ant.* 11(2), 210–28.

(1992b). 'Practical aspects of grape-growing and the ideology of Greek viticulture', in Wells, B. (ed.), 161–66.

(1995). *The Other Greeks: The Family Farm and the Agrarian Roots of Western Civilization.* New York, NY: Free Press.

Harding, P. (1985). *From the End of the Peloponnesian War to the Battle of Ipsus. Translated Documents of Greece and Rome* 2. Cambridge: Cambridge University Press.

Harris, E. M., Lewis, D. M., and Woolmer, M. (eds) (2016). *The Ancient Greek Economy: Markets, Households and City-States.* Cambridge: Cambridge University Press.

Harris, W. V. (2013). 'Defining and detecting Mediterranean deforestation, 800 BCE to 700 CE', in Harris, W. V. (ed.), 173–94.

Harris, W. V. (ed.) (2013). *The Ancient Mediterranean Environment between Science and History. Columbia Studies in the Classical Tradition* 39. Leiden: Brill.

Harrison, A. R. W. (1968). *The Law of Athens Volume I: The Family and Property.* Oxford: Oxford University Press.

Hasebroek, J. (1931). *Griechische Wirtschafts- und Gesellschaftsgeschichte.* Tübingen: J. C. B. Mohr.

Hastings, M. and Jenkins, S. (1997). *Battle for the Falklands. Revised edn.* London: Norton.

Hatcher, J. and Bailey, M. (2001) *Modelling the Middle Ages: The History and Theory of England's Economic Development.* Oxford: Oxford University Press.

Hayami, Y. (2001). *From the Poverty to the Wealth of Nations, 2nd edn.* New York, NY: Oxford University Press.

Henige, D. (1998). *Numbers from Nowhere: The American Indian Contact Population Debate.* Norman, OK: University of Oklahoma Press.

Herlihy, D. and Klapisch-Zuber, C. (1985). *Tuscans and their Families: A Study of the Florentine Catasto of 1427.* New Haven, CT: Yale University Press.

Hignett, C. (1952) *A History of the Athenian Constitution to the End of the Fifth Century* BC. Oxford: Oxford University Press.

Bibliography

Hin, S. (2013). *The Demography of Roman Italy*. Cambridge: Cambridge University Press.

(2016). 'Revisiting urban graveyard theory: migrant flows in Hellenistic and Roman Athens', in De Ligt, L. and Tacomoa, L. (eds) *Migration and Mobility in the Early Roman Empire*, Brill: Leiden, 234–63.

Hoepfner, W. and Schwandner, E.-L. (1994). *Haus und Stadt im klassischen Griechenland*. Munich: Deutscher Kunstverlag.

Holladay, A. J. and Poole, J. C. (1979). 'Thucydides and the plague of Athens', *CQ* 29, 282–300.

(1982). 'Thucydides and the plague: a footnote', *CQ* 32, 235–6.

(1984). 'Thucydides and the plague: a further footnote', *CQ* 34, 483–5.

Holleran, C. and Pudsey, A. (eds) (2011). *Demography and the Graeco-Roman World: New Insights and Approaches*. Cambridge: Cambridge University Press.

Hollingsworth, T. H. (1969). *Historical Demography*. London: Hodder & Stoughton.

Hopkins, M. K. (1966). 'On the probable age structure of the Roman population', *Population Studies* 20 (2), 245–64.

(1983). 'Introduction', in Garnsey, P., Hopkins, M. K., and Whittaker, C. R. (eds), *Trade in the Ancient Economy*, London: Chatto & Windus, ix–xxv.

(1987), 'Graveyards for historians', in Hinard, F. (ed), *La mort, les morts et l'au-delà dans le monde Romain*. Caen: University of Caen Press: 113–26.

Hoppa, R. D. and Vaupel, J. W. (2002). 'The Rostock Manifesto for paleodemography: the way from stage to age', in Hoppa, R. D. and Vaupel, J. W. (eds), *Paleodemography: Age Distributions from Skeletal Samples,* Cambridge Studies in Biological and Evolutionary Anthropology 31. Cambridge: Cambridge University Press, 1–8.

Horden, P. and Purcell, N. (2000). *The Corrupting Sea: A Study of Mediterranean History*. Oxford: Blackwell.

Hornblower, J. (1981). *Hieronymus of Cardia*. Oxford: Oxford University Press.

Hornblower, S. (1991). *A Commentary on Thucydides:* Volume 1, Books I–III. Oxford: Oxford University Press.

How, W. W. and Wells, J. (1912). *A Commentary on Herodotus with Introduction and Appendixes* (2 vols). Oxford: Oxford University Press.

Hughes, J. D. (2014). *Environmental Problems of the Greeks and Romans: Ecology in the Ancient Mediterranean*. Baltimore, MD: Johns Hopkins University Press.

Hume, D. (1752). *Political Discourses*. Edinburgh: Kincaid & Donaldson.

Humphrey, C. and Hugh-Jones, S. (eds) (1992). *Barter, Exchange and Value: An Anthropological Approach*. Cambridge: Cambridge University Press.

Humphreys, S. C. (1978). *Anthropology and the Greeks*. London: Routledge & Kegan Paul.

Hunt, P. (1998). *Slaves, Warfare and Ideology in the Greek Historians*. Cambridge: Cambridge University Press.

Bibliography

(2007). 'Military forces' in Sabin, P., Van Wees, H., and Whitby, W. (eds), 108–46.

Ingalls, W. (2002). 'Demography and dowries: perspectives on female infanticide in classical Greece', *Phoenix* 56 (3/4), 246–54.

Isager, S. and Skydsgaard, J. E. (1992). *Ancient Greek Agriculture: An Introduction*. London: Routledge.

Jameson, M. (1977–8). 'Agriculture and slavery in classical Athens', *CJ* 73(2), 122–45.

(1988). 'Sacrifice and animal husbandry in classical Greece', in Whittaker, C. R. (ed.), 87–119.

(1992). 'Agricultural labour in ancient Greece', in Wells, B. (ed.), 135–46.

(1994). 'Class in the ancient Greek countryside', in Doukellis, P. N. and Mendoni, L. (eds), *Structures rurales et sociétés antiques*, Paris: Les Belles Lettres, 55–63.

(2002). 'On Paul Cartledge, *The Political Economy of Greek Slavery*', in Cartledge, P., Cohen, E., and Foxhall, L. (eds), 167–74.

Jardé, A. (1925). *Les céréales dans l'antiquité grecque*. I. *La production*. Paris: Éditions de Boccard.

Jones, A. H. M. (1957). *Athenian Democracy*. Oxford: Blackwell.

Jones, D. W. (2014). *Economic Theory and the Ancient Mediterranean*. Chichester: Wiley Blackwell.

Jones, N. F. (2004). *Rural Athens under the Democracy*. Philadelphia, PA: University of Pennsylvania Press.

Jordan, B. (2003). 'Slaves among the frogs', *L'Antiquité Classique* 72, 41–53.

(2010). 'The Sicilian expedition was a Potemkin fleet', *CQ* 50(1), 63–79.

Kagan, D. and Viggiano, G. (2013a). 'The hoplite debate', in Kagan, D. and Viggiano, G. (eds), 1–56.

Kagan, D. and Viggiano, G. (eds) (2013b) *Men of Bronze: Hoplite Warfare in Ancient Greece*. Princeton, NJ: Princeton University Press.

Kallet, L. (2013). 'The origins of the Athenian economic *archē*', *JHS* 133, 43–60.

Kallet-Marx, L. (1993). *Money, Expense and Naval Power in Thucydides' History* 1–5.24. Berkeley, CA: University of California Press.

Kellogg, D. L. (2013). *Marathon Fighters and Men of Maple: Ancient Acharnai*. Oxford: Oxford University Press.

Keen, A. (1993). "Grain for Athens': notes on the importance of the Hellespontine route in Athenian foreign policy before the Peloponnesian War', *Electronic Antiquity: Communicating the Classics* 1(6).

Krentz, P. (2013). 'Hoplite hell: how hoplites fought', in Kagan, D. and Viggiano, G. (eds), 134–56.

Kron, G. (2005). 'Anthropometry, physical anthropology, and the reconstruction of ancient health, nutrition and living standards', *Historia* 54, 68–83.

(2011). 'The distribution of wealth at Athens in comparative perspective', *ZPE* 179, 129–38.

Bibliography

Kurke, L. (1999). *Coins, Bodies, Games and Gold: The Politics of Meaning in Archaic Greece*. Princeton, NJ: Princeton University Press.

Lagia, A. (2015). 'Diet and the polis: an istopic study of diet in Athens and Laurion during the Classical, Hellenistic and Imperial Roman periods', in Papathanasiou, A., Richards, M. P., and Fox, S. C. (eds) *Archaeodiet in the Greek World: Dietary Reconstruction from Stable Isotope Analysis Hesperia Supplement* 49, Princeton, NJ: Princeton University Press, 119–41.

Laing, D. R. (1965). *A New Interpretation of the Athenian Naval Catalogue: IG* II² 1951. Unpublished dissertation, University of Cincinnati.

Lambert, S. D. (ed.) (2011). *Sociable Man: Essays on Ancient Greek Social Behaviour in Honour of Nick Fisher*. Swansea: Classical Press of Wales.

Lancaster, H. O. (1990). *Expectations of Life: A Study in the Demography, Statistics, and History of World Mortality*. New York, NY: Springer Verlag.

Lane, F. C. (1934). *Venetian Ships and Shipbuilders of the Renaissance*. Baltimore, MD: Johns Hopkins University Press.

(1973). *Venice: A Maritime Republic*. Baltimore, MD: Johns Hopkins University Press.

Langmuir, A. D. et al. (1985). 'The Thucydides syndrome: a new hypothesis for the cause of the plague of Athens', *New England Journal of Medicine* 313, 1027–30.

Lapini, W. (1997). 'Les hoplites athéniennes de 431 (Thuc. 2.13.6)', *Mnemosyne* 50, 257–70.

Launaro, A. (2011). *Peasants and Slaves: The Rural Population of Roman Italy (200 BC to AD100)*. Cambridge: Cambridge University Press.

Lewis, D. M. (2016). 'The market for slaves in the fifth and fourth century Aegean: Achaemenid Anatolia as a case study', in Harris, E., Lewis, D., and Woolmer, M. (eds), 316–36.

Littman, R. J. (2009). 'The plague of Athens: epidemiology and paleopathology', *Mount Sinai Journal of Medicine* 76(5), 456–67.

Littman, R. J. and Littman, M. L. (1969). 'The Athenian plague: smallpox', *TAPhA* 100, 261–75.

Lo Cascio, E. (1994). 'The size of the Roman population: Beloch and the meaning of the Augustan census figures', *JRS* 84, 23–40.

(1999). 'Popolazione e risorse agricole nell'Italia del II secolo a. C.', in Vera, D. (ed.), *Demografia, sistemi agrari, regimi alimentari: atti el convegno internazionale di studi*, Bari: Edipuglia, 217–45.

(2001). 'La population', *Pallas* 55, 179–98.

Lohmann, H. (1991) 'Zur Prosopographie und Demographie der attischen Landgemeinde Atene', in Olshausen, E. and Sonnabend, H. (eds), *Stuttgarte Kolloquium zur historischen Geographie des Altertums* 2. Bonn: Rudolf Habelt, 203–58.

(1992). 'Agriculture and country life in classical Attica', in Wells, B. (ed.), 29–57.

(1993). *Atene: Forschungen zu Siedlungs- und Wirtschaftsstruktur des klassichen Attika*. Cologne: Böhlau.

Bibliography

Loomis, W. (1998) *Wages, Welfare Costs and Inflation in Classical Athens*. Ann Arbor, MI: University of Michigan Press.

MacDougall, P. (1987). *The Chatham Dockyard Story*. Rainham: Meresborough Books.

(2012). *Chatham Dockyard: The Rise and Fall of a Military Industrial Complex*. Stroud: The History Press.

MacKinnon, M. (2014). 'Animals, economics and culture in the Athenian Agora: comparative zoological investigations', *Hesperia* 83, 189–255.

Markle, M. M. (1985), 'Jury pay and assembly pay at Athens', in Cartledge, P. and Harvey, F. (eds), 265–97.

Matson, F. R. (1972). 'Ceramic studies', in McDonald, W. A. and Rapp, G. R. (eds), *The Minnesota Messenia Expedition: Reconstructing a Bronze Age Regional Environment*. Minneapolis, MN: University of Minnesota Press, 200–24.

Mattingly, D. J. (1996). 'First fruit? The olive in the Roman world', in Salmon, J. and Shipley, G. (eds), 213–53.

Mattingly, D. J. and Salmon, J. (eds) (2001). *Economies Beyond Agriculture in the Classical World*. London: Routledge.

McCloskey, D. (1998). *The Rhetoric of Economics (2nd edn)*. Madison, WI: University of Wisconsin Press.

McNeill, W. H. (1976). *Plagues and Peoples*. Garden City, NY: Anchor Press.

Meiggs, R. (1972). *The Athenian Empire*. Oxford: Oxford University Press.

(1982). *Trees and Timber in the Ancient Mediterranean World*. Oxford: Oxford University Press.

Meikle, S. (1995a). *Aristotle's Economic Thought*. Oxford: Oxford University Press.

(1995b). 'Modernism, economics and the ancient economy', *PCPhS* 41, 174–91.

Meyer, E. (2010). *Metics and the Athenian Phialai-Inscriptions: A Study in Athenian Epigraphy and Law*. Stuttgart: Steiner.

Miller, M. (1997). *Athens and Persia in the Fifth Century BC: A Study in Cultural Receptivity*. Cambridge: Cambridge University Press.

Millett, P. (1991). *Lending and Borrowing in Ancient Athens*. Cambridge: Cambridge University Press.

(1993). 'Warfare, economy and democracy in classical Athens', in Rich, J. and Shipley, G. (eds) *War and Society in the Greek World* London: Routledge, 177–96.

(2000a). 'Mogens Hansen and the labelling of Athenian democracy', in Flensted-Jensen, P., Nielsen, T.H., and Rubinstein, L. (eds), *Polis and Politics. Studies in Ancient Greek History Presented to Mogens Herman Hansen on his Sixtieth Birthday*, August 20, 2000, Copenhagen: Museum Tusculanum Press, 337–62.

(2000b). 'The economy', in Osborne, R., (ed.) *Classical Greece*, Oxford: Oxford University Press, 23–51.

Mitchell-Boyask, R. (2008). *Plague and the Athenian Imagination: Drama, History, and the Cult of Asclepius*. Cambridge: Cambridge University Press.

Bibliography

Moreno, A. (2007). *Feeding the Democracy: The Athenian Grain Supply in the Fifth and Fourth Centuries* BC. Oxford: Oxford University Press.

Morley, N. (1996). *Metropolis and Hinterland: The City of Rome and the Italian Economy* 200 BC–AD 200. Cambridge: Cambridge University Press.

Morris, I. (1987). *Burial and Ancient Society: The Rise of the Greek City-State.* Cambridge: Cambridge University Press.

(1994a). 'The Athenian economy twenty years after *The Ancient Economy*' (Review of Cohen 1992), *C Phil.* 89, 351–66.

(1994b). 'Archaeologies of Greece', in Morris, I. (ed.) *Classical Greece: Ancient Histories and Modern Archaeologies.* Cambridge: Cambridge University Press, 8–47.

(1999). 'Foreword', in Finley, M. I., *The Ancient Economy (updated 3rd edn)*, Berkeley, CA: University of California Press, ix–xxxvi.

(2002). 'Hard surfaces', in Cartledge, P., Cohen E., and Foxhall, L. (eds), 8–43.

(2007). 'Early Iron Age Greece', in *CEH*, 211–41.

(2009). 'The greater Athenian state', in Morris, I. and Scheidel, W. (eds) *The Dynamics of Ancient Empires*, Oxford: Oxford University Press, 99–177.

(2010). *Why the West Rules – For Now: The Patterns of History and What They Reveal About the Future.* New York, NY: Farrar, Straus and Giroux.

(2013). *The Measure of Civilization: How Social Development Decides the Fate of Nations.* Princeton, NJ: Princeton University Press.

Morrison, J. S., Coates, J. F., and Rankov, N. B. (2000). *The Athenian Trireme: The History and Reconstruction of an Ancient Greek Warship (2nd edn).* Cambridge: Cambridge University Press.

Mossé, C. (1962). *La fin de la démocratie athénienne: aspects sociaux et politiques du déclin de la cité grecque au IVe siècle avant J.-C.* Paris: Presses universitaires de France.

(1972). 'La vie économique d'Athènes au IV siècle: crise ou renouveau?', in Sartori, F. (ed.) *Praelectiones Patavinae.* Rome: L'Erma di Bretschneider, 135–44.

(1973). 'Le statut des paysans en Attique au IVe siècle', in Finley, M. I. (ed.), *Problèmes de la terre en Grèce ancienne.* Paris: Mouton, 179–86.

Munn, M. and Munn, M. Z. (1989). 'The Stanford Skourta Plain Project: the 1987 and 1988 seasons of survey on the Attic–Boiotian frontier', *AJA* 93, 274–5.

(1990). 'On the frontiers of Attica and Boiotia: the results of the Stanford Skourta Plain Project', in Schachter, A. (ed.), *Essays in the Topography, History and Culture of Boiotia.* Montreal: McGill University, 32–40.

Nafissi, M. (2005). *Ancient Athens and Modern Ideology: Value, Theory and Evidence in Historical Sciences.* Max Weber, Karl Polanyi and Moses Finley. London: Institute of Classical Studies.

Naiden, F. S. (2013). *Smoke Signals for the Gods: Ancient Greek Sacrifice from the Archaic through Roman Periods.* Oxford: Oxford University Press.

Napier, W. (1857). *The Life and Opinions of General Sir Charles James Napier* (4 vols). London: John Murray.

Bibliography

Newell, C. (1988). *Methods and Models in Demography*. London: Belhaven Press.

Oakley, J. H. and Sinos, R. H. (1993). *The Wedding in Ancient Athens*. Madison, WI: University of Wisconsin Press.

Ober, J. (1985). *Fortress Attica: Defense of the Athenian Land Frontier, 404–322 BC*. Brill: Leiden.

(2008). *Democracy and Knowledge*. Princeton, NJ: Princeton University Press.

(2015). *The Rise and Fall of Classical Greece*. Princeton, NJ: Princeton University Press.

O'Connor, S. (2013). 'The daily grain consumption of classical Greek sailors and soldiers', *Chiron* 43, 327–56.

Ogilvie, S. (2007) '"Whatever is, is right"? Economic institutions in pre-industrial Europe', *Economic History Review* 60(4), 649–84.

Oliver, G. J. (2007). *War, Food and Politics in Early Hellenistic Athens*. Oxford: Oxford University Press.

Olson, S. D. (1991). 'Firewood and charcoal in classical Athens', *Hesperia* 60, 411–20.

Osborne, R. G. (1985). *Demos: The Discovery of Classical Attika*. Cambridge: Cambridge University Press.

(1987). *Classical Landscape with Figures. The Ancient Greek City and Its Countryside*. London: G. Philip.

(1988). 'Social and economic implications of the leasing of land and property in classical and Hellenistic Greece', *Chiron* 18, 279–323.

(1991). 'Pride and prejudice, sense and subsistence: exchange and society in the Greek city', in Rich, J. and Wallace-Hadrill, A. (eds), *City and Country in the Ancient World*, London: Routledge, 119–46.

(1992). '"Is it a farm?" The definition of agricultural sites and settlements in ancient Greece', in Wells, B. (ed.), 21–7.

(1995). 'The economics and politics of slavery at Athens', in Powell, A. (ed.), *The Greek World*, London: Routledge, 27–43.

(1996). 'Pots, trade and the archaic Greek economy', *Antiquity* 70, 31–44.

(1997). Review of Lohmann 1993. *Gnomon* 69, 243–47.

(2004). 'Demography and survey', in Alcock, S. E. and Cherry, J. F. (eds), 163–72.

Osborne, R. G. (ed.) (2000). *Classical Greece*. Oxford: Oxford University Press.

Papagrigorakis, M. J., Yapijakis, C., Synodinos, C. N., and Batziotopoulou-Valavani, E. (2006a). 'DNA examination of ancient dental pulp incriminates typhoid fever as a probable cause of the Plague of Athens', *International Journal of Infectious Diseases* 10(3), 206–14.

(2006b). 'Insufficient phylogenetic analysis may not exclude candidacy of typhoid fever as a probable cause of the Plague of Athens (reply to Shapiro et al.)', *International Journal of Infectious Diseases* 10(4), 334–5.

Papalas, A. (2012). 'The reconstructed trireme Olympias and her critics', in Rankov, B. (ed.), 101–8.

Papazarkadas, N. (2011). *Sacred and Public Land in Ancient Athens*. Oxford: Oxford University Press.

Bibliography

Parker, R. (1994). 'Athenian religion abroad', in Hornblower, S. and Osborne, R. (eds), *Ritual, Finance, Politics. Democratic Accounts Rendered to D.M. Lewis.* Oxford: Oxford University Press, 339–46.

(1996). 'Sacrifice, Greek', in Hornblower, S. and Spawforth, A. (eds), *The Oxford Classical Dictionary.* Oxford: Oxford University Press, 1344.

(2005). *Polytheism and Society at Athens.* Oxford: Oxford University Press.

Parkin, T. (1992). *Demography and Roman Society.* Baltimore, MD: Johns Hopkins University Press.

Patterson, C. (1981). *Pericles' Citizenship Law of 451–450 BC.* Salem, NH: Arno Press.

(2005). 'Athenian citizenship law', in Cohen, C. and Gagarin, M. (eds), *The Cambridge Companion to Greek Law.* Cambridge: Cambridge University Press, 267–89.

(2007). 'Other sorts: slaves, foreigners and women', in Samons, L. (ed.), *The Cambridge Companion to the Age of Pericles.* Cambridge: Cambridge University Press, 153–78.

Patterson, O. (1982). *Slavery and Social Death: A Comparative Study.* Cambridge, MA: Harvard University Press.

(2008). 'Slavery, gender and work in the pre-modern world and early Greece: a cross-cultural comparison', in Dal Lago, E. and Katsari, C. (eds), 32–69.

Pečírka, J. (1976). 'The crisis of the Athenian polis in the fourth century BC', *Eirene* 14, 5–29.

Persson, K. (1988). *Pre-Industrial Economic Growth: Social Organisation and Technical Progress in Europe.* Blackwell: Oxford.

(2010). *An Economic History of Europe: Knowledge, Institutions and Growth, 600 to the Present.* Cambridge: Cambridge University Press.

Piggott, S. (1976). *Ruins in a Landscape: Essays in Antiquarianism.* Edinburgh: Edinburgh University Press.

Pleket, H. W. (1976). Review of Finley 1973. *Mnemosyne* 29, 208–16.

Polanyi, K. (1944). *The Great Transformation: The Political and Economic Origins of Our Times.* New York, NY: Farrar & Rinehart.

Polanyi, K., Arensberg, C. M., and Pearson, H. W. (eds) (1957). *Trade and Market in the Early Empires: Economies in History and Theory.* Glencoe, IL: Free Press.

Polle, F. (1887), 'Zu Thukydides', *Neue Jahrbücher für Philologie und Paedagogik* 135, 109–11.

Pomeroy, S. (1975). *Goddesses, Whores, Wives and Slaves: Women in Classical Antiquity.* New York, NY: Schocken Books.

(1989). 'Slavery in the light of Xenophon's *Oeconomicus*', *Index* 17, 11–18.

(1994). *Xenophon Oeconomicus: A Social and Historical Commentary.* Oxford: Oxford University Press.

Postan, M. (1973a). *Essays on Medieval Agriculture and General Problems of the Medieval Economy.* Cambridge: Cambridge University Press.

(1973b). *Medieval Trade and Finance.* Cambridge: Cambridge University Press.

Bibliography

Potts, S. (2011). 'Co-operation, competition and clients: the social dynamics of the Athenian navy', in Lambert, S. (ed.), 45–66.

Price, S. and Nixon, L. (2005). 'Ancient Greek agricultural terraces: evidence from texts and archaeological survey', *AJA* 109, 665–94.

Pritchard, D. M. (2015). *Public Spending and Democracy in Classical Athens*. Austin, TX: University of Texas Press.

Pritchett, W. K. (1956). 'The Attic Stelai, part 2', *Hesperia* 25, 178–328.

(1971). *The Greek State at War: Part* I. (Originally published as Ancient Greek Military Practices). Berkeley, CA: University of California Press.

(1991). *The Greek State at War. Part* V. Berkeley, CA: University of California Press.

Raaflaub, K. (1999). 'Archaic and classical Greece', in Raaflaub, K. and Rosenstein, N. (eds), *War and Society in the Ancient and Medieval Worlds: Asia, the Mediterranean, Europe, and Mesoamerica*. Cambridge, MA: Harvard University Press, 129–61.

Rackham, O. (1982). 'Land-use and the native vegetation of Greece', in Bell, M. and Limbrey, S. (eds), *Archaeological Aspects of Woodland Ecology (*BAR *International Series* 146*)*, Oxford: British Archaeological Reports, 177–98.

(1983). 'Observations on the historical ecology of Boiotia', *ABSA* 78, 291–351.

Rankov, B. (ed.) (2012). *Trireme* Olympias:*The Final Report*. Oxford: Oxbow Books.

Rathbone, D. (1990). 'Villages, land and population in Graeco-Roman Egypt', *PCPhS* 36, 103–42.

(1991). *Economic Rationalism and Rural Society in Third-Century* AD *Egypt: The Heroninos Archive and the Appianus Estate*. Cambridge: Cambridge University Press.

Rathbone, D. and Von Reden, S. (2015). 'Mediterranean grain prices in classical antiquity', in Van Der Spek, R. J., Van Leeuwen, B., and Van Zanden, J. L. (eds), *A History of Market Performance: From Ancient Babylonia to the Modern World*. London: Routledge, 149–235.

Ray, D. (1998). *Development Economics*. Princeton, NJ: Princeton University Press.

Reeve, M. (1968). 'Review of Roussel, L. (1966) (Pseudo-)Lysias, *L'Invalide*. Paris', *CR* 18(2), 235–6.

Rhodes, P. J. (1980). 'Epheboi, bouleutai and the population of Athens', *ZPE* 38, 191–201.

(1981). *Commentary on the Aristotelian* Athenaion Politeia. Oxford: Clarendon Press.

(1988). *Thucydides History* II:*Edited with Translation and Commentary*. Warminster: Aris & Philips.

(1992). 'The Athenian revolution', *CAH* 4, 62–95.

(2010). *A History of the Classical Greek World:* 478–323 BC. Chichester: Wiley-Blackwell.

Bibliography

Rhodes, P. J. and Osborne, R. (2003). *Greek Historical Inscriptions 404–323 BC.* Oxford: Oxford University Press.

Rihll, T. (1993). 'War, slavery and settlement in early Greece', in Rich, J. and Shipley, G. (eds), *War and Society in the Greek World.* London: Routledge, 77–107.

(2001). 'Making money in classical Athens', in Mattingly, D., and Salmon, J. (eds), 115–42.

(2011). 'Classical Athens', in Bradley, K. and Cartledge, P. (eds), *The Cambridge World History of Slavery, Vol.* 1. Cambridge: Cambridge University Press, 48–73.

Rosivach, V. J. (1994). *The System of Public Sacrifice in Fourth-Century Athens.* Atlanta, GA: Scholars Press.

Rostovtzeff, M. I. (1933). Review of Hasebroek, J. (1931). *Zeitschrift für die gesamte Staatswissenschaft* 92, 333–9.

(1941). *The Social and Economic History of the Hellenistic World.* Oxford: Oxford University Press.

Roth, J. P. (2007). 'War', in Sabin, P. Van Wees, H., and Whitby, H. (eds), 368–98.

Runnels, C. N. and Van Andel, T. H. (1987). *Beyond the Acropolis: A Rural Greek Past.* Stanford, CA: Stanford University Press.

Ruschenbusch, E. (1979). *Athenische Innenpolitik im 5. Jahrhundert v. Chr: Ideologie oder Pragmatismus?* Bamberg: Aku Fotodruck.

(1981). 'Epheben, Bouleuten und die Bürgerzahl von Athen um 330 v. Chr', *ZPE* 41, 103–5.

(1984). 'Zum letzten Mal: Die Bürgerzahl im 4. Jh v. Chr.', *ZPE* 54, 253–70.

Sabin, P., Van Wees, H., and Whitby, H. (2007). *The Cambridge History of Greek and Roman Warfare. Volume I: Greece, the Hellenistic World and the Rise of Rome.* Cambridge: Cambridge University Press.

Sahlins, M. D. (1972). *Stone Age Economics.* Chicago, IL: Aldine Atherton.

De Ste Croix, G. E. M. (1966). 'The estate of Phainippus (Ps. Dem. xlii)', in Badian, E. (ed.), *Ancient Society and Institutions: Studies Presented to Victor Ehrenberg.* Oxford: Blackwell, 109–14.

(1981). *The Class Struggle in the Ancient Greek World.* London: Duckworth.

Sallares, R. (1991). *The Ecology of the Ancient Greek World.* London: Duckworth.

(2002). *Malaria and Rome: A History of Malaria in Ancient Italy.* Oxford: Oxford University Press.

Saller, R. (2002) 'Framing the debate over growth in the ancient economy', in Scheidel, W. and Von Reden, S. (eds), *The Ancient Economy*, Edinburgh: Edinburgh University Press, 251–69.

(2012) 'Human capital and economic growth', in Scheidel, W. (ed.), *The Cambridge Companion to the Roman Economy*, Cambridge: Cambridge University Press, 71–86.

Salmon, J. (2001). 'Temples the measures of men: public building in the Greek economy', in Mattingly, D. J. and Salmon, J. (eds), 195–208.

Bibliography

Salmon, J. and Shipley, G. (eds) (1996). *Human Landscapes in Classical Antiquity: Environment and Culture*. London: Routledge.

Samuelson, P. and Nordhaus, W. (2009). *Economics (19th edn)*. New York, NY: McGraw Hill.

Sargent, R. L. (1924). *The Size of the Slave Population at Athens During the Fifth and Fourth Centuries Before Christ*. Urbana, IL: University of Illinois Press.

Sarpaki, A. (1992). 'The palaeoethnobotanical approach: the Mediterranean triad, or is it a quartet?', in Wells, B. (ed.), 61–76.

Sbonias, K. (1999). 'Introduction to issues in demography and survey', in Bintliff, J. and Sbonias, K. (eds), *The Archaeology of Mediterranean Landscapes 1: Reconstructing Past Population Trends in Mediterranean Europe (3000 BC–AD 1800)*, Oxford: Oxbow Books, 1–20.

(1999). 'Investigating the interface between regional survey, historical demography, and paleodemography', in Bintliff, J. and Sbonias, K. (eds), 219–34.

Schaps, D. (2004). *The Invention of Coinage and the Monetization of Ancient Greece*. Ann Arbor, MI: University of Michigan Press.

(2011). *Handbook for Classical Research*. London: Routledge.

Scheidel, W. (1995). 'The most silent women of Greece and Rome: rural labour and women's life in the ancient world', *Greece and Rome* 42, 202–17; 43, 1–10.

(1996). *Measuring Sex, Age and Death in the Roman Empire: Explorations in Ancient Demography*. Ann Arbor, MI: University of Michigan Press.

(2001a). 'Roman age structure: evidence and models', *JRS* 91, 1–26.

(2001b). 'Progress and problems in Roman demography', in Scheidel, W. (ed.), *Debating Roman Demography*. Leiden: Brill, 1–82.

(2001c). *Death on the Nile: Disease and the Demography of Roman Egypt*. Leiden: Brill.

(2002). 'A model of demographic and economic change in Roman Egypt after the Antonine plague', *JRA* 15, 97–114.

(2003). 'The Greek demographic expansion: models and comparisons', *JHS* 123, 120–40.

(2005). 'Real slave prices and the relative cost of slave labor in the Greco-Roman world', *Ancient Society* 35, 1–17.

(2007). 'Demography', in Scheidel, W., Morris, I., and Saller, R. (eds), *The Cambridge Economic History of the Greco-Roman World*. Cambridge: Cambridge University Press, 38–86.

(2008). 'The comparative economics of slavery in the Greco-Roman world', in Dal Lago, E. and Katsari, C. (eds), 105–26.

(2017). *The Great Leveller: Violence and the History of Inequality from the Stone Age to the Twenty-First Century*. Princeton, NJ: Princeton University Press.

Schofield, R. S. and Wrigley, E. A. (1979). 'Infant and child mortality in England in the late Tudor and early Stuart period', in Webster, C. (ed.), *Health*,

Bibliography

Medicine and Mortality in the Sixteenth Century. Cambridge: Cambridge University Press, 61–95.

Schwartz, A. (2013). 'Large weapons, small Greeks: the practical limitations of hoplite weapons and equipment', in Kagan, D. and Viggiano, G. (eds), 157–75.

Shapiro, B., Rambaut, A., and Gilbert, M. T. P. (2006). 'No proof that typhoid caused the Plague of Athens (a reply to Papagrigorakis et al.)', *International Journal of Infectious Diseases* 10(4), 334–5.

Shepherd, R. (1993). *Ancient Mining*. London: Elsevier.

Shryock, H. S. and Siegel, J. S. (1976). *The Methods and Materials of Demography*. Washington, DC: US Bureau of the Census.

Sinclair, R. K. (1988). *Democracy and Participation in Athens*. Cambridge: Cambridge University Press.

Snodgrass, A. M. (1977). *Archaeology and the Rise of the Greek State*. Cambridge: Cambridge University Press.

(1983). 'Two demographic notes', in Hägg, R. (ed.), *The Greek Renaissance of the Eighth Century* BC. Stockholm: Svenska Institutet i Athen, 167–71.

Sommerstein, A. H. (1984). 'Aristophanes and the demon Poverty', *CQ* 34(2), 314–33.

Spence, I. (1993). *The Cavalry of Classical Greece*. Oxford: Oxford University Press.

Strauss, B. (1986). *Athens After the Peloponnesian War: Class, Faction and Policy* 403–386 BC. London: Croom Helm.

(1993) *Fathers and Sons in Athens: Ideology and Society in the Era of the Peloponnesian War*. Princeton, NJ: Princeton University Press.

(1996). 'The Athenian trireme, school of democracy', in Ober, J. and Hedrick, C. (eds), *Dēmokratia: A Conversation on Democracies, Ancient and Modern*. Princeton, NJ: Princeton University Press, 313–25.

(2000). 'Perspectives on the death of fifth-century Athenian seamen', in Van Wees, H. (ed.), *War and Violence in Ancient Greece*. London: Duckworth, 261–83.

Tandy, D. W. (1997). *Warriors into Traders: The Power of the Market in Early Greece*. Berkeley, CA: University of California Press.

Taylor, C. E. (2005). *Participation in Athenian Democracy*. Unpublished PhD thesis, University of Cambridge.

(2017). *Poverty, Wealth, and Well-Being: Experiencing Penia in Democratic Athens*. Oxford: Oxford University Press.

Taylor, C. E. and Vlassopoulous, K. (eds) (2015). *Communities and Networks in the Ancient Greek World*. Oxford: Oxford University Press.

Thompson, H. A. (1980). 'Stone, tile and timber: commerce in building materials in classical Athens', *Expedition* 22(3), 12–26.

Thür, G. (1989). 'Wo wohnen die Metöken?', in Schuller, S., Hoepfner, W., and Schwandner, E. (eds), *Demokratie und Architektur: der hippodamische Städtebau und die Entstehung der Demokratie: Konstanzer Symposion vom 17. bis 19. Juli 1987*, Munich: Deutscher Kunstverlag, 117–21.

Bibliography

Tilley, A. (2012). 'An unauthentic reconstruction', in Rankov, B. (ed.), 121–32.

Todd, S. C. (2007). *A Commentary on Lysias, Speeches 1–11.* Oxford: Oxford University Press.

Trevett, J. (1992). *Apollodorus the Son of Pasion.* Oxford: Oxford University Press.

UN (2004). *Inequality, Growth, and Poverty in an Era of Liberalization and Globalization.* Oxford: Oxford University Press.

Vaughn, P. (1991). 'The identification and retrieval of the hoplite battle-dead', in Hanson, V. D. (ed.), *Hoplites: The Classical Greek Battle Experience.* London: Routledge, 38–62.

Van Wees, H. (1995). 'Politics and the battlefield: ideology in Greek warfare', in Powell, A. (ed.), *The Greek World.* London: Routledge, 153–78.

(2001). 'The myth of the middle-class army: military and social status in ancient Athens', in Bekker-Nielsen, T. and Hannestad, L. (eds), *War as a Cultural and Social Force: Essays on Warfare in Antiquity.* Copenhagen: Det Kongelige Danske Videnskabernes Selskab, 45–71.

(2004). *Greek Warfare: Myths and Realities.* London: Duckworth.

(2006). 'Mass and elite in Solon's Athens: the property classes revisited', in Blok, J. and Lardinois, A. (eds), 351–89.

(2011). 'Demetrius and Draco: Athens' property classes and population in and before 317 BC', *JHS* 131, 95–114.

(2013a). 'Farmers and hoplites: models of historical development', in Kagan, D. and Viggiano, G. (eds), 222–55.

(2013b). *Ships and Silver, Taxes and Tribute: A Fiscal History of Archaic Athens.* London: I. B. Tauris.

Veal, R. (2013). 'Fuelling ancient Mediterranean cities: a framework for charcoal research', in Harris, W. V. (ed.), 37–58.

Von Reden, S. (1995). *Exchange in Ancient Greece.* London: Routledge.

(2007). 'Classical Greece: Consumption', *CEH*, 385–406.

(2015). *Antike Wirtschaft. Enzyclopädie der griechisch-römischen Antike* 10. Oldenbourg: De Gruyter.

Waley, D. (1968). *The Italian City-Republics.* London: Weidenfeld & Nicolson.

Walker, D. and Raoult, D. (2011) 'Typhus Group Rickettioses', in Guerrant, R., Walker, D., and Weller, P. (eds), *Tropical Infectious Diseases (3rd edn).* Edinburgh: Saunders Elsevier, 329–33.

Wallinga, H. T. (1982). 'The trireme and its crew', in Den Boeft, J. and Kessels, A. H. M. (eds), *Actus: Studies in Honor of H. L. W. Nelson.* Utrecht: Instituut voor Klassieke Talen, 463–82.

(1993). *Ships and Sea-Power before the Great Persian War: The Ancestry of the Ancient Trireme (Mnemos. Suppl. 121).* Leiden: Brill.

War Office, (1916). *Field Service Pocket Book 1914 (Reprinted with Amendments 1916).* London: HMSO.

Watson, J. (2010). 'The origin of metic status at Athens', *Cambridge Classical Journal* 56, 259–78.

Bibliography

Weber, M. (1968). *Economy and Society.* Edited by G. Roth and C. Wittich. New York, NY: Bedminster Press.

(1976). *The Agrarian Sociology of Ancient Civilisations.* Translated by R. I. Frank. London: New Left Books.

Wells, B. (ed.) (1992). *Agriculture in Ancient Greece.* Proceedings of the Seventh International Symposium at the Swedish Institute at Athens, 16–17th May 1990. Stockholm: Svenska Institutet i Athen.

Welwei, K. W. (1974). *Unfreie im antiken Kriegsdienst* I. Wiesbaden: Steiner.

Welskopf, E. C. (ed.) (1974). *Hellenische Poleis: Krise, Wandlung, Wirkung* (4 vols). Berlin: Akademie-Verlag.

Whitehead, D. (1977). *The Ideology of the Athenian Metic.* Cambridge: Cambridge Philological Society.

Whitby, M. (1998). 'The grain trade of Athens in the fourth century BC', in Parkins, H. M. and Smith, C. J. (eds), *Trade, Traders and the Ancient City.* London: Routledge, 102–28.

Whittaker, C. R. (ed.) (1988). *Pastoral Economies in Classical Antiquity.* Cambridge: Cambridge Philological Society.

Wood, E. M. (1983). 'Agricultural slavery in classical Athens', *AJAH* 8(1), 1–47.

(1988). *Peasant-Citizen and Slave: The Foundations of Athenian Democracy.* London: Verso.

Woods, R. (2007). 'Ancient and early modern mortality: experience and understanding I', *Economic History Review* 60(2), 373–99.

Wrenhaven, K. (2009). 'The identity of the "wool-workers" in the Attic manumissions', *Hesperia* 78, 367–86.

Wrigley, E. A. (1969). *Population and History.* London: Weidenfeld & Nicolson.

Wrigley, E. A., Davies, R. S, Oeppen, J. E., and Schofield, R. S. (1997). *English Population History from Family Reconstitution, 1580–1837.* Cambridge: Cambridge University Press.

Zelnick-Abramovitz, R. (2005). *Not Wholly Free: The Concept of Manumission and the Status of Manumitted Slaves in the Ancient Greek World* (Mnemos. Suppl. 266). Leiden: Brill.

(2013). *Taxing Freedom in Thessalian Manumission Inscriptions (Mnemos. Suppl. 361).* Leiden: Brill.

INDEX

Acton, P., 95
Adeimantos, 219
Aeschines, 64
age classes, 10, 74
Agesilaus, 54
agriculture, 176–9
Agyrrhius, 234–5
Aigospotamoi, battle of, 163, 172
Allbaugh, L., 185, 190
Andocides, 234–5, 241
Angel, J. L., 12
animal husbandry, 178–9
animal sacrifice, 196–9
Antipater, 47
arbitrators, 10, 15, 33
archaeology, 46
archers, 68, 71
Archilochus, 180
Arginusae, battle of, 104, 131, 163, 240
Aristides, 35, 36
Aristophanes, 58, 96, 135–6, 180, 240,
    242–3
    Ecclesiazusae, 47
Aristotle, 37, 122, 127, 172–3, 188, 209
army
    Athenian, 10, 15, 45, 47, 51–61, 64
    Spartan, 54
Arsenale, 128–30, 200
Artemis, 197–8
Athenaeus, 91, 193
Athenaion Politeia, 2, 72–3, 236
Athenian army, 63
Attic Stelai, 201, 206, 219

Badian, E., 6
Bailey, M., 6,
Beloch, J., 14, 69, 88, 93
Bissa, E., 7, 93, 128, 174–8, 194, 200–1
Black Death, 215–16
Black Sea, 173

Boeotia, 202
Boserup, E., 107
Brasidas, 135
Braun, T., 180
Brea, 219–20
Brenner debate, 4–5, 6
Bresson, A., 7, 37, 59–60, 155,
Burn, A. R., 16

*Cambridge Economic History of the Greco-
    Roman World*, 3–4, 7
Carthage, 172
Cato the Elder, 181, 189, 190,
cavalry, 15, 52, 78, 108, 164, 171, 182, 236
census, 41
    Athenian, 47–8, 122–3
    India, 16
    Italy, 14
Cephalus, 128
Chabrias, 53
Chaeronea, battle of, 57, 73, 91
Chalkis, 40,
Chartists, physical force, 151
Chatham dockyard, 130–1
cheese, 188
children, 14, 19
Christ, M., 57–8
citizenship law of 451/0, 22, 34, 61, 67–8,
    144, 147, 155, 169, 236
Cleisthenic constitution, 62–3, 142
Clerc, M., 123–4
cleruchs, 40–1
Cohen, E. E., 2, 6, 210, 223–4, 226,
    227, 240
colonies, 163
Columella, 194–5
Conon, 104
Conophagos, C. E., 97, 202, 203
Corcyra, 53, 231
Corinthians, 79

Index

Cornelius Nepos, 64
Coronea, battle of, 54
Council of 500, 10, 32, 45, 47, 49–50, 51,
    56–7, 63, 142, 143, 157
cows, 237
Crete, 185, 190,
Ctesicles, 90–1, 95, 123

Davies, J. K., 33, 209, 213–15, 218–22
De Ste Croix, G. E. M., 4–6, 106, 108, 220
Decelea, 167, 181
Decree of Themistocles, 64–7
Delium, battle of, 73–4
demes, 58, 62–3, 196, 197, 222
  Acharnai, 58
  Atene, 62, 85, 228–9
  Decelea, 92, 109, 233, 236, 239
  Erkhia, 196, 197
  Euonymon, 33, 178–9, 194, 225
  Laurion, 97
  Marathon, 196, 197
  Thorikos, 183, 196
Demetrius of Phaleron, 47, 48, 91,
    122–3, 125
Democleides, 219
demographic transition, 22, 28
Demosthenes, 47, 56, 57, 98, 102, 206, 212
Demotionidai, 236
Denmark, 212
Dexileos, 12
diaitetai. See arbitrators
dikasts, 100
Diocles of Carystus, 188
Diodorus Siculus, 47–8, 51–4, 55, 69,
    72, 162
donkeys, 202
Duncan-Jones, R., 124, 211

Edwards, M., 75
Egypt, 36, 67, 113, 115, 157, 172,
    173
eisphora, 208, 242
Eleusis, 115
England, 15
ephebes, 10, 15, 33, 45, 49–50, 72–3
Ephialtes, 142
Erechtheum, 115–17
Euboea, 40, 181, 237–8
Euripides, 34–6

fallowing, 178–9
Fawcett, P., 41
figs, 188
Finley, M. I., 4, 6, 7
First World War, 14
Fisher, N., 93, 106
flax, 200
fleet
  Athenian, 43–5, 52–3, 64–7, 76–83,
    104–5, 121, 125, 128–31, 143,
    159–60, 199–201, 219, 231, 237, 246
  Spartan, 234
Florence, republic of, 214–16, 218
Food and Agriculture Organisation, 184,
    186, 187
Forbes, H., 182, 183–6, 190, 193, 201
Four Hundred, 239
Foxhall, L., 178, 182, 183–6, 191–3, 207,
    209–12, 215, 217, 219, 221
France, 21
fuel, 199, 201–4

Gabrielsen, V., 200
Galen, 188
Gallant, T., 178, 188, 189
Garlan, Y., 106
Garnsey, P., 166, 178, 180, 186–7, 195
Germany, 212
Gini coefficients, 211–12
goats, 196–9
Golden, M., 9
Goldthwaite, R., 216
Gomme, A. W., 1, 2, 11, 13–16, 31–2, 70,
    88, 92, 99, 141, 143, 155, 165, 244
grain consumption, 174–87
grain price, 235
grain supply, Athenian, 42–3
Grain Tax Law, 117
Grmek, M., 59

Hagnias, 33
Hagnon, 162
Halstead, P., 110, 118, 178
Hansen, M. H., 1, 2, 9, 11, 18–26, 30–3,
    38–61, 82, 88, 93, 124, 125–6, 139,
    140–1, 142–4, 145, 154–5, 161–3,
    166, 168–9, 175, 176, 207, 214,
Hanson, V. D., 75, 93, 232
Harrison, A. R. W., 34–5

Index

Index

olives, 178, 181, 193
Olson, D., 204
Orcs, 46
Osborne, R., 18, 86, 88, 110–12, 118,
    207–13, 217, 223, 228, 235
oxen, 182, 196–9, 219, 235, 237, 238

palaeodemography, 13
Papagrigorakis, M., 164
Parkin, T., 3, 27, 29
Patterson, C., 2, 18, 22, 61, 67–8, 141,
    144–5, 155, 169
Pausanias, 197
Peloponnesian War, 7, 13, 25, 34, 35, 37,
    68–84, 91–2, 104–5, 132, 140, 158,
    169, 170, 172, 183, 199, 203, 216, 222,
    229, 231, 233, 245, 246
pentecontaetia, 66, 67–8
Pericles, 67, 68, 74, 79, 82
perioikoi, 121
Persia, 51
Persian War, 63–7, 84, 140, 142, 152,
    156, 159
Phaenippus, 206, 209
Phantocles, 219, 220
Philip II of Macedon, 57, 243
Philochorus, 67
pigs, 196–9, 238
Piraeus, 57, 128–31, 146
pitch, 200
plague of Athens, 36, 160, 161, 163–7, 171,
    172, 246
Plataea, 25, 63–4
Plataea, battle of, 24, 64, 142, 157
Plato, 35, 172–3, 189, 209
Plutarch, 47–8, 67, 188, 193
Polanyi, K., 218
Polemarchus, 98, 126
Polybius, 54, 55
Pomeroy, S., 33–7
Potidaea, siege of, 74, 162, 165
prices, 208, 211
property classes, 103, 219–20
Pylos, 109

quadriremes, 54

Rackham, O., 202–4
Rathbone, D., 3

Rhodes, P. J., 32, 80, 93, 124
Rihll, T., 202–3
Roman empire, 14, 16, 20, 22–4, 112, 211
Rosivach, V., 196–9
Roth, J., 162
Ruschenbusch, E., 2, 47, 214

Salaminioi, 198, 199
Salamis, battle of, 64–7, 142, 150
Sallares, R., 10, 105, 144–5, 148–54, 156,
    164, 165–6, 172, 194–5
Saller, R., 3
Samos, 25
Sargent, R., 90, 92, 93–5, 106, 176
Sbonias, K., 87
Schaps, D., 7
Scheidel, W., 3, 28, 29, 31, 93, 107, 112–18,
    119–20, 145–9, 154, 171, 216–18
Schwartz, A., 60
Scythian archers, 97
Second Punic War, 172
Second World War, 157
Sestos, 157
sex ratio, 14
sex structure, 33–7
sheep, 196–9, 238
shipyards, 53, 128–31, 232
Sicilian Expedition, 162, 166, 172
Sicily, 34, 35, 239
Sinclair, R. K., 2,
skeletal remains
    human, 12–13, 186
Skourta plain, 85
Skydsgaard, J. E., 94, 118, 178,
slaves, 9, 66–7, 76, 81, 89–120, 137–8, 146,
    160, 167, 176, 181, 189, 190, 235, 237,
    238, 239–40, 242
smallpox, 163, 166–7
Snodgrass, A., 148, 153
Socrates, 35–6, 179, 181, 189
Strauss, B., 2, 8, 82, 140–1, 142, 161–3,
    165, 230–8, 241–3, 245
Sundt, E., 157
survey archaeology, 84–8, 148, 206
symmories, 102
syssitia (Spartan), 188, 193

Tandy. D., 148
taxes, 234–5

Index

Taylor, C., 230
terracing, 178
Thasos, 194, 219
Theophrastus, 180
Theseus, 197
thetes, 71
Thibron, 237
Thirty Tyrants, 82
Thrace, 220
Thucydides, 13, 14, 52, 67–84, 91–2,
    99–100, 108–9, 122, 123–4, 135–6,
    142–4, 149, 152, 154, 162, 163–7,
    169, 171, 199, 219, 224, 225,
    229–30, 237
timber, 199–201
Timotheus, 53
Todd, S., 95
tombstones, 12, 16
tribes, 197
tribute, 246
trierarchs, 64, 65, 207
trierarchy, 242
triremes, 64–7, 68
    Olympias, 129, 199

Paralos and *Salaminia*, 78
Troezen, 66, 159
typhoid, 164
typhus, 164, 166

United Kingdom, 212, 215, 227
United States of America, 14, 157, 212

Van Wees, H., 41, 66, 75, 101, 103, 144
Venice, republic of, 128–30, 200
Viggiano, M., 75

Wales, 15
Watson, J., 127–8, 149
Whitehead, D., 90, 122, 123–4, 132–6, 168
wine, 178, 181, 188, 189, 193–5
women, 14, 93, 134, 138, 165–6, 194, 240
Wood, E. M., 93, 105, 106–10
Wrigley, E. A., 28, 29

Xenophon, 35, 53, 55, 97, 98, 109, 136–7,
    162, 168, 181, 206, 224

Zelnick-Abramovitz, R., 89

CPSIA information can be obtained
at www.ICGtesting.com
Printed in the USA
LVHW080533280520
656720LV00012B/187